# A History of Company C 50th Pennsylvania Veteran Volunteer Infantry Regiment

# A History of Company C 50th Pennsylvania Veteran Volunteer Infantry Regiment

From the Camp, the Battlefield and the Prison Pen, 1861–1865

J. Stuart Richards

The History Press

Published by The History Press
Charleston, SC
www.historypress.net



*Cover Image:* 50th Pennsylvania at Beaufort, South Carolina. *Courtesy the Library of Congress.*

First published 2006

Manufactured in the United States

ISBN 1.59629.089.7

Library of Congress Cataloging-in-Publication Data

A history of Company C, 50th Pennsylvania Veteran Volunteer Infantry Regiment : from the camp, the battlefield and the prison pen, 1861-1865 / edited by J. Stuart Richards.
p. cm.
Includes bibliographical references.
ISBN 1-59629-089-7 (alk. paper)
1. United States. Army. Pennsylvania Infantry Regiment, 50th (1861-1865). Company C. 2. Pennsylvania--History--Civil War, 1861-1865--Regimental histories. 3. United States--History--Civil War, 1861-1865--Regimental histories. 4. Pennsylvania--History--Civil War, 1861-1865--Personal narratives. 5. United States--History--Civil War, 1861-1865--Personal narratives. 6. United States--History--Civil War, 1861-1865--Campaigns. 7. United States. Army. Pennsylvania Infantry Regiment, 50th (1861-1865). Company C--Biography. 8. Schuylkill Haven (Pa.)--History, Military--19th century. 9. Soldiers--Pennsylvania--Schuylkill Haven--Biography. I. Richards, J. Stuart, 1949-
E527.550th .H57 2006
973.7'448--dc22
2006007411

This book is dedicated to Margaret Piacine, my mother in-law and my friend, who always supported me on all my ventures. And to my wife Danielle who has encouraged this and all efforts in preserving history, and for listening and reading about all the military history that has been my interest, and most of all for her time spent correcting what didn't make sense in the manuscript to something that was readable. Her insights were of the utmost value. And to my grandson Nathaniel Dixon, who has a wonderful military lineage from the Revolutionary War to the present war on terrorism. May he never forget those who have sacrificed for their country.

And to the men of Company C, 50th Pennsylvania Volunteers, who helped save our Union and preserved our heritage and way of life.

# Contents

# Introduction

Schuylkill County, Pennsylvania, sent to the Civil War one soldier for every seven inhabitants. In one week, from the seventeenth to the twenty-fourth of April 1861, the county supplied twenty-three companies of volunteers for a total of 1,795 soldiers. During the course of the war, Schuylkill County supplied over 4,000 men to 101 Pennsylvania regiments and companies, 70 different state regiments, the regular army, navy, marine corps and signal corps. During the initial bugle call, the county called to arms two full companies and had the honor of having the National Light Infantry and the Washington Artillerists among the first five companies of First Defenders who arrived in Washington April 18, 1861. They arrived a day ahead of any other troops in response to the call of Abraham Lincoln for volunteers to defend the Union, issued after the fall of Fort Sumter.

On Saturday, April 20, 1861, three days after the First Defenders left for the front, four additional Schuylkill County companies, the Ringgold Rifles of Minersville, the Scotts Artillery of Schuylkill Haven, the Minersville Artillerists and the Port Clinton Artillery, were assigned to the 5th Pennsylvania Infantry. The following Monday, April 22, 1861, eight more Schuylkill County companies answered the call of the president and left the county for the fray. The companies that left on April 22 were the Tower Guards, Pottsville, assigned to the 6th Regiment; the Nagle Guards, Pottsville, assigned to the 6th Regiment; the Wynkoop Artillery, Silver Creek, assigned to the 16th Regiment; the Keystone Rifles, Port Carbon, assigned to the 6th Regiment; the Washington Yeagers, Pottsville, assigned to the 6th Regiment; the Scott Rifles, Tamaqua, assigned to the 10th Regiment; the Jackson Guards, Tamaqua, assigned to the 16th Regiment, and the German Light Infantry, Tamaqua, assigned to the 16th Regiment.

On Wednesday, April 24, 1861, the Union Guards of Pottsville, made up of firemen from the Hydraulian Fire Company, and the Schuylkill Guards of Minersville departed for the front. The Good Intent Fire Company from Pottsville also enlisted the majority of their members.

Schuylkill County is not unique in its civilian contributions to the Civil War—many small communities supplied men to fill the regiments of the Union army. But I choose the community of Schuylkill Haven, Pennsylvania, and the men of Company C, 50th Regiment of Pennsylvania Veteran Volunteers for their unique composition. They were primarily men who worked on and around the Schuylkill Canal. They served as veteran volunteers and—their most interesting aspect—they had among their ranks two Medal of Honor recipients. Quite an accomplishment for a small community.

Schuylkill Haven is located in the lower portion of Schuylkill County in east-central Pennsylvania. The beauty of this area is striking. If you stand atop Blue Mountain and look to the north, your eyes will behold a vast expanse of rolling mountains. In the near distance is Second Mountain, a beautiful round range running east and west. Cutting through the Second Mountain is the Schuylkill River and the West Branch River. Beyond Second Mountain is Sharp Mountain, and at the base of Blue Mountain, before Sharp Mountain, lies Long Run and a vast area of farmland. Following Long Run eastward will bring the traveler to a small community sitting peacefully upon the banks of the Schuylkill River. This tranquil refuge is the town of Schuylkill Haven.

From the time of the French and Indian War people have inhabited this area of rolling hills and rich farmland. Access to the Schuylkill River is easy as it winds its way south toward Philadelphia, and over the ensuing years Schuylkill Haven grew to become one of the major ports along the prosperous Schuylkill Canal. By 1840, when the canal was opened, Schuylkill Haven was large enough to become known as a borough. The Schuylkill Canal provided the main system of transportation for the coal industry from the anthracite coalfields. It began in Port Carbon, northeast of Pottsville, and ran south to Philadelphia. The canal consisted of an extensive system of docks and locks that raised or lowered the canal boats, depending upon the terrain and elevation of the surrounding land, making for an easy passage of the heavily loaded boats. Boats ran daily both, north and south.

A large number of men who lived in and around Schuylkill Haven were employed as boat builders, boatmen and lock tenders. Schuylkill Haven's population was 988 people in 1840, and by 1860 over 1,800 people lived in the community. The increase in population was a result of the growth of the Schuylkill Canal and the railroad and the increasing shipments of coal from the anthracite coalfields to the north. During the Civil War almost all the coal shipped out of the southern and middle Pennsylvania coalfields passed through Schuylkill Haven.

Like most communities during the 1840s and 1850s, Schuylkill Haven had its own military militia unit. In the early part of 1850, Schuylkill Haven's first military unit was organized and led by Captain Henry Hesser. This small unit's existence was short-lived and ended through the 1850s, when a new unit was organized calling themselves the Scotts artillerists. The unit drilled regularly in Schuylkill Haven.

On Saturday, April 13, 1861, the people of Schuylkill Haven were alarmed at the news that Southern secessionists had put Fort Sumter, near Charleston, South Carolina, under siege and were firing artillery at the fort. The news of this devastating event was slow in coming. People flocked to the railroad station where the telegraph was located in hopes of getting some new information. The telegraph, at the time, was in its infancy and not very reliable. Most people had to wait until the evening passenger train arrived from Philadelphia. When the news arrived, nothing could be taken as the truth. Rumors were running wild. Stories of major victories and disastrous defeats were the talk of the town.

Patriotism was at a high level during the months of April and May 1861. On April 20, at the railroad car shops owned by the Philadelphia & Reading Railroad, employees of the company raised a large American flag, rousing the spirit of the community. A large flag was also raised at the Michael Bassler home on the highest point of Schuylkill Haven. Patriotic speeches were being made daily. Local bands were playing patriotic airs. On June 27, a 115-foot-high pole was raised, bearing an eagle and a wooden cannon pointing toward the south.

When Fort Sumter was fired upon, the Scotts artillerists had volunteered themselves for active duty. When completely filled out, the company went to Harrisburg and volunteered their service to the United States. On April 21, 1861, the Scotts artillerists were mustered in United States service as Company F, 5th Regiment of Pennsylvania Volunteers.

The volunteer soldiers dressed in civilian clothes and, despite no military experience, were marched to the state arsenal at Harrisburg and issued old, worn-out smoothbore muskets. Each man was issued twenty rounds of ball and cartridges but, having no accoutrements such as cartridge boxes, belts and percussion cap pouches, the men were required to carry the ammunition loosely in their pockets.

On the evening of April 21, the men boarded a train and were moved in the direction of Baltimore. But during the night, orders were changed and the regiment was returned to Harrisburg. This time their orders were to proceed to Philadelphia, where they arrived on April 22. The next morning the regiment moved to Perryville by rail and then by steamboat to Annapolis, Maryland. The men remained in Annapolis performing guard duty. On April 26 the regiment marched to Annapolis Junction and were put in a rudimentary position in the hope that they could defend Baltimore in case of an attack by advancing Rebel units. The regiment remained in this area until May 9. On May 7, the men finally received their state uniforms consisting of a blue four-button sack coat and dark blue trousers. The men from Schuylkill Haven performed mostly provost and guard duty for their remaining time on active duty. On July 25 the regiment was ordered back to Harrisburg, where it was mustered out and the men returned home to Schuylkill Haven.

On the return of the men of the 5th Regiment to Schuylkill Haven, Lieutenant Daniel F. Burket, late of the 5th Regiment, opened up a recruiting station at the town hall and began actively recruiting volunteers from Schuylkill Haven and the surrounding communities to serve for three years. After recruiting ninety-four men,

Burket organized and put the men in military formation and marched them to the railroad station. They traveled to Camp Curtin in Harrisburg and were immediately assigned as Company C, 50th Pennsylvania Volunteer Infantry, with Daniel Burket as their captain, under the command of thirty-nine-year-old Colonel Benjamin C. Christ, a resident of nearby Minersville and former Schuylkill County sheriff.

Throughout the entire war, Company C was an almost all–Schuylkill Haven company. Also in the 50th Pennsylvania was another company from Schuylkill County, Company A, composed of men from Minersville and the surrounding area of western Schuylkill County. Company I also included a number of men from Schuylkill County.

Nearly half of the men who enlisted in Company C were boatmen and canal workers. There were three types of boatmen that worked the canal: a river boatman, who usually carried coal to Philadelphia and remained in the Philadelphia area to winter over; the company boatman, who worked directly for the canal company and whose boat and a team of mules were supplied by the company; and the individual boatman, who also worked directly for the canal company but owned his own boat and team of mules. Most of the men of Company C were individual boatmen. Among the boatmen from Schuylkill County in Company C were Captain Charles E. Brown, an individual boatman who rose from private to captain in command of Company C, and Corporal Henry Hill, the two men in the company who earned the Medal of Honor for heroic feats during the war.

Not all of the men in Company C listed as boatmen came from Schuylkill Haven. Some lived in Pottsville and the surrounding area and others lived throughout Berks County. The men who worked the canal and captained the boats were well known for their toughness—they were used to hard work and exposure to inclement weather. They were well versed in how to defend themselves against river thieves that tried to steal their goods. The traits these tough river men or boatmen brought to Company C would see them through the hard and troubled times ahead.

Company C of the 50th Regiment was in thirty-six regular battles during its enlistment. During the siege at Petersburg the boys were under constant fire day and night. Captain Charles E. Brown was quoted in the *Schuylkill Haven Call* newspaper in 1916 as saying of his company, "We had a fine company of soldiers when we went to the battlefield in 1861 as ever listed in an army and our losses were great. There were many interesting things that happened to this company during the war. With all the narrow escapes I experienced, God was surely merciful to me, that I am here in the world today."

Corporal John Doudle, who served from August 14, 1861, to June 3, 1865, on the battlefield and in Andersonville prison wrote of his company: "I cannot go without giving the boys of Company C, and also the regiment, my heartfelt thanks, as they were as brave a set of boys as ever trod upon southern soil. And I hope when us few survivors that are left will explain the hardships and what we endured on many a weary march on the battlefield, or in the prison pen, and to our children let it be handed down to our children's children, that, when we are laid to rest, they will be awake to their duty and trust, and see that our graves will be kept green."

As Captain Joseph Levan, veteran of this proud regiment, stated, the story of the 50th Pennsylvania is

> A story of daring, bravery, death and sorrow, pain and suffering, enduring courage without a parallel. A story of gallant comrades, falling beneath the hard blows of the enemy, how the sounds of columns, the sound of the bugle above the roar of the cannon, the shouts of the boys, the charge sweeping like whirl wind, the flank movements sometimes routed and sometimes compelled to retire. Seeing those long lines of gray and solid columns of blue, hearing the booming of the big guns, the rush of the artillery, the rattle of the musketry, and the sharp crack of the skirmisher. Those long and weary marches, through snow and rain over muddy and dusty roads. How we rallied at the word of command, and again and again faced that brave and skillful foe. There is one debt the Government can never pay, that is the debt of gratitude it owes its soldiers.

In distances traveled, in the variety of service and in the extremes of heat and cold to which they were subjected, it may be doubted whether any other organizations of Pennsylvania troops equaled or approached the 50th Pennsylvania Veteran Volunteer Infantry. The total number of miles traveled by this regiment on rail, foot and water amounted to over twelve thousand, according to statistics gathered on the Civil War.

In 1916 Captain Charles Brown wrote the history of his time spent in the 50th PVVI for the *Schuylkill Haven Call* newspaper. Another version of the history of the boys of Company C was written by Corporal John Doudle of Schuylkill Haven, which was later published in the *Pottsville Daily Republican* in June of 1908. Included in his book is a narrative written by Lieutenant Colonel Samuel K. Schwenk, originally a lieutenant and captain of Company A, the other Schuylkill Country company, and a later member of the Field and Staff of the regiment. Schwenk provides an interesting narrative of the movements of the entire 50th Regiment from Second Bull Run to Antietam.

> *Author's Note*
> *In editing this work it was my wish to allow the reader to feel and read what the common soldier lived in his daily life in camp, combat and prison. It is a work written by the men who lived this experience; it is told their words, through letters home, personal narratives and official reports. This book is not another overview of the war by another Civil War historian. It is as if you were sitting on a porch listening to an old Civil War veteran reminisce about the war, his likes, his dislikes, his fears and memories of his comrades in arms who shared this great moment in his life.*

# A Brief History of Company C 50th Pennsylvania Veteran Volunteer Infantry

Company C of the 50th Regiment was recruited in Schuylkill Haven, Schuylkill County, Pennsylvania. Its organization took place on September 9, 1861, with Daniel F. Burket as the company commander. On October 2 the company went to Washington, and thence to Annapolis on October 9. On the nineteenth it sailed on transports for the Carolinas.

On the night of November 1, a gale was encountered off of Cape Hatteras and one of their vessels was saved from loss by the efforts of the men of Company C after the masts had been cut away, everything thrown overboard and the ship had been abandoned by the crew.

The company first encamped near Hilton Head, but on December 6 it went to Beaufort, where, on the night after arrival, it had its first fight with the rebels whom they helped drive from the island. On January 1, 1862, they were engaged in force for the first time at the battle of Coosaw, where a rebel fort was destroyed.

In the demonstration on Charleston in May 1862, Colonel Benjamin Christ with Company C, along with the regiment and some other troops of the brigade, went to Pocotaligo to burn the railroad bridge there. The only access to the place was a narrow causeway through a marsh and a bridge from which the plank had been removed. The bridge was not burned and a large force was drawn from Charleston.

In July the company was ordered to Fortress Monroe, and thence to the support of General John Pope in Virginia. It was engaged for two days at the battle of Second Bull Run, and the company suffered with two men killed, ten wounded and five missing. But the boys drove the enemy in every encounter. The company was severely shelled near Centreville and was also actively engaged in the battle of Chantilly. It was again engaged at South Mountain, Maryland, on September 14, and Antietam on September 17, 1862. At Fredericksburg the company was not actively engaged but witnessed the whole battle.

After General Ambrose Burnside was superseded in Virginia, the 50th went west and took part in the siege of Vicksburg, and after the fall of that place was with General William T. Sherman in his campaign to Jackson. In the action at Jackson, Lieutenant Colonel Thomas S. Brenholtz commanding the regiment was killed.

On August 10, 1863, the company returned to Kentucky and thence to Knoxville. The company was very short on men—in fact the whole regiment had only eighty men fit for duty, nearly all of whom were suffering from malaria. The rest were in hospitals. In October the company was sent with the corps to repel the invasion of east Tennessee. It saw minor action at this place. The company then went to aid in checking the advance of General James Longstreet from Chattanooga but was compelled to fall back with the regiment. The company fought hard at Campbell's Station where the enemy was held back for over seven hours.

On November 29 the company assisted in the defense of Fort Saunders and was skirmishing to the rear of the enemy after the siege was raised. While camping at Blaine's Crossroads, almost the entire company re-enlisted on January 1. Shortly thereafter the men were ordered to move to Nicholasville, a distance of two hundred miles, which was accomplished in ten days. The sufferings of the company on this march were almost unbearable.

After returning home to Schuylkill Haven for a short furlough the men returned to the field again in March 1864. On March 5 the company reached the field at the Wilderness, where it was once again engaged in heavy fighting and suffered heavy casualties killed, wounded and missing. The company was again engaged in battle at the Spotsylvania Court House, where it was involved in a charge with its brigade and carried the heights, once again suffering heavy losses. On March 20 they went to Annapolis, where their numbers were bolstered by recruitment.

For more than a month in the area around Petersburg, Virginia, the company was engaged in picket duty. On August 19 the company was engaged near Weldon Railroad. The company remained actively engaged all around the Petersburg area for the remainder of the year, then went into winter camp in November, where it remained till the spring of 1865. In April of 1865 the company was the first Union regiment to enter Petersburg. The company also participated in the ceremony of laying the cornerstone of the National Monument at Gettysburg, and finally returned home to Schuylkill Haven and was mustered out on June 6, 1865. Throughout its service the company suffered eleven men killed, twenty-five wounded and eleven men missing.

# 1861

*If anything happens to you, the United States will care for you.*

—*Colonel Welch, United States Army*

Since April 12 and the firing on Fort Sumter the patriotic spirit of the people of Schuylkill County was at a high pitch. Many units from around the county had already marched off to the seat of war. On April 15 President Lincoln issued the proclamation for troops, and in Pottsville the Washington Artillerists and the National Light Infantry immediately volunteered and marched off in the defense of the country. Two days later they were involved in a fracas while marching through Baltimore on their way to Washington. They, along with three other companies, earned the title of the "First Defenders" for being the first to arrive in the defense of the capital.

By April 24, over 1,850 men had left the county for the war. During this time, work continued for the many men who were still remaining at home. While many still held hope that this rebellion would end very soon, the patriotic fever was still high. Women organized aid societies, politicians gave motivational speeches. In every issue of the *Pottsville Miners' Journal* there was nothing but war news—who was serving, what regiments were being formed, news of far-off engagements with the Rebel forces. Then, on July 22, 1861, news arrived that the Union army had been defeated at Manassas Junction and people milled about the streets of Schuylkill Haven discussing this very disturbing news.

Just a few days later twenty-year-old Charles E. Brown found himself on his boat in the Schuylkill Canal. Brown had plied his trade of canal boating for about five years and at this time was captain of his own boat.

## Charles E. Brown, Civilian Boatman

Schuylkill Haven, Pennsylvania, July 1861

> One day in July 1861, I was lying in the canal in front of Charles Mecks store with my boat. I had just finished being loaded and I was washing it off when my friend Levi Eckert came along side and said, "Come on Brown, lets go and enlist." "Do you mean it?" I said. Levi said, "Sure!" I was barefooted at the time and I dropped my bucket and mop and jumped up on the shore and went up to the steps of the town hall. We both put our names down, we then commenced to drill outside of the building. While drilling they kept tramping on my bare feet so I quit, went back to the boat and got my stuff and was ready to drill the next day with my shoes on.

At the time of Brown's enlistment, Daniel Burket from Schuylkill Haven was raising a company to go off to war. All over the young country recruiting offices like the one in the town hall of Schuylkill Haven were set up. When Burket's company was filled to its quota they departed Schuylkill Haven and traveled to Harrisburg were they were assigned a regiment. All through the month of August men were recruited.

The recruiting process was the same in almost every town during the early portion of the war. Men such as Daniel Burket followed the procedure for mustering in a company. The new recruit would give his full name, age, height, weight, color of eyes, complexion and color of hair and he would either sign his name or make his mark on the initial mustering roll.

When Burket's regiment reached Harrisburg, they rendezvoused at Camp Curtin.

## Private Charles E. Brown

Camp Curtin, Harrisburg, Pennsylvania, September 1861

> In a few days we left Schuylkill Haven for Harrisburg, and were sent to Camp Curtin, and in a short time we found out that the barracks were full of all kinds of filth. In time we were put on camp guard when it was our turn. At one post the guard would hand you an old flintlock musket, all bent, then at the next post the guard would hand you just the barrel of the gun, and at the next post you would get only a big club. This is what we had to stand guard with at Camp Curtin.

On April 14, 1861, President Abraham Lincoln called for seventy-five thousand volunteers to come to the aid of the Union. In Pennsylvania, Governor Andrew Curtin called on the citizens of that state to enlist. Men and organized companies of militia from throughout the state arrived in Harrisburg and offered their services. It soon became apparent that a military camp would have to be organized to handle the thousands of men arriving in the area. The grounds of the Dauphin County Agricultural Society, located in the northern outlaying area of Harrisburg, were selected as the site for the camp. It was between Reel's Lane on the north, the Pennsylvania Railroad tracks on the east, Maclay Street on the south and Fifth Street on the west. On April 18, Major Joseph Knipe opened the camp and called it Camp Curtin.

Throughout the war years over three hundred thousand men passed through Camp Curtin. At the end of the war, the camp was used as a mustering-out point for thousands of troops on their way home. Camp Curtin was officially closed on November 11, 1865.

While at Camp Curtin a new recruit very quickly learned the rudiments of military training and life. He was instructed by the drill manual of the day, called the "School of the Soldier," teaching the fundamentals of close order drilling. He was taught to drill by the squad, company, battalion and regiment. The new recruit was also taught how to carry, load and fire a firearm—for many of the men this was their first encounter with a rifle or musket. The recruit would learn the workings of his company, how to march in columns, how to deploy in line of battle. He would begin to see who was a good soldier and who was to be avoided. He had his first look at his officers—the men who would lead him in combat, the men who would be responsible for him and his comrades.

While at Camp Curtin the men would receive their first uniforms, though because of the great influx of men to the camp many of the regiments were not fully equipped and the men drilled in the civilian clothes they arrived in. At some point the regiment was issued the standard uniform of the Union soldier: sky blue wool trousers, a dark blue four-button sack coat, leather army shoes, wool socks, cotton drawers and a muslin shirt. The soldier would be assigned to a line regiment. A regiment in the Union army consisted of ten companies, lettered A through K (the letter J was not used because it resembled the letter I too closely).

A full regiment included 1,025 officers and men. The Field and Staff of the regiment included the following men: one colonel, one lieutenant colonel, one major, one sergeant major, one quartermaster sergeant, one commissary sergeant, one adjutant, one quartermaster, one surgeon, two assistant surgeons, one chaplain, one hospital steward and two musicians. A standard company comprised one captain, one first lieutenant, one second lieutenant, one first sergeant, four sergeants, eight corporals, two musicians, one wagoner and eighty-two privates.

Throughout the month of August and into early September 1861, the 50th Pennsylvania Volunteer Infantry drilled regularly and on September 9, 1861, was mustered into Federal service. One of the first recruits from Schuylkill Haven who had enlisted in Daniel Burket's company was Private John Doudle.

## Private John Doudle

Camp Curtin, Harrisburg, Pennsylvania, September 1861

> On the 9th day of September, 1861 we were organized and mustered into the United States Service, for three years, with a bounty of one hundred dollars, at

the expiration of our term. The companies of the Fiftieth Regiment Pennsylvania Volunteers, were recruited as follows, A and C and part of I from Schuylkill County, B, E and part of H from Berks, D from Susquehanna, F from Lancaster, G and K from Bradford, part of H from Chester and part of I from Luzerne: by choice of the following field officers, Colonel Benjamin C. Christ, of Minersville, Schuylkill County; Lieutenant Colonel Thomas S. Brenholtz, of Berks county; Major Edward Overton, Of Towanda, Bradford County; Adjutant John A. Rodgers of Lancaster county; Quartermaster, Dr. Alfred Jones, of Schuylkill County; Surgeon, David J. McKibban, Schuylkill County; Asst. Surgeon, Joseph Vickers; Sgt. Major Henry Laub of Reading, Berks County; Hospital Steward Alexander Shaffer, Private of Company G.

On the first of October Andrew Curtin, governor of the state, presented the regiment a beautiful silk flag, which was received by Col. Christ, who returned to the authorities of the state his most grateful thanks, assuring the Governor that the confidence reposed in the men of the fiftieth regiment of it incentives to prompt duty, and that while there was a man left standing or an arm to be raised to strike a blow, that the flag would be borne aloft in defiance, and all foes that might assail it.

## Private Charles E. Brown

Camp Curtin, Harrisburg, Pennsylvania, September 1861

While at Camp Curtin our clothing began to give out, the state didn't have any to give us, so they secured some old rubbers for us and some military clothing. On the 9th day of September Colonel Welch mustered us into the United States service, and he said we would be paid in silver and gold. We were only paid once in silver and gold, and that was our first pay. At this time he also said, "If anything happens to you, the United States will care for you or any person depending on you."

On October 2, 1861, the regiment took the train at Harrisburg and went to Washington, D.C., and into camp at Kalarama Heights, overlooking the city. Kalarama Heights was in the northwest area of Washington, and at the time of the Civil War wealthy landowners built their homes there. It gave an excellent view of the city and of the Potomac River. Certainly an excellent place for a military camp. The first night the men were in camp a fierce storm came in, wrecking the camp and blowing down all the tents (which the men hadn't learned how to put back up yet).

Rudimentary things like learning how to set up tents would soon become a thing of the past for the regiment. While encamped on the Heights the men drilled, posted guards and were in the very process of learning the basics of military life. They learned basic military tactics—the same tactics used since the Mexican War in 1846.

On the first morning after their arrival a detail was made up for picket duty. After the guard was formed, Colonel Christ called the regiment together and delivered a stern counsel to the men on the dangers of carelessness and inattention to duty, also reciting the punishment for sleeping on post, as laid down in the manual. Corporal Doudle remembered Christ's warning as he pointed toward the sun, "As sure as yonder luminary shines; the picket found sleeping on his post will be shot."

On October 9, 1861, the regiment broke camp and returned to Washington, and then on to Annapolis, Maryland. Here it was quartered in the naval buildings along the bay until the eleventh. The regiment was then assigned to Brigadier General Isaac I. Stevens's brigade of Major General Thomas W. Sherman's corps. The regiment went into camp a short distance from the town, where it would remain until October 19. During their stay in the different camps the men drilled by regiment, company and squad, quickly learning the basics of an infantry regiment on the march, in the field and in combat. The officers and men had to quickly learn these skills. As the majority of the enlisted men were volunteers and had no prior service experience, nothing concerning military tactics or drill was familiar to them.

On October 14, 1861, Winfield Scott ordered Brigadier General Thomas W. Sherman to command the forces headed for the South Carolina expedition. Included in this plan were a naval blockade of the Southern ports and a recapture of the seacoast fortifications. Winfield Scott's sealed orders were:

> *HEADQUARTERS OF THE ARMY,*
> *Brig. Gen. THOMAS SHERMAN, Washington, October 14, 1861.*
> *U. S. Volunteers:*
> *Sir: You have been selected to command the land portion of a joint expedition with a naval squadron, and selected on account of its importance. A short letter of general instructions you have already received from the War Department, and are fully impressed with the principal objects of the expedition. Wishing to leave you a wide margin of discretion, I have but little to add, and that little relates to the principles which govern co-operation in joint expeditions. No land officer can be subjected in strictness to the orders of any sea officer until placed on ship to serve as a marine, and no sea officer under the orders of a land officer unless placed in some fortification to assist in its defense or before it to assist in its capture. But land troops embarked in vessels of war for transportation merely will be considered, in respect to naval commanders, as passengers, subject, of course, to the internal regulations of the vessel.*
>
> *Cordiality and deference on the part of our land forces towards those of our Navy in the service in question need scarcely to be urged. Hearty reciprocity cannot fail to be the result. To this end free and frequent conferences between the joint commanders are recommended. Accordingly the President, Commander-in-Chief of the Army and Navy, requires and expects*

*the most effective and cordial co-operation between the commanders of the expedition, their officers and men, and will hold all, in proportion to rank, to a strict and severe responsibility for any failure to preserve harmony and to secure all the objects of the joint expedition.*

*You will take care to maintain strict order and discipline among your troops, not to neglect opportunities of making the prescribed returns to the Adjutant-General, and to report to him every incident of importance that may occur to your command.*

*I am, with great respect,*
*WINFIELD SCOTT.*

On the midmorning of October 19 the 50th Pennsylvania marched to the wharf and commenced to embark on steamers tied up to the pier. Companies A, B, C, D and E, under the command of Colonel Christ, embarked on the steamer *Winfield Scott*. Companies F, G, H and K, under the command of Lieutenant Colonel T.S. Brenholtz, embarked with the 100th Pennsylvania Volunteer Regiment on the *Ocean Queen*. The vessels shoved off and set sail for Hampton Roads, Virginia. Arriving there on the twenty-ninth, the vessels dropped anchor and waited in the harbor until the following day. On the night of October 30, under the command of Commodore Samuel F. DuPont and General Thomas Sherman, the fleet weighed anchor and put out to sea. The fleet consisted of fifty-one vessels and moved out in three columns. More than 12,500 men were involved in this combined effort. Sailing under sealed orders, the men knew nothing of their destination. With just over three weeks of military training and service the boys were embarking on their great adventure and moving deep into Rebel territory. The trip out to sea would be a memorable one for these boatmen from Schuylkill Haven.

## Private Charles E. Brown

At Sea, October 1861

We sailed in three columns. The transports were in the middle and the *Wabash* was our flagship, she was a three decker and had nothing on her but old style pop guns. There were between fifty and one hundred vessels in the fleet. We had all kinds of vessels. We had side-wheel tug boats, old ferry, and double-end boats. The latter were built to go up narrow streams to bring cotton and come down again without turning around.

We struck the Gulf Stream and ran into a terrible storm, and then every vessel had to take care of herself. I learned that we lost half of our fleet. Our ship had eight feet of water, we had no fire or steam, and started drifting helplessly in the ocean. We threw over board everything that was loose. We even cut down the masts to try and save the ship.

The gunboat *Bienville* came to us and tried to get us off, but she only got a few off then gave it up. The mate then made a speech to us and told us he had been in three wrecks before this but none as bad as this one, but if we would all obey him he would save us. Then by his good management and Captain Burket, of Schuylkill Haven, the water in the hold was taken by use of hogsheads. Then we got up steam. It then developed that we had a Rebel Captain and he tried to run away from the gunboat and take us to Charleston harbor and there surrender us to the Rebels. However, the gunboat *Bienville* fired several solid shots across our bow, causing us to stop.

## Private John Doudle

At Sea, October 1861

A beautiful scene was presented on the morning of the 31st as the sun shone brilliantly out over the world of water, which seemed to be ag tated by some unseen poyer, one moment down in the hollow between two great waves.

On the 1st of November, while rounding the Cape Hatteras, the *Winfield Scott* sprung a leak. She was a light structure and was not sea worthy and was built to run from Philadelphia to Boston, but was chartered buy the Government to carry the troops. The Gulf Stream was too much for her. Little did we know while on board of her and in mid ocean that there was eight or ten feet of water in her hold. Until we were informed of the fact, and which we soon found out, we got barrels and rigged them by ropes and pulleys and put a barrel down in all the hatchways, and by two men going down and filling them and then the men on deck hoisted them up and dumped them overboard. We cut down our masts and threw our muskets and tents, wood, coal and provisions overboard. We did this to lighten the vessel. So we worked this way for two days; when the *Bienville* came to us, they thought we were a Rebel blockade-runner, when the Captain of our vessel spoke through his trumpet and told him who we were. They thought to rescue us from the *Scott*, but it was impossible to do so, as the sea was running mountains high. We tied ropes around our waists, in case we were thrown overboard and [they] could rescue us with lines. The two vessels came together several times and several of our men caught hold of the rigging of the *Bienville* and landed safe on her decks. The Captains of the two vessels came to the conclusion that coming together would injure our vessels and towed us into Hilton Head or Port Royal, S.C.

These are the names of the men who got over on the *Bienville* during the storm: Elias Berger, James Saylor, and the first mate of our vessel. Lieut. H.S. Rush had his wife on our vessel going south for the betterment of her health. The sailors launched a small boat and landed her safe on the *Bienville*. Berger and

Saylor were from Company C. The first mate was put in irons, and when we landed at Port Royal he was dishonorably discharged from the United States service for deserting his vessel in time of danger.

It is interesting to note that the saving of the vessel came about through the efforts of Captain D.F. Burket, of Schuylkill Haven, himself a canal boatman with years of experience. Because of Burket, and no doubt many of the 50th canal boatmen, the *Winfield Scott* was saved.

The steamer *Winfield Scott* was 182 feet long with a 31-foot beam, 49 feet wide and had three 42-inch boilers. Her cabin could hold eighty-four passengers. She was, as Doudle said, unfit for sea duty, especially in the notorious Cape Hatteras area of the Atlantic.

The USS *Bienville* that attempted to rescue the troops from the *Scott* was a 1,558-ton side-wheel steamer, 253 feet long with an armament of eight 32-pounders. She was built in 1861.

As the fleet arrived off the coast of South Carolina at Port Royal, General Sherman wrote his report to Winfield Scott. Taken from the official records is part of General Sherman's report of the initial stages of the expedition.

> *Reports of Brig. Gen. Thomas TV. Sherman, U.S.A.*
> *HEADQUARTERS EXPEDITIONARY CORPS,*
> *Port Royal, S. C., November 8, 1861.*
> *SIR: I have the honor to report that the force under my command embarked at Annapolis, Md., on the 21st October, and arrived at Hampton Roads, Va., on the 22d. In consequence of the delay in the arrival of some of our transports and the unfavorable state of the weather the fleet was unable to set out for the Southern coast until the 29th, when, under convoy of a naval squadron, in command of Commodore DuPont, and after the most mature consideration of the objects of the expedition by that flag-officer and myself; it was agreed to first reduce any works that might be found at Port Royal, S.C., and thus open the finest harbor on the coast that exists south of Hatteras. It was calculated to reach Port Royal in five days at most, but in consequence of adverse winds and a perilous storm on the day and night of the 1st November the fleet arrived at Port Royal bar not till the 4th, and then but in part, for it had been almost entirely dispersed by the gale, and the vessels have been straggling in up to this date. The transport steamers Union, Belvidere, Osceola and Peerless have not arrived. Two of them are known to be lost, and it is probable that all are. It is gratifying, however, to say that none of the troop transports connected with the land forces were lost, though the Winfield Scott had to sacrifice her whole cargo and the Roanoke a portion of her cargo to save the lives of the regiments on board. The former will be unable to again put to sea. The vessels connected with the naval portion of the fleet have also suffered much and some have been lost.*

Arriving at Port Royal on the fourth of November, the troop transport waited for the orders to land their troops. Waiting onboard the *Scott*, the men of the $50^{th}$ watched the preparations for a landing.

## Private Charles E. Brown

Port Royal, South Carolina, November 1861

We are on the ocean outside of Hilton Head. The fleet is coming from every direction and are all gathering here. The armored vessels are getting ready to bombard Hilton Head. The vessels begin bombarding the Rebel forts on both sides of the harbor. The vessels were going around in a ring and when they got opposite a fort they would fire a broadside and then move on. We are lying out in the ocean watching the bombardment.

It was fine to watch this bombardment and still finer to watch the surrender of the Rebels. The marines were landed and took possession of the forts. The transports then steamed into the harbor and the soldiers were landed. As soon as we left our ship they ran her on a sand bar with a full head of steam and abandoned her. The Captain of our vessel they took north and placed him in prison.

## Private John Doudle

Port Royal, South Carolina, November 1861

The fleet commanded by Commodore Dupont consisted of fifty vessels of which two transports were lost and a great deal of damage done to the fleet and their cargoes. Not with standing the storm having dispersed the fleet, one vessel after another began to come into the harbor of Port Royal. On November $3^{rd}$, in the afternoon, five Rebel gunboats boldly steamed down the bay, and attacked the gunboats of Dupont's fleet, but after an hours shelling, Commodore Tatnall, of the Rebel fleet was glad to fly back again, faster than he came forth! On the following Thursday about seven o'clock or there about, a clear calm morning the *Wabash* and several other gunboats were busily at work shelling not only the Rebel gunboats but also the batteries on the shore. At 2 o'clock P.M. the Rebels were in utter rout and spiking their guns, and in an hours time the stars and stripes floated on Fort Walker. As the emblem of liberty was run up the flagstaff, shout after shout burst from the soldiers and sailors who had witnessed the combat. The troops landed on the Island and we were employed in building breastworks and doing picket duty.

The $50^{th}$ remained at Port Royal until December 6, when they received orders to take a steamer and go to Beaufort to take possession of the island. That night the boys of Company C would "see the elephant," soldier slang for being in combat. Company C suffered its first casualty, Private Jacob Guertler, a boatman from Schuylkill Haven, but he was not seriously wounded.

## Private John Doudle

Beaufort, South Carolina, December 1861

> We were sent by steamer to Beaufort S.C. to take possession of the Island. When we arrived at night, pickets were thrown out under the command of Captain J.B. Brandt of Company A, and marched about two miles from the town, on a place called the Shell road. They met a squad of Rebel cavalry with which a short engagement took place, wounding a Captain Barnwell of the Rebel Army and Jacob Getler [Guertler] of our Company C. We then proceeded to Port Royal Ferry and to different parts of the island to do picket duty, which was the principal work we did while on the island.

In a letter written to the *Pottsville Miners' Journal* Corporal Robert Bechtel of Company C from Schuylkill Haven, the acting company clerk, informed the readers of the whereabouts of the 50th regiment and Company C and of their first engagement with the enemy.

## Corporal Robert Bechtel

Beaufort, South Carolina, December 20, 1861

> Editors, *Miners' Journal:*
> I suppose it will prove quite interesting to our Schuylkill County friends to hear how our Pennsylvania troops are progressing here. We left Hilton Head on the 6th of this month, for Beaufort, and arrived here that same evening, on the Steamer *Ben Duford.* We immediately sent out picket guards. They got about two miles out of town when they met some Rebel cavalry. The Rebels no sooner saw them than they wheeled around crying with an oath. "Turn back, here are the Yankees" and fled. Our boys fired on them but they succeeded in shooting the Rebel captain through the shoulders. The Rebels fired one pistol shot, which took effect in the shoulder of Jacob Guertler, of Schuylkill Haven. The ball just passed through the skin. It therefore did him no harm whatever, not even as much as to excuse him from drill the next day. The picket guard was sent out under the command of Captain Burket of Co. C 50th Pa. Rgt. They again fell in with some Rebels. The Rebels fired upon them and fled. They however, did not succeed in hurting any of our boys. The third day the whole regiment marched out to have a brush with the cowards; but we could not find one on the whole Island, as there has not been one on it since. I do not think that there will be any on it again in a hurry, until they become good Union men.

The town of Beaufort is, I suppose, one of the finest little places in the south, and was chiefly inhabited by wealthy persons, who have plantations in the neighboring country. It has some fine houses in it, and by going through them one can readily tell that they were owned by persons who were in easy circumstances. They have left a large part of their furniture behind and other things, which came very handy to our soldiers. It would indeed do our Schuylkill County friends' hearts good to walk through our camp and see the tents, for there are a great many of them equal to some of our Schuylkill County parlors. Why we think we have a badly furnished tent. If we have no Scotch carpet, three or four cushioned chairs, a sofa, a looking glass, a few oil paintings, a pile of food, books etc. Indeed I do not think that there are many soldiers who wish to be home.

Our regiment with the New York 79th Highlanders are out at the ferry, waiting for a good chance, and the first thing the Rebels still know will be on the mainland. The other day a Company of the Michigan 8th went over and took six of the Rebel pickets prisoner, without losing a man. We also took six prisoners on Lady's Island just opposite this. Our Colonel Christ had quite a conversation with some Rebel officers, (for one can speak across the river). They asked the Colonel if we would come over and take supper with them. Our Colonel replied that we had not eaten all the turkeys and chickens on this Island yet, but as soon as we had we would come over and eat what they had.

There is no more news of any importance at present, but you will hear from us soon again.

Corp. R. Bechtel
Co. C 50th Pa. Regt. 3d Brigade, Sherman's Division.
Expeditionary Corps, Beaufort, S.C.

## Private Charles E. Brown

Beaufort, South Carolina, December 1861

A few days after we landed, preparations were made to go to Beaufort, South Carolina, and take Beaufort Island. We landed and drove the Rebels off the island. We had but one man wounded. We were about eight or nine months on this island but we had plenty to do. We went over to the main land many times and we tried to cut off the Charleston and Savannah railroad, but never succeeded in doing this. At Gardner's Corner they got in our rear and we had a hard time to get it back. We had lots of trouble while we were there. Lieutenant Brumm was our first lieut. He received orders from General Stevens to go over to Gardner's Corner about four or five miles from the river and find out how many Rebels were there. He picked me and a man from Lebanon [George Friestein] and a negro for a guide and we started before daylight, stole across the river and that evening we came in sight of their picket post, two cavalry men. Our Negro guide became excited and ran, and the cavalrymen mounted and rode to Gardner's Corner. They then came after us, but it was night and we went into the marsh. That evening Lieut. Brumm went into their camp and secured the information we were after. We then started home and it took us two nights and two days to get back across the river. We had to remain in the marsh day and night as they were hunting us with a Company of cavalrymen. When we got to camp we were so full of wood ticks that you could not put your finger between them.

## Private John Doudle

Beaufort, South Carolina, December 1861

On December 9th, three companies under command of Lieut. Col. Brenholtz moved out the Shell road. Company A was left at the fork of the Shell and Seabrook road, while a half dozen were posted on the causeway to observe the enemy's movement. Soon after, six or eight shots were fired by the enemy and an effort was made by them to burn a house on the end of the causeway. Companies E and K advanced to the ferry and commenced firing at the Rebels, while Lieutenant Ransom's Battery opened fire upon the enemy's Breastworks and drove them away on the opposite side of the river. As the enemy had control of the flat boats in which they would come occasionally and rob our picket posts, two men out of Company K volunteered to swim over the river and capture and bring back the boats on our side, which they did, when a man on horseback came galloping down on the Rebel side holding a flag of truce in his hand. Lieutenant Col. Brenholtz had a long conversation with him, but as it does not amount to much, I will not relate it. But it was ascertained afterwards that the object of the flag of truce was to gain time to take Captain Barnwell, who had been wounded by our pickets, to a place of safety. While on Beaufort Island we were continually on the run, as there would be reports coming into headquarters that the enemy was preparing to land on the island, or that they were on it and driving our pickets from their posts, and when the troops would go out, there would be nothing about it. But never the less it was our duty to be on the alert at all times, as we knew that we were in the enemy's country.

On December 11th the enemy was discovered throwing up breastworks on the opposite side of the river near the ferry. A messenger was at once sent to General Stevens who immediately ordered the Regiment, the Battery and the Seventy-Ninth New York to the ferry, where they arrived on the morning of the 12th. The batteries opened fire and drove them away, and a small force went over to discover the enemy's position. They were obliged to beat a hasty retreat, as they were in considerable force.

On the 14th Lt. Col Brenhotz and Lieut. Kellog and four men of Company K started in a small boat to the sound the channel with a few of ascertaining whether and to what extent it had been obstructed. They found the channel clear and a depth of from fourteen feet of water except at one point about two miles north of the ferry the enemy had driven spikes and sunk some logs, the obstruction extending about twenty feet into the channel. They found the channel of sufficient width for large boats to pass through.

On the 21st of December the portion of the regiment that had been placed under the command of Lieut. Col. Brenholtz and stationed at the ferry was relieved and ordered back to Beaufort, and on Christmas day the soldiers got up a ball on the regimental camp ground, and invitations were issued to the officers. A violin, drum and three brass horns were the instruments used, and the officers and soldiers tripped the light fantastic toe.

## Captain D.F. Burket

Beaufort, South Carolina, December 27, 1861

Editors *Miners' Journal:*

You cannot imagine how happy we are when the Journal arrives in camp, for the boys all love to read your valuable paper. My Company is in good health. I have only lost two men, Swartz and Halhn both of whom died at Fortress Monroe, before we left for the great expedition to Hilton Head, S.C. I am happy to say that my men are always ready when called on. We were in the advance on this Island to Port Royal Ferry, but had not advanced more than three miles when we were fired upon and were compelled to send for reinforcements. On their arrival, General Stevens and Col. Christ, with 800 of his men, and two pieces of artillery, soon drove the Rebels from the island. The next day we marched back again and laid here some ten days, when we were ordered to march in double quick time too the Ferry. When we arrived at the Ferry, the Union gunboat *Mayflower* passed us, and at the same time the Rebels opened a tremendous fire on her. The shells flew over our heads, all too high, the boys stood like statues, ready to obey the commands of their beloved colonel.

Yours. Capt. D.F. Burket

P.S. Jacob Guertler was wounded during the advance, but is well again.

## Corporal R. Bechtel

Beaufort, South Carolina, December 30, 1861

[To the *Pottsville Miners' Journal*]

Christmas was duly celebrated at this place, and I am sure soldiers never have enjoyed themselves more than the members of the Pennsylvania Fiftieth did on this occasion. About 10 o'clock in the forenoon, the following notice was posted on a pole: "Grand Military Ball, to be held on Parade Ground of the Fiftieth this afternoon, at 2 o'clock.The band of the New York 79th Highland Regt., will be present, also a string band. Floor Manager, Capt. Deale. Assistants, Capt. Burket, Capt Harmon, Capt. Telfoird, Capt. Buzzard, Capt. Brant, Capt. Dolanias, Capt. Ingram, Capt. Parker and Capt. Dimock. All Lieutenants are invited, and the Col and all other field officers, non commissioned officers and privates are also earnestly requested to be present at the grand entertainment."This caused a little excitement, and before 1 o'clock the ground was crowded with soldiers. At 2 o'clock the band arrived, and the grand march was played.There were of course, no ladies present, and therefore, some of the gentlemen had to personate the ladies.The fun was indeed glorious. At 4'oclock, one of the boys managed to get a black lady up to the ring. We had to do considerable coaxing before we could get her to dance. She finally, concluded that she would take a step. We asked her what tune she would like. She said that she could dance a Highland fling, "wid any culered pussions in de town of Beaufort."The band struck up, and she began her dance, I tell you she brought those "Mud Hooks" of hers down the right way. You can't imagine the faces of the boys.They were one grin, and remained so until she stopped. Champagne bottles were handled quite freely, during the occasion, but no body was drunk everything passed off pleasantly, and by 9 o'clock that night, every soldier was enjoying sweet repose. So ended Christmas day among the soldiers of General Stevens Brigade at Beaufort South Carolina.

There is no news of any importance at present. We will soon receive our new uniforms, which consist of a dress coat, light blue pants and an infantry cap. The regiment is enjoying good health.There are very few in the hospital. As for our Colonel, there is not another one in the service who is loved more by his men than Colonel Christ, and I believe that the 50th regiment is as well drilled as any other in the field. You may depend upon it that the 50th is going to work its way through, as long as they have Colonel Christ at their head. You will hear from us soon again.

As the year 1861 came to a close, the boys of Company C looked back proudly at their time from muster through their campaigning in South Carolina. The regiment was in good spirits. The 50th was one of the healthiest regiments on duty in the Carolinas after 114 days of service since being mustered. Other regiments in the division had many men reporting daily for sick call, while C Company had few or none reporting.

On the last day of the year the regiment was called out on dress parade and listened as Colonel Benjamin C. Christ ordered the men to fill their haversacks with rations enough for forty-eight hours, clean and put their weapons in order and be prepared to fall out at midnight. Fateful 1862 was just hours away.

# 1862

*Honor and shame from no condition rise; act well your part, there all the honor lies.*
—*Pottsville Miners' Journal*

As the New Year rolled in, the 50th Pennsylvania and the boys of Company C were still on Beaufort Island awaiting orders to move. At five o'clock on the afternoon of January 1 the regiment formed up in columns of companies and set out on the march. Over the next couple of hours, the boys would fight in the first battle of 1862, recorded in the regiment's history as the "Fight at the Coosaw River," but also known as the battle of Port Royal Ferry.

## Corporal Robert Bechtel

January 1, 1862

We marched out about 7 miles towards the ferry, where we laid until 3 o'clock in the morning, when we marched out to the ferry brick yard. We there embarked in flat boats to cross over to the main land, there being already two regiments over there belonging to our Brigade, the New York 79th Highlanders and the Michigan 8th. As soon as our regiment landed the Brigade advanced, under our Patriotic General Isaac I. Stevens, each regiment being formed in line of battle. We had not marched out more than a quarter of a mile before the General sent Company A of the Michigan 8th in deploy as skirmishers while the rest of us marched in opposite directions, the Rebels firing into us with a masked battery just as hard as they could pelt. We dodged the shells as best as we could, and the cowards only succeeded in wounding two men. We marched up near the fort that we had taken from them, and there rested for a few minutes, at the same time watching the actions of the Michigan skirmishers. I tell you they are brave boys. They moved forward and crept up until they could see the whites of the Rebels eyes. They then gave three cheers and fired, killing a great many of the Rebels. The first five companies of our regiment were next ordered ahead. We proceeded toward the woods; halted and sent out some skirmishers. We were then ordered to fall back and let the gunboats shell the Rebels out. But the order was countermanded and we advanced a little further ahead and halted. At the same moment we received word that a large body of Rebels was advancing. Col. Christ immediately sent out a squad of skirmishers to reconnoiter. They were not gone long, before they returned and reported it to be true. We then advanced at the double quick until we got within reach of them. We halted and fired a volley of musketry, killing a great many of them. At the same time we heard the great pivot guns of the *Pembina* and the *Ottawa* roar, landing two shells in the midst of them. Such a sight I never beheld before, it was indeed horrible. The air was full of hands, feet, legs and heads etc. flying about. One could see anything but a whole man. Even the horses turned summersaults. Those two shells did great execution. How many men were killed by them, we cannot say but the number must have been great. They then retreated in bad order. Col. Christ was anxious to follow them but the General thought it not best to do so, for fear they might have some more masked batteries back in the woods. The Rebels then sent a man in with a flag of truce and asked permission to bury their dead. The General gave them one hour to bury their dead and bring back a man whom they had shot and taken prisoner, he being one of the skirmishers belonging to Company A of the Michigan regiment. They immediately brought back the prisoner and commenced to bury their dead. They were burying over an hour, and hauled two cart loads away, and left some five or six laying on the field. Among them was one who was wounded very badly, but who was still living. The surgeons asked his name and where he was from, He said his name was Vallandingham, and he was first cousin of Congressman Vallandingham, of Ohio. The surgeons told him he could not live over an hour or so. They then asked him the strength of the Rebels, but he would not tell them. We then marched down to the fort and rested for the night. We took from the Rebels a few guns, one of them a large siege gun. We also captured all the ammunition they had in the fort. They had the siege gun spiked, but we un-spiked it in a half an hour. We then took it over the ferry, and sent it down to Beaufort. When our surgeons were out hunting up the dead and wounded, the cowardly Rebels fired on our red flag, which is the hospital flag. This angered our General and he told them if they did not immediately leave he would cut them to pieces. To revenge himself for the act which they had done, he ordered us to burn every house that was there and soon every house was in flames, Having done all that we were ordered, we started back again for Beaufort. General Sherman only ordered us to drive the enemy from the fort, but we now have driven them back as far as we wish for the present and have taken their fort, guns, horses, cows and ammunition.

January 2, 1862

> But we must now leave the effects of the battle to tell you of our brave colonel, for I can tell you with an honest heart, there is not a braver officer fighting for the Union. He never says go, and just following and he knows at all times what he is doing. He did not seem to care about the Rebel firing, than he would mind so many boys firing at us with pop guns. When the General sent us out to attack the enemy on their right he halted saying, "Boys we could not have got into a nicer little arrangement, and if you only obey the commands rightly, we will come out all right. I am not afraid of your spunk; the only trouble I have is to keep you back." The captains of the gunboats said they never saw such fellows like us. They said the shells they fired at the enemy were just as liable to kill us as the enemy. They said they never saw men so eager to get into a fight as we were, and that Col. Christ and his Regiment would wade through hell, if they thought they could find any secessionists there.
>
> This is all I can tell you about the battle, but you can rely on this, that there was only one killed and eight wounded on our side. We have not yet found out what exactly the number was on the Rebel side, but it was great, we can let you know in a few days.

The fight at the Coosaw River was the first large-scale action in which the boys were engaged and the memories of this fight were something to write home about. It seems the horrible devastation of the Rebel force by gunfire from the gunboats remained vivid in the minds of the men. Private James Saylor, another canal boatman from Schuylkill Haven, wrote this engrossing letter to the editor of the *Pottsville Miners' Journal.*

## Private James Saylor

Beaufort, South Carolina, January 2, 1862

> On Christmas we had a ball in the Beaufort Arsenal Hall, and the boys enjoyed it very much. After that we had drill pretty much all the time. On the evening of the 31st, we got orders to march to the Ferry with 48 hours rations in our haversacks; canteens full of water. The Colonel said "I don't want any man who can't go ten miles, without resting." We marched out, and laid on our arms until 3 o'clock in the morning, when we marched down to the brick yard about five miles distant, where we were to cross to the main land. About 10 o'clock our boats came to take us across. We got over without any trouble and I stood on the main land of South Carolina. However we did not stand long before we were formed into line of battle. Our forces consisted of the N.Y. 79th, Penna. 90th, Michigan 8th, Penna. Roundheads, N.Y. 47th and 48th in all six regiments number about 5,000 men all told. We were on the advance, the 79th first and the 50th next. We had not gone far, before we smelt something warm. The Rebels had masked a battery and we had to march under the fore of their guns. It was anything but pleasant. I have heard C [Col. Benjamin

C. Christ]. our leader say how he used to dodge the balls in Mexico. Some of the men got down on all fours sometimes, for shells flew like hail among us. Strange to say, none were hurt by the shelling. It seemed as though there was some power that protected us through the battle. You may judge what was expected, when the Brigade surgeon had orders to have quarters ready for seven hundred wounded men. However we did not know until we got back to camp. Our loss was five killed and wounded. That of the Rebels we cannot ascertained [*sic*]. We saw legs and arms flying in all directions. The gunboats were shelling them at the same time. As we had no battery with us we could not advance. I believe it was not the intention to follow them, but to destroy the fortifications, which they were erecting.

The 50th regiment acted bravely. The General and the Commodore say they never saw men stand shelling like ours did. You may think I am giving ourselves to much praise; but I don't say more than is actually true. We charged on a body of infantry and the way things did fly was cautious. We got possession of the fort and captured one large gun. They ran and let it behind. It was spiked, but we soon had it all right and it is now in Beaufort. We also got a lot of ammunition, some horses, destroyed all the works and burned the buildings. After the battle we sent out our litter for the dead and wounded, and the Rebels fired upon us again. They afterwards sent in a flag of truce to get their dead and the General gave them one hour to do it in. They could not however bury all the dead in time or haul them away, so we buried some of them the next day. After destroying everything we could we retired in good order and are in camp once more. We did not lose a single man of our regiment. The Michigan regiment lost the most, and all honor to those brave boys, for braver men never existed.

A friend of Colonel Christ's sent a copy of the colonel's official report of the battle to the *Pottsville Miners' Journal*.

*THE BATTLE OF PORT ROYAL, S.C.*
*Official report of Colonel Benjamin C. Christ commanding the 50th Regiment of Pennsylvania Volunteers.*
*Beaufort, S.C., January 2, 1862.*
*SIR:*
*I respectfully submit the following: According to Special Orders, No. —, I left our encampment at Beaufort at 5.30 O'clock p.m. December 31, 1861, with four companies of my command, viz, C, B, F, and K, and proceeded along the shell road in the direction of Port Royal Ferry to the cross-roads, where I was joined by Companies A and H. We then proceeded along the shell road to the 6-mile post, where we bivouacked until 2.30 o'clock a.m. January, 1862, when I again took up my line of march, under the direction*

*of a guide, to a point on Coosaw Creek. From this latter point I was ordered by the general commanding to a point called the Brick-yard, on the upper end of Port Royal Island, and as soon as boats were furnished me to push across Coosaw River and land at the Adams house, where I arrived at 12.30 p. m., and immediately formed a junction with Companies A, B, and I, under command of Lieutenant Colonel Brenholtz, who had reached this point from Beaufort by boats. The whole regiment then took their position in the center of the brigade, and proceeded with it under heavy cannonading of the enemy over a narrow causeway and along a road leading to the fort at Port Royal Ferry. When within three-quarters of a mile of the fort I was ordered to move with the right wing of my command (I was on the enemy's right, with a view to support Colonel Fenton, of the Eighth Michigan, who was gallantly leading his command in the face of a battery on the enemy's left. I accordingly moved forward, taking them) Precaution to throw out small skirmishing parties, the better to watch the movements of the enemy and to guard against surprise. After moving forward about 300 yards my advance was fired upon by the enemy from a wood on our left. I called in my skirmishers, and immediately put my command on a double-quick until within good musket range, when I discovered from 400 to 500 of the enemy forming line of battle and evidently preparing to give us a warm reception. I, however, anticipated his movement; amid before his line was completed mine was formed and ready for action. I immediately commenced firing, I believe with telling effect, for at the third volley the enemy broke and beat a hasty retreat towards the woods.*

*I again rapidly pushed forward, with a view to cut off his retreat and prevent a junction with the main body, when I was arrested in my further progress by shells from our gunboats, which now came pouring in among them, making sad havoc in their already decimated ranks. After firing one more volley at their broken and disordered ranks we retired about 200 yards out of range of the gunboats, and were subsequently ordered to take a position near the fort, where we bivouacked for the night, and to-day, January 2, re-crossed the Coosaw, and reached our encampment at 5 o'clock p.m.*

*Although the whole of my command were within range of the enemy's cannon for a half hour and a portion of them within 100 yards of a detachment of his* [the enemy's] *infantry, and for some time sustained a heavy fire, I have no killed to report and none wounded save M. Werdenhammer, of Company B, a slight wound on the right foot, and Ensign Herbert, wounded in the leg by a spent piece of shell.*

*I cannot close this report without expressing my decided approbation of the conduct of the officers and men of my command—to the officers for anticipating almost every order, thereby rendering my portion of the work comparatively easy and to the men for their strict attention and prompt compliance with every command.*

*All of which is respectfully submitted.*

*B.C. CHRIST, Colonel, Commanding Fiftieth Regiment*

*Pennsylvania Volunteers.*

Upon the return of the regiment to their camp, Colonel Christ gave his congratulations to the officers and men of his command. Corporal Robert Bechtel recollected the speech.

## Corporal Robert Bechtel

Near Port Royal, January 3, 1862

"Men of the fiftieth: I congratulate you on your safe return to camp. I suppose you will be astonished when I tell you that the Brigade Surgeon received orders to have accommodations for over 700 wounded. (The eyes of the soldiers looked very big as the Colonel said this.) I also congratulate myself on being so fortunate as to have command of this Regiment. We have received praise from high authorities and those persons who spoke ill of us cannot but speak well of us now. We have shown them that we are soldiers. I am satisfied that I have as good a set of men as ever volunteered to fight for their country. We also have the honor of being the men who first desecrated the sacred soil of South Carolina, by planting the Stars and Stripes again on it, and by being the men who planted that banner first on the mainland."

We then gave him three cheers, and the Colonel proposed three more for the Stars and Stripes. The Colonel then said, "I am now satisfied that I have brave men battle, and I know that they will stand by me as long as there is a man left. Attention Battalion, Shoulder Arms! Present Arms! Shoulder Arms! Order Arms! Parade Rest! Parade is dismissed." And the Colonel went to his quarters amid the cheers of his men.

## First Sergeant William H. Mennig

January 13, 1862

*[From the editor, Pottsville Miners' Journal]*

*The first part of this letter contains some structures in rather strong language, of parties in this county whom, it is alleged, by the writer, speak unkindly of the some of the volunteers. We assure the writer that the person who uses language derogatory in the honor or disinterestedness of our brave boys, now facing in the field the foes of the Republic, is not worthy of serious notice, especially in public print. We therefore, suppress that portion of our correspondent's letter, assuring him that.*

*"Honor and shame from no condition rise;*
*Act well your part, there all the honor lies"*

Editors, *Miners' Journal:*

We are all well here, and in good spirits; in fact the 50th I think is one of the healthiest regiments in the service. We have been in service now for five months and have but ten deaths in the regiment. While almost all companies in other regiments have from 15 to 20 men on their daily sick report, our report yesterday morning was sick, this numbering two.

We continue to receive the Journal weekly, for which we are all very thankful, as it seems like meeting an old friend. By the time the copies go the rounds of the Company, they are pretty well worn, in consequence of repeated handling.

## Private John Doudle

**Beaufort, South Carolina, January 1862**

The town of Beaufort is situated on an island and is a very pretty place. As we were informed, it was a summer resort for the aristocracy of the city of Charleston and vicinity. The distance from Beaufort to Port Royal Ferry is ten miles with a beautiful shell road. In it was a handsome church and jail, and in almost every house a piano. Some of the officers came to the conclusion that they would ship these pianos home to the north. And were in the act of shipping them home when on the vessel, when General I.I. Stevens was informed of the fact. He sent a detail and dumped them into the river.

As I said, Beaufort is a pleasant place and as we were informed, a summer resort. The town was evacuated with the exception of one man, and he took the oath of allegiance to the Federal Government and went into business, store keeping selling little necessary items to the soldiers. Capt. D.F. Burket raised the stars and stripes, the next morning when we landed, upon one of the buildings he gave a short address to the boys, informing us of the dangers we were in at the present moment not knowing how soon the enemy would come and drive us into the river or take us prisoner or take the town again. He congratulated the boys upon how nobly they repulsed the enemy the night before and the first blood that was spilt was from his Company C. while we were fixing our tents to make our selves more comfortable, the darkies came in from the plantations which they took procession of after the Rebels had fled. When the Union man of war *Wabash* made her appearance at Hilton Head, Tatnal's fleet having also skipped, they wanted to see the Yankees, and were all dressed up in their best as they termed it, but dear reader, you can imagine how they were clad being slaves, but I must say that they were mannerly, but ignorant in regard to money or education, and as jovial as a set of coons you never saw. They would sing, dance, clap their hands and enjoy themselves highly. Oysters were in abundance. They opened them and when the soldiers would teach them Uncle Sam's money they got soused to saying five cents that all the produce that they would bring into camp such as hoe cakes, or milk would be "Five Cents" Sir. Often the soldiers would take their hoe cakes away from them and pretend to break them and not pay them, they would say "If you don't tuk it don't brock it."

When we were on the island a few months they soon became intelligent and while we remained upon the island they knew how as much as we did and report us to headquarters for the least offense.

## The Fight at Pocotaligo Bridge

On May 29, 1862, General Stevens was ordered to join up with General David Hunter and make reconnaissance against Charleston. Colonel Christ and the 50th Pennsylvania, two companies of the 1st Massachusetts Cavalry and a small detachment of artillery were ordered to move to the mainland. Their orders were to march toward the railroad bridge at Pocotaligo and burn it.

The men left Beaufort in the early evening and crossed in the dimming light. Near old Pocotaligo, the enemy was waiting in strength. The men had to advance through a very marshy causeway along a narrow stream for almost a quarter of a mile. The men could not cross the bridge spanning the stream because the Rebels had removed the planks. It became apparent that the only way to dislodge the enemy was by fording the stream. Heavy firing erupted and the only way to dislodge the enemy was by a frontal attack.

Captain Charles Parker, of Company H, 50th Pennsylvania, volunteered to charge across the bridge. He succeeded and Colonel Brenholtz of the 50th had the bridge re-planked; six companies crossed. The enemy fell back into a wooded area were the Massachusetts Cavalry could not operate. The infantry elements were too fatigued to keep on the pressure. The men were running out of ammunition, and the long delay had helped secure a stronger hold by the Rebels who were quickly reinforced. It was decided to fall back. In the attack, Captain Parker was killed. During the retreat back to Beaufort, the temperature was extremely high causing the men to suffer severe heat prostration. The expedition failed to attain its goal. The loss to the regiment was four killed and nine wounded.

## Private John Doudle

Pocotaligo, South Carolina, May–June 1862

On the 29th of May we received orders to have rations for twenty-four hours and each man to carry sixty rounds of cartridges; we were to move upon the main land and advance toward Pocotaligo and burn the railroad bridge, the distance being 24 miles from Beaufort, and between marching and fighting by the time we arrived at Pocotaligo the Rebels were well fortified and numerous. Also the place was very swampy, and narrow thoroughfares. We were not able to accomplish our object. We skirmished with the enemy for several hours, and not successful; we then returned to Beaufort. Small detachments of the enemy's cavalry followed us as far as Gardners Corner. We met a detachment of the 8th Michigan Volunteers and a detachment of the 79th New York Volunteers, who had been ordered out as a reserve. As soon as we reached the ferry we commenced to cross over. We arrived at the ferry about eleven o'clock. And about three of four we were all on this side of the Coosaw. During the engagement the regiment lost two killed and nine wounded. What the enemy's loss was I am unable to say. We captured two prisoners, one of them being wounded. In our Company Jacob Herbst was wounded. Scouting parities would cross the Coosaw River and destroy Rebel property, and ascertain the enemy's strength, which often resulted in daring results. Between drilling and doing picket duty, and running to the ferry every now and then, we had our hands full.

One day orders came to detail six men out of each Company to go over to Lady's Island. A small Island opposite Beaufort, as there was an abundance of everything, such as cattle, hogs, horses, turkeys, chickens etc. I and Charles E. Brown, Elias Berger, Samuel Losch, Alex Garret and Stoughten Kieghnor were chosen. We remained on the island for a few weeks and lived very high, we had our roast turkeys everyday, and had a fine horse to ride, and lived in high style. Uncle Sam's rations were no place alongside of the living, and we enjoyed it highly.

## Colonel Benjamin C. Christ

Pocotaligo, South Carolina, May 29, 1862

From the Official Records

DEAR GENERAL: After a spirited engagement, which lasted two hours, we succeeded in driving the enemy from their cover, and the cavalry is now in full pursuit. We have 2 killed and 5 wounded. I regret to say that Captain Parker is one of the killed. We will proceed at once to the railroad. The battery has just arrived. We should have some ambulances to bring our dead and wounded.

Yours, respectfully,<br>
B.C. CHRIST,<br>
Colonel, Fiftieth Pennsylvania Volunteers<br>
General STEVENS, Beaufort, S.C.

P. S.—I have just learned from a wounded prisoner that their loss is severe and that their force was at least 800.

Pocotaligo, May 29, 1862

SIR: Upon investigation I find that the men have not over 12 rounds of cartridges on the average. I also learn from Negroes that the desperate stand made by the enemy at this point was in the expectation of reinforcements from Grahamville and McPhersouville. At the latter place it is said they have 600, and they expected a larger force from the former.

After consulting with the officers, and in view of your orders to avoid a general engagement, I have considered discretion the better part of valor, and leave 2.30 o'clock for Beaufort.

Yours,
B. C. CHRIST

Beaufort, South Carolina, May 30, 1862

SIR: In pursuance to orders I left Beaufort at 10.30 o'clock on the evening of the 28th with my regiment and one Company of the Eighth Michigan Volunteers, Captain Doyle, and one Company of the Seventy-ninth New York Volunteers, Captain Elliott, and proceeded to Port Royal Ferry. We succeeded in getting on the main-land by daylight, and immediately took up my line of march for Pocotaligo via Garden's Corners. About 2 miles from the ferry we commenced driving in the enemy's pickets, and did so three times before we reached Garden's Corners. At this point I left Company E, Lieutenant Lantz commanding, and at this point also Major Higginson, First Massachusetts Cavalry, reported to me with 80 men and horses. I again took up my line of march for Pocotaligo via the Sheldon road, and save the driving in of the enemy's pickets several times, which caused us considerable delay, we reached Pocotaligo without further interruption.

Here the enemy had chosen a most favorable position, and we suffered the casualties (which I will mention hereafter) in a successful effort to dislodge him. As you reach Pocotaligo, you do so over a causeway about a quarter of a mile in length, flanked partly on either side by a marsh, and through which passes a stream. About 80 yards from the end of the causeway over this stream was a bridge about 15 feet wide, which the enemy had so far destroyed as to make it impassable save by passing over a the string pieces, about 6 inches wide. On the opposite side of the marsh from Pocotaligo there is a narrow strip of woods. Through this we skirmished, and then ascertained that the enemy was posted under cover of trees and ditches within good rifle-range on either side of the causeway. Some small firing now ensued with very little effect on either side. It however became evident that in order to dislodge the enemy we must have a nearer range for our arms, and the lamented Captain Parker then volunteered to take his Company across the stream on the string pieces and let them drop into a ditch on our right, where they would be partially under cover. This movement was successful.

After some considerable time I succeeded in passing over about 300 men, under command of Lieutenant-Colonel Brenholtz, who gradually approached the opposite side of the marsh and succeeded in dislodging the enemy on our right, which was followed by a charge on the left, when the enemy commenced a rapid retreat to the woods. As soon as it could be done I had the bridge re-laid, and immediately ordered the cavalry in pursuit, but the enemy having taken refuge in a wood where cavalry could not operate successfully I had to pursue him with infantry, but unfortunately the men were so jaded and worn-out with their long march of 24 miles that they could not pursue him as rapidly as he retreated.

At this time Lieutenant Cannon, with a section of the Connecticut battery, reported himself, having just arrived on the ground. In my judgment, if the artillery had been on the ground when the action commenced we could have dislodged the enemy in a very short time and proceeded to accomplish the object of the expedition; but the action itself lasted nearly two hours, and by the time I could recall the companies in pursuit of the enemy and again get ready to move more than three hours had elapsed; besides, the men had so much reduced their ammunition that I was not willing to risk another engagement, which I had every reason to expect awaited me at the railroad to where the enemy had retreated, and, as I had been informed by the negroes, they were sure to meet re-enforcements from McPhersonville and Grahamville.

In view of the positive orders I received to return to Port Royal Island during the night, and to avoid, if possible, bringing on a general engagement, and with reduced ammunition, I deemed it prudent to retire, and accordingly arrived at Port Royal Ferry at 11 o'clock p. m. Small detachments of cavalry followed us as far as Garden's Corners, when the outer pickets of Company E repulsed them by unhorsing one of their number. At Garden's Corners I met a detachment of the Eighth Michigan Regiment, Lieutenant-Colonel Graves commanding, and a detachment of the Seventy-ninth New York, to cross over, and by 3 o'clock [morning] the entire force was on this side the Coosaw River.

Our loss during the engagement was 2 killed and 9 wounded, for details of which I respectfully refer you to the accompanying report of Dr. Siemens, regimental surgeon. What the enemy's loss is it is difficult to say, but from all I can learn it must be much greater than ours. We captured 2 prisoners, one of which I have already sent to head-quarters, and the other is in the hospital, wounded. It is also difficult to state the force of the enemy, but it could not have been less than from 600 to 800. There were six companies of mounted riflemen, besides infantry, among which were a considerable number of colored men. Among the killed is Capt. Charles A. Parker, Company H, who fell while gallantly cheering his men to duty.

Before leaving Pocotaligo I had the bridge over that river destroyed. My object in this was that in any future expedition to this point it would prevent the enemy from cutting off our retreat by sending forces from Grahamnville.

I regret to state that on yesterday morning, near Stewart's plantation, Lieutenant Rush, Company B, was dangerously wounded by the accidental discharge of his pistol.

I cannot speak too highly of the conduct of both officers and men under my command. They proved themselves soldiers not only in name but in deed. I gratefully acknowledge the assistance of Colonel Brenholtz Major Overton, and Adjutant Rodgers, of the Fiftieth Pennsylvania Volunteers; Major Higginson, of the First Massachusetts Cavalry, and of Lieutenant Lyons, aide-de-camp to Gereral Stevens.

All of, which is respectfully submitted.

B.C. CHRIST,

Colonel, Commanding Fiftieth Regiment Pa. Vols.

On July 10, 1862, the regiment received orders to move north. The men regretted leaving their pleasant camp at Beaufort. The regiment formed up and marched to Hilton Head. Here they were sent north to Newport News, Virginia. On July 28 the men boarded a small steamer called the *Merrimac*. According to Charles Brown, "the *Merrimac* brought us North, and we had a better time going than coming," referring to the regiment's trip south, back in October of 1861.

The regiment was ordered to Fortress Monroe and was incorporated into the 9th Corps under General Ambrose Burnside. Burnside had just returned from a successful campaign in North Carolina.

## Private John Doudle

Newport News, Virginia, July 1862

On the 10th of July, 1862 we left our pleasant camp at Beaufort, S.C. and proceeded north, arriving at Newport News, Va. On the 12th, where it encamped and was assigned to the Second Brigade, First Division of the Ninth Army Corps. Our Colonel B.C. Christ was appointed Brigade Commander. Company and Regimental drill were constantly kept up until the 28th, when we were put on the steamer *Merrimac* and conveyed to Aquia Creek, Va. where we arrived on the 30th, taking cars for Falmouth. Here we encamped until the 2nd of August, when we were transferred to the other side of the river, [Rappahannock] and encamped on St. Mary's Heights.

## First Sergeant William H Mennig

Near Fredericksburg, Virginia, August 9, 1862

Editors, *Miners' Journal:*

...We left our camping ground at Newport News on the 3d inst. Went on board of the new steam transport *Merrimac*, and on the same evening ran out to Fortress Monroe, where we anchored until the next afternoon when we weighed anchor and steamed up the Chesapeake Bay. By daylight next morning we had made the mouth of the Potomac River, up which we turned and that same evening arrived at Aquia Creek where we again came to anchor. Here we landed the next day [August 6] and in the afternoon of the same day took the cars for Fredericksburg, where we are now.

Fredericksburg is on the banks of the Rappahannock River, distant some 65 miles from Washington via the Potomac River, and about 160 miles from Richmond. I cannot tell you much about the town as I have not been in it, and cannot go there, although we are only about one mile off, and can see the tops of the houses over a little hill and across the river to our right.

When we first came here a party of our boys went out one night on a scouting expedition. They did not go far before they met a party of seceders whom they immediately captured and drove into camp. Our commander however ordered them released and told the boys they were only poor unoffending inhabitants of the farms in this vicinity, and they were quite harmless. This did not quite suit our boys, and they determined at least to make them take the oath. But as they refused to do this, two [of] them were killed upon the spot. Our officers seeing that what was done could not be undone, determined to make the best of it, and ordered the boys to skin them, cut them up and the next morning we cooked them for our breakfast. But don't be alarmed, and turn palm, Messers. Editors nor think us cannibals, for they were no human beings of whom I have been writing, only steers.

Our brave Colonel is at present acting Brigadier General and General Stevens, former Brigadier, is acting Major General. I think he deserves promotion, for certainly is a good General and brave man.

Since writing the above we have crossed the Rappahannock, marched through the village of Fredericksburg and two miles over the hills (for this country is all hills) where we are now encamped. The town of Fredericksburg is [a] miserable, dirty, straggling place, and had before the war broke out a population of 800 whites, but like all other Southern towns of which the northern mudsills hold possession it is most deserted by its white inhabitants.

I do not know how long we will stay here, but undoubtedly not very long. Of course if we knew the exact time of our departure it would not do to write about it. For if I wrote it and you published it we would both be in Fort Warren or Fort Lafayette in double quick time, but this may write that we are all anxious for a move, which will bring us in contact with the enemy. We are all anxious for a chance to

"Strike! Till the last armed foe expires!
Strike! For our altars and our fires!
Strike! For the green graves of our sires,
God and native land!"

Glory Hallelujah! We have marching orders again, light marching, which almost always means something and so I must stop writing. Hip! Hip! Hurrah!!

## Private John Doudle

Marching in Virginia, August 1862

On the 13th we broke camp north of Fredericksburg, and marched through the town and crossed the Rappahannock below the railroad, and filed left through the town of Falmouth, and on to Culpepper Court House, thence to Raccoon Ford on the Rapidan where we remained until the 17th, then pulled out and fell back to the Rappahannock River. Every day seemed to have some slight skirmish in store for our forces, many which the regiment participated in, as at Kelly's ford on the Rappahannock, where companies D and H were cut off. However through the careful management of Captain G.Z. Dimock, who commanded the detachment, they succeeded in regaining our lines and joined the regiment after nearly a weeks absence.

On the first day after arriving in the Bull Run area, Colonel Christ's brigade was attached to Major General Carl Schurz's division of General Franz Siegel's corps. Shortly, the regiment would be engaged with the Rebels.

On August 28, 1862, Confederate Major General Thomas J. Jackson attacked Union forces under the command of Major General John Pope near the Warrenton Turnpike close to the old battlefield of Bull Run. The fighting lasted several hours at the Brawner Farm resulting in no gains for either side. On entering this engagement near Gainesville, Virginia, the following day, the men of the 50th Pennsylvania marched and sang in tune with the regimental drum corps to the tune of "The Red, White and Blue."

General Pope ordered attacks made against the Rebels positioned near an unfinished railroad cut. The attacks were severe and many casualties were suffered on both sides.

## Lieutenant Samuel K. Schwenk

From a Narrative Published in the *Pottsville Miners' Journal*, October 18, 1862

To relieve some of the fearful anxiety and painful suspense that must prevail respecting the conduct and safety of their friends in the army, I take advantage of this opportunity to inform them, through the columns of your paper, of the loss my regiment sustained, and the particulars of the several actions in which the regiment has been engaged. The account of our march and scouts along the Rappahannock to Manassas would probably prove more interesting to your readers than the realities of the same were to us; but other duties still prevent me from giving full details. Our Division under the late gallant Gen. Stevens marched from Fredericksburg, Va. on the morning of the 13th, ult; marched and counter marched guided by the enemy's movements, waded creeks and rivers; bivouacked in fields and woods, and after a series of tiresome days and nights, reached the famous and identified battlefield of Bull Run on Friday August, 29th, at 1 P.M. "Christ's Brigade" was immediately ordered forward through thick woods and took position in line of battle along the embankment of an unfinished railroad near the end of the woods. The enemy occupied a high hill in front between which and the woods was a deep ravine, about a thousand yards wide. The Skirmishers soon opened a brisk rifle fire "communication" with the enemy sharpshooters, some of whom were posted on high trees on the opposite hill, but in several instances were brought to the ground by the balls from our side. They laid there for over two hours, in the meantime the battle was raging furious like on the left. It was coming closer and more furious until about 5 P.M. when several regiments broke and fell back in confusion. The Rebels out flanked the 50th and in a minute's time were under heavy fire from both the front and rear. At this critical moment Colonel Christ rode along from the left flank and heroically ordered the whole line to advance over the bank. Every man simultaneously sprang up and fixed bayonets and off started the brigade lead by their brave commander Colonel Benjamin Christ. Through the woods below with a vociferous cheer that made the air vocal and the woods around reverberate. Reaching the foot of the hill, we "right flanked" and marched to the rear around the edge of the woods. The brigade came out in good order but suffered a heavy loss, and after caring for the wounded we bivouacked on the field. The boys of Company C were fully involved in the fighting around Manassas and the major retreat of the Union Army. Firing continued along the lines till 9 P.M. when the Rebels were again driven through the field beyond the railroad, from the woods, and pressed hard by our forces on the heights beyond. Night and darkness impeded the further progress of our army.

## Private John Doudle

Marching in Virginia, August 1862

As we passed Manassas Junction on the 28th of August, every man seemed to feel as he looked upon the forms of dead Rebels lying here and there, that the time for action had come. Passing along one of the elevations adjacent to Bull Run, the contest at Gainesville could be distinctly heard. In a few hours afterward the regiment entered the engagement, and the day ended with the following casualties: Killed Jerry Boles Co. K, Wounded Ira, A. Tomkins, private of Company G.

Bull Run, Virginia, August 1862

August 29th the regiment again entered the battle, the contest being severe, the regiment lost 4 men killed, 15 men wounded and 5 captured. Company C lost Henry Northrup who was killed and George Schwenk and George Simpson wounded, Henry Deibler and Jacob Guertler were captured.

In the second day's fight at Bull Run, the regiment had a smaller number of casualties but the fighting was harder, according to Captain Dimock. During the engagement Brigadier General Stevens's brigade drove the Rebels back very quickly. At this point in the fight, the men in Company C thought they had secured a victory. General Stevens ordered Colonel Christ to front his men toward the enemy coming out of the woods. Colonel Christ set his brigade at rest, also thinking they had just secured a victory. Early in the evening with the fading light, Colonel Christ was given a warning to get his brigade out of the area immediately. Both wings of the army were driven back, leaving Christ's brigade in the center of a developing horseshoe. The brigade made a quick retreat.

On August 30, General Longstreet arrived on the field and attacked, completely crushing the Union left and driving them back over Bull Run, nearly causing another disaster like the one that had occurred at Manassas in 1861.

## Corporal Charles Brown

Bull Run, Virginia, August 1862

We began our retreat and had to fight and retreat at the same time. Lee was after us with his entire army. I saw General Pope in his shirt sleeves helping to build the road to get our cannon and wagons over so we could retreat back to Thoroughfare Gap. There we held them for a few days and then General Poe had orders to fall back on the first Bull Run battle ground and there make a stand. McClellan's army was supposed to come up and help. The battle began on August 29th, 1862, and on the following day it ended. None of McClellan's troops came to help us. It was the hardest fought battle and biggest loss of men I was ever in. Pope's entire army was destroyed. General Pope was the best general I ever fought under. I saw him on the battle line every half hour during the two days fight, encouraging his men.

## Private John Doudle
Chantilly, Virginia, September 1862

The regiment was again engaged on the 30th of August. We advanced into a wood where we attacked the Rebels, when a severe engagement took place. The 50th composed part of General Reno's command. We drove them from their position, but about dusk the Rebels massed their columns, and advanced upon our troops with overwhelming force, and drove us from the field. Our losses in the regiment on this day were 4 killed, 14 wounded and 6 captured. In Company C we lost, Killed, George Hiney, Wounded, Jonas W. Krammer, Darius Milberg, Franklin Wise, Edward Mariand, Franklin Fox, Captured Edward Marian, Adam Schwenk. When our forces were driven from the field at Bull Run, very little rest we received that night. And besides our wagon trains were in danger of being captured by the enemy. On the 31st a heavy storm set in, but Jackson pushed forward toward Fairfax to turn the Union right. Pope sent McDowell, Heintselman and Reno in that direction to attack about the 2nd of September. But the heads of the two forces came in contact just before dark on the 1st of September. Stevens Brigade was first attacked. The 50th regiment, being in advance, was one of the first engaged. During the engagement rain descended in a deluge. The thunder was deafening. After a short engagement the enemy fled from the field.

Our troops marched about a mile into a field, and started large fires, thinking we would remain for the night and renew the battle the next morning, being as [we] were drenched to the skin by the heavy rains of the previous evening we received orders to in about an hours time to fall into line, and off we started marching all night, arriving at Fairfax early the next morning.

The Company wounded during this engagement at Chantilly were Private Garett Kerrigan, Private Peter Paul, Private John Martin, Private Frank Sharon, and Private Samuel Hoffman. When we arrived at Fairfax Courthouse we rested for a few hours, when the line of march was again taken up, arriving at Alexandria on the 2nd and resting for a few days, and then we proceeded to Washington City.

## Lieutenant Colonel Samuel K. Schwenk
Bull Run, Virginia, 1862

On Saturday morning August 30th, the thrilling roar of artillery and clamorous volleys of musketry wakened the weary soldier at an early hour it answered all the purpose of "reveille" and the sound was much louder and more distinct. The cannonading was severe at intervals, the enemy replying with heavy rifled pieces until 2 o'clock, when the infantry fire was again commenced, and soon became general and fierce along the right. We were held in reserve, changing position, till

> late in the afternoon. A line advanced in the centre through the wood in which the enemy had a battery and a large force of infantry, and was driven back in disorder, coming on to us. Our brigade now marched forward in splendid style, with a yell and fearless of the enemy's ruinous fire, advanced about ½ mile, halted, and returned rapid and destructive volleys, which soon sent back the Rebels over the same ground they had driven our troops not long before. After it got dark, we knew we were entirely surrounded. The battle was continued hot and bloody till the enemy forced McDowell's left, he was on our left, and the left of the army through the woods. We were ordered to retire, and marched off the field to the rear of the batteries stationed on the heights, cannonading the woods and plains to the left. This was at five o'clock. The enemy now came through the edge of the woods on our left, advancing into open space, but was mowed down column after column and driven back into the woods, by the murderous showers of grape and canister from all the batteries stationed on the heights commanding the plains. The battle now became general along the whole line. The artillery fairly shook the country about, and its accurate shots proved fatal to many a Rebel. The battlefield presented a scene of carnage and pity. The dead and wounded in great numbers were scattered over the ground. We rested several hours behind the batteries, waiting for ammunition, but none could be procured. All this time we were under a severe fire from the Rebel artillery, and about 8 o'clock a volley of musketry was poured into our ranks and we had no cartridges for a return fire, which caused momentary confusion, but the men soon rallied and fell back to Centerville Heights.

As the Union forces fell back from Bull Run, General Jackson made a wide flanking march in the hope of cutting off their retreat. On September 1, Jackson sent his men against the divisions of Major General Philip Kearny and Major General Isaac Stevens at the Chantilly Plantation near Ox Hill. Rain poured down on the troops, drenching them to the bone. With the crash of thunder above and blinding lightning all around them, the boys were caught in a fierce fight.

## Lieutenant Colonel Samuel K. Schwenk

Bull Run, Virginia, August 1862

> All was quiet during the night, and Sunday morning dawned on the weary and unmolested lines of both armies. We were again in the advance, where Stevens commonly was, but did not become engaged. The batteries which we supported exchanged a few random shots with the enemy, which was all that disturbed the tranquility of the day. In the evening we were relived by fresh troops, and marched back to Centerville, where we had a goods night rest.

On Monday morning information was received at Centerville that Rebels were appearing on our right in force to capture our supply trains and cut off communications between the army and Washington. To prevent the effect of this design, Reno's command was ordered to Fairfax Court House to reconnoiter and drive back the enemy. Steven's Division was in the advance, and while cautiously pursuing its line of march, and examine . .the woods to the right and left was fired upon by the Rebels who were concealed in the woods. Stevens immediately drew up his command in battle array to repel the attack of the enemy now hid in the thick woods and cornfields. Christ's Brigade was on the left, and marched steadily forward, while the enemy kept up a brisk fire from the woods wounding many of our men. But fearless of the bullets that came whistling around our heads like a hail storm, the line advanced bold and determined, and upon reaching the crest of the hill in front of the woods, opened a destructive fire, pouring swift and ruinous volleys into the Rebel ranks, which soon forced them to retire.

After driving the enemy out of the cornfield to the left of the woods, we advanced into a ravine in the center of the field, continuing to fire till all our ammunition (50 rounds) was exhausted. There being no troops to relive us, and two regiments on the right breaking in disorder, Col. Brenholtz gallantly ordered the 50th "to fix bayonet" and charge the Rebels out through the woods. This order was nobly responded to by the men, but the enemy hearing his stern command, and, as a prisoner had said, "afraid of the deadly weapons," fell back before we reached him with the bayonet. The battle lasted from four to eight o'clock through a heavy rainstorm of thunder and lighting, which caused a brief lull in the action. Our regiment held the enemy in check for about one hour without a cartridge, Kearney's troops took our place and we marched to the rear wet and tired, and rested on our laurels, which, on a cold night, was a poor substitute for a woolen blanket. In this fight General Stevens, the beloved hero, met his death while gallantly bearing in his own hands the colors of the 79th New York Regiment, trying to rally the men for a charge. Captain Stevens, son of the General and acting Adjutant General of the division, was also wounded in the arm. After General Stevens was killed, Col. Christ, acting Brigadier, assumed command of the Division, and nobly performed the important duties of a Major General. The enemy's loss was heavy in this fight. Their dead lay in furrows over the cornfield, where we sent the first volleys among them. Our loss in killed is slight, but we had many wounded. The next day we fell back toward Alexandria, and encamped two miles from that city.

## Corporal Charles Brown

Chantilly, Virginia, September 1862

> We commenced to build our fires to cook our coffee. But we are all mixed up! The Rebels are cooking their coffee on the same fire with our men. At about 10 o'clock everybody is asleep.
>
> I awakened five of our Company and told them to come along with me. We had to stay away from the road and get away and when we got to Bull Run it was not a big stream but just about six to eight feet in the earth. I took hold of a sapling and let myself down to the bottom and grasped some roots and then pulled myself up the other side. I said to my companions, "Come on, and get over." They refused and stated they would not go. I left them and they all died in the Rebel prison. I traveled through brush all night and into the morning. Next I was near our skirmish line. I lay behind the grave of a soldier that was killed in the first battle of Bull Run. It was not long until the Rebel skirmish line came into sight, but we held our ground and during the day I went back to Chantilly and there I found who in the regiment escaped from the battle.
>
> On the1st of September General Longstreet tried to get between us and Washington and cut off our retreat. Our army moved in front of him and the Battle of Chantilly commenced. We fought hard until in the night we lost a large number of men. We lost the two best Generals in the Army, General Stevens was shot with the colors of the of the 79th New York Highlanders in his hands. Then his son picked them up and he was shot, but he recovered. When the battle was over General Carney [Kearny] was putting pickets out and he rode in the Rebel lines and they shot him. General Longstreet sent a man over to tell us he had General Carney in his lines, that he was dead and we should send someone over to bring him back. We brought his body to our side, placed it in an ambulance and sent it to Washington. Generals Carney and Stevens were all in one class at West Point and were in the Mexican war together.

During the Battle of Chantilly, in a heavy thunderstorm and dangerous lightning strikes, General Isaac Stevens, attempting to encourage the men of his old regiment, the 79th New York Highlanders, had grabbed the flag from a wounded color sergeant and held it high, shouting, "Highlanders, My Highlanders follow your General!" Along with the Highlanders, the 50th Pennsylvania and 28th Massachusetts charged forward. Through the heavy rain and loud thunderclaps and the roar of battle, the men moved forward. As the force reached a wooded area, General Stevens fell to the ground, still clutching the colors, with a musket ball in his head.

Union General Philip Kearny was also killed in the fight. General Pope ordered his forces to retreat toward Washington. With General Pope no longer a threat to the Confederate forces, General Robert E. Lee marched westward and up into Maryland.

## Corporal Charles Brown

In Camp Near Washington, D.C., September 1862

> Following the battle we built fires and pretended we were going to remain all night. Instead of this though we retreated for Washington as fast as possible, when daylight came the last of us was on our way to Washington. We camped for a few days around Washington. General McClellan was made Commander of the Army of the Potomac at this time and he re-organized the army.

During the battles of Second Bull Run and Chantilly, the 50th Pennsylvania regiment suffered its most casualties up to this point.

While in camp near Washington, D.C., Sergeant William H. Mennig wrote a very graphic letter to the *Pottsville Miners' Journal* detailing the work done by Company C and the fighting at Second Manassas.

## First Sergeant William H. Mennig

Near Washington, D.C., September 9, 1862

> Editors, *Miners' Journal:*
>
> During the last four weeks we have been continually on the move and have seen some lively times both on the march and on the field of battle. I will give you a short account of our experience. We left Fredericksburg on the 13th of August, and marched to Culpepper Court house where we stopped two days, and then came to a right about and went back to the Rappahannock River by a forced march or skedaddle. (If you can understand that better.) We arrived at Barnard's Ford on the Rappahannock, about 4 o'clock in the afternoon, but did not pause long on its banks. We started to ford the river as soon as we had divested ourselves of our shoes, and other clothing. We left the river some two miles in our rear, and then stopped for the night. The next day we proceeded up the river to a place called Mount Holly, and thence to Rappahannock Station. At the latter place we (that is our forces and the Rebels) had several days fighting, but as it was mostly artillery fighting across the river and at long range, of course the infantry did not get much show at them. One fine morning we left in disgust, and came on to Warrenton. From thence we proceeded to Manassas Junction and Bull Run, where we soon succeeded in picking up a fuss with Stonewall Jackson and his "Merry men." On Friday the 29th of August, we were marched down through thick woods, and at the bottom of the woods a kind of railroad embankment was thrown up the whole length of the woods. On the inside of the bank and on the side of the woods there was a ditch about four or five feet deep, and on the outside of the bank or railroad was a steep bank of about twenty

feet down into the level fields below. In the ditch on the inside of the embankment is the spot we were placed, and immediately sent skirmishers out in front of us. Our regiment laid here some two hours without seeing a Rebel, but all this time the fight was raging furiously on our left, and further up the woods. At last the bullets came whistling around our own ears, and it was soon ascertained that most of them came from our rear. The truth was some of the regiments on our left had broken, and the enemy had outflanked us and got in our rear. At the same time those in front of us had begun to show themselves putting us between the two fires. For a moment there was confusion, and I was afraid we were going to have a regular panic. The enemy in our rear we could not see any as they were in thick woods behind us, and those in our front would have been our match. At this moment Colonel Christ came galloping up and ordered the whole line to forward over the bank. The men thought they were to charge on the enemy in our front, and started with a cheer, fixing their bayonets as they went over the bank. Col. Christ's intention however was to pass around the point of the woods and thus get out from between the two fires which were pouring in upon us, and when we got down the hill or bank he gave the command to "right flank" but owing to the noise of musketry and the cheers of our own men, half of the men did not hear the command, [and] still thinking they were to charge on the Rebels ran up a considerable distance before they perceived their mistake. Our lines were broken, and we came out of the woods in anything but good military order. In this affair the loss of our Company was two men wounded.

We had nothing more to do on Friday and Saturday forenoon and part of the afternoon passed away without our getting in. We were beginning to think there was nothing for us to do for that day, when we were ordered to fall in. In less than it takes me to write it every man was in his place, and we moved down towards the same woods in which we had the fight the day previous. The Rebels had planted a battery there and we were to silence it. We advanced into the woods and after a few volleys succeeded in doing so. We however, were warmly opposed by a strong body of infantry and fought until our ammunition gave out. Then we fell back giving our place too fresh troops. This closed our second days fighting. In the evening the whole army fell back towards Centerville [*sic*], and on Sunday we laid on a hill about three quarters of a mile from that place. Nothing happened to us on this day with the exception of having a few shells thrown over our heads by the enemy, who had closely followed us up. Our artillery soon opened on them and silenced them. On Monday morning we fell back behind the village of Centerville and here we thought we would have several days rest, as we were completely worn out, but in the afternoon we again fell in and started for Fairfax. We did not go far before it was ascertained that a large body of Rebels was hovering around our baggage train, probably waiting for nightfall to make a dash and capture all or part of the train. So

General Stevens' Division to which we belong was ordered up to drive them back, and it was not long before we got a pop at them. We met them in the woods, and the 79th N.Y. Regt. Opened the ball. It did not take long for the "Old 50th" to get in and we poured it into them hot and heavy for about one hour, driving the enemy a distance of about two miles. Part of the time we were on one side of a corn field, and the enemy on the other, and the way we made the corn stalks fly between us was a caution. Our Company went into the fight with from 50 to 60 rounds of cartridges, and I do not think a man brought out more than two or three rounds. During the fight our battery fired shells directly over our heads and a shell bursting directly above us knocked down the flag bearer, slightly wounding him in the arm. We had advanced a considerable distance up in the corn field and were ordered to fall back to the fence out of danger from our own guns which gave rise I suppose to the story of the New York Tribune that one of the regiments in our division retreated and they blamed this division for General Stevens' death. The General was a brave old man and was beloved by his whole division who would have laid down his life for him. The same correspondent for the Tribune brags ups Kearney's Division and talks as if they had saved the day, while the truth is they did not get there until the fight was nearly or quite over. Far be it for me to detract anything from the well-earned laurels of the brave men of Kearney's Division. My opinion is that they are a brave body of men, but I say let justice be done to all. Kearney and Stevens both ost their lives in this fight. The nation lost two heroes and the army two brave and able commanders.

The loss of our Company in the last fight was five men wounded and our entire loss in the three days fight was ten wounded (one of which has since died) and five missing. The names of the wounded are as follows: George W. Hiney (who has since died), George Schwenk, Corporal Jonas Kremer, George Simpson, Peter Paul, Samuel Hoffman, Garrett Garrigan, Ben Knarr, Dennis Mellery, and John Martin. The names of the missing are Jacob Getler [Guertler], Charles Knarr, Franklin Wise, Edward Marland and Henry M. Deibler.

At present we are encamped on the outskirts of Washington City D.C. We will however not stay here for very long [as] we are under marching orders now. So good bye for the present, we are ready to go Whenever they want us.

The men mentioned in William Menning's letter who were missing were captured and sent behind Confederate lines, and in all probability marched south toward Richmond. Sometime in early October they were paroled and sent to Camp Parole in Annapolis. Here they would be exchanged for Confederate prisoners. Jacob Guertler was severely wounded in 1864. Charles Knarr, Edward Marland and Henry Diebler returned to the company and mustered out in 1865 with the rest of the regiment. Franklin Wise was exchanged, but he was wounded seriously and was discharged.

# September 1862

*"Col. Christ and his regiment would wade through hell, if they thought they could find any secessionists there."*

At eight o'clock on the morning of September 7, 1862, the boys of Company C broke down their tents, gathered their accoutrements and muskets, formed into columns of fours and took to the march. Marching nearly twelve hours the boys arrived at Leesborough, Maryland, and halted by seven that evening. Resting until six thirty on the morning of the ninth, the boys once again took up the march and moved to Brookville, Maryland, where they went into camp about two o'clock that afternoon. On the eleventh, getting up to an early reveille, the boys marched out toward New Market and encamped at Forer's Creek. Resting overnight they once again took up the march and arrived later in the day at Monocacy, about two miles from Fredrick Maryland. The next day, the boys marched to within one and a half miles of Middletown.

On September 14, the boys moved with the division to South Mountain, marching up the Boonsborough Road. Here they engaged the Rebels once again. The enemy was strong in force and held an important position along the top of the mountain. The Rebel artillery was placed in such a manner as to cover the road on which the 50th was advancing. The boys, in total defiance of the Rebel artillery, marched straight into the fire of grape and canister. They were determined to take this position at all costs. About noon, Colonel Christ's brigade, consisting of the 79th New York, 8th and 17th Michigan, 28th Massachusetts and the 50th Pennsylvania, was in the advance.

Their orders were to advance to the field on top of the mountain. While deploying, the brigade came under heavy fire, causing four of the regiments to break in confusion. The 50th gallantly held their ground. General Orlando B. Willcox placed the 50th in position, stating to Colonel Edward Overton, "Take the Fiftieth; it's better than two ordinary regiments."

The 17th Michigan was a new regiment and under all this fire was inspired by the steadfastness of the 50th. Under a rallying cry from their officers, the 17th drove the Rebels from behind a stone fence at the points of their bayonets.

The 50th was soon ordered to support the left flank of General Jacob D. Cox's forces and rallied in the woods to the left of the road. The remainder of the brigade moved farther to the right. After entering the woods, the boys of Company C lay down quietly while taking fire from the Rebel artillery. They waited in the woods for over one hour, watching as General Cox's division made several gallant charges through the woods, repulsing the enemy with great loss. The firing ceased about nine o'clock, when the Rebels were in full-scale retreat. The boys held their arms through the evening and into early Monday morning. Later that day the boys gathered up their equipment and marched up the mountain.

## Lieutenant Colonel Samuel K. Schwenk

Company A, Field and Staff, September 1862

> We crossed the Potomac, and after a repose of four days near Washington, the enemy's advance into Maryland required us to move in that direction. The Rebels had ventured as far as Monrovia, but retreated as our army approached, without the least display of their boasted "Southern Chivalry." At Monocacy River, near Fredrick City, they disputed our further advance. A brief artillery fight ensued, which resulted in a victory to our batteries and we crossed unmolested.

## Private John Doudle

On the March, September 1862

> After our arrival in Washington, the 50th regiment was placed in the First Brigade, First Division, Ninth Army Corps, with our Colonel Benjamin C. Christ commanding the brigade; General Wilcox commanding the Division. General J.L. Reno commanding the Corps. And A.E. Burnsides [*sic*], commanding the right wing of the Army of the Potomac.
>
> On the 3rd of September, with the Ninth Corps, the regiment moved out on the Seventh Street Road and encamped outside the line of the defenses of the city of Washington, where it remained for several days and then with the right wing of the Army of the Potomac marched on to Fredrick City and took an active part in the battles of South Mountain and Antietam.
>
> Judging by the loss sustained by the regiment in the engagement at South Mountain, September 14th, it might be supposed that it did little service, not a single man was killed and only two men were wounded in the regiment: Privates Henry Kline of Co. E and Partial Kennedy of Co. K.

## Lieutenant Colonel Samuel K. Schwenk

Company A, Field and Staff, On the March, September 1862

On Friday September the 12th in the evening the heads of the Union column passed through Fredrick City, capturing about 500 prisoners. To most of the citizens the appearance of our army seemed as a relief from the bondage. In many instances they showed acts of kindness and bursts of enthusiasm. And as we advanced driving the Rebel horde before us, the beautiful banner of our country, under whose folds millions have found a home was unfurled in the gentile breeze of "My Maryland." On Saturday night we crossed over the mountains into Middletown. On Sunday morning we reached South Mountain where the enemy in strong force held an advantageous position along the top of the mountain, having batteries placed so as to rake the road of our approach.

## Corporal Charles E. Brown

South Mountain, Maryland, September 1862

We then started for South Mountain, Maryland. As we got closer to South Mountain we could hear the guns they were using on the South Mountain.

## Private John Doudle

South Mountain, Maryland, September 1862

On the afternoon of the 15th, the regiment, with other troops of the Ninth Corps, assisted in burying the Rebel dead, which having fled they left them on the field, and we also buried our own dead, after which we were marched to what is known as the Rhorersville and Sharpsburg road towards Antietam Creek.

## Corporal Charles E. Brown

South Mountain, Maryland, September 1862

On September 15th 1862 we went up South Mountain. The shot and shell were flying in every direction. All of the Rebel batteries were directing their fire on the road. We went to the right of the road in order to avoid their shot and shell. We crept up to the top of the mountain and over the rocks and through the brush until we got close to the Rebels. We then lay down behind a stone fence and they turned their batteries on us. Their fire knocked the limbs from the trees and the limbs fell on us. We had to help one another to get out from under them. A Michigan regiment followed us up the Mountain. They had never been [in] action before and they came right up the road. I believe the Rebels killed half of them before they got to the top of the mountain. The balance of this regiment was brave and they went for the Rebels and drove them off the top of the mountain. By the time darkness came on, the battle was almost over. In this engagement we lost another Mexican General. His name was General Park and he was a very good one.

On the night of the 16th we put out pickets for the night and I am one of them. I am stationed in a thick wood and the dead and the wounded Rebels are lying [so] thick about me that I can hardly walk. When daylight came there were no Rebels about. We then followed the Rebels, we can hear loud cannonading in our front.

## Lieutenant Samuel K. Schwenk

Company A, Field and Staff, South Mountain, Maryland, September 16, 1862

Our men however, in defiance of the enemy's advantages, marched forward under fire of shell and grape and canister, determined to take the chosen position at all hazards. At about noon, Christ's Brigade, in the advance, consisting of the 79th New York, 8th and 17th Michigan, 28th Massachusetts and the 50th Pennsylvania Volunteer Regiments, were ordered to a field near the top of the mountain, and while deploying, the enemy opened their batteries upon us from the woods, at a short range, producing a tremendous storm of shell, grape and solid shot. The fire was murderous and perfectly terrible, causing four regiments to break in confusion, but the 50th regiment stood its ground, gallantly holding their ground, and as Burnside said, "Saved the day." The 17th Michigan, a new regiment, seeing our men stand, promptly rallied under a frightful fire, and afterwards fought and charged like veterans, driving the Rebels from behind the stone fences at the point of the bayonet. Col. Christ behaved nobly, and with his bold efforts soon reformed his brigade. Our regiment was then ordered to support the left flank of General Cox's forces in the woods to the left of the road, the remainder of the brigade going further to the right. After entering the woods we laid quietly and rested over an hour under the fire of the Rebel batteries. General Cox's Division made three gallant charges through the woods, repulsing the enemy with great slaughter. In a charge the 11th and 23rd Ohio regiments met the 11th and 23rd North Carolina regiments who fought desperately, but the "Ohio Numbers" were too good for the "North Carolina similar." The Rebels made several charges trying to turn our left flank and take a battery. They came up with boisterous cheers of "Hurrah," but the destructive volleys of Infantry and fatal shower of grape and canister that was poured among their ranks returned them groaning with at least a loss of half of their men. Firing ceased at 9 P.M. when the enemy was everywhere defeated and rapidly retreating. We remained in line, under arms till Monday morning when McClellan was in pursuit.

## Private John Doudle

South Mountain, Maryland, September 1862

On the night of the 16th of September we were put on picket duty, we occupied a position on the extreme left front of the Corps. On the morning of the 17th we had a fine view of the battle, though a few miles distant.

The regiment remained on picket duty the night of the sixteenth, with the Company C boys receiving sporadic fire through out the night. The enemy suffered heavy casualties and the dead and wounded Rebels were left lying all over the mountain. Returning to the first brigade and forming up, the boys moved out about seven o'clock on the morning of September 17. The 50th Pennsylvania pushed on toward Antietam Creek.

*From the Official Records, Concerning the Movements of the Division*
*September 17, 1862*
*The division marched to Antietam Creek, crossed to the west bank by the stone bridge, and took position on Rodman's right and on both sides of the road, toward Sharpsburg, and engaged the enemy at 5 P.M. Charged up the hill toward the village, broke the Rebel lines, driving them in confusion from their position opposite front, and held the position till ordered by General Burnside to fall back a short distance, holding the west bank of the Antietam, near a ford, and the road to the bridge.*

On Wednesday morning the fight commenced at daylight. The boys were under fire most of the morning. About one o'clock, the regiment crossed the Antietam and marched off to the right under the cover of a hill on the opposite side of the bridge. Christ's brigade now held the extreme right of Burnside's army. After resting for a short period of time, the brigade was ordered to advance.

The boys moved off into a hail of bullets and shell. They reached the top, gaining more ground than the left wing or the center wing, and had to halt and wait for the other wings to catch up. Colonel Christ, realizing what had happened, ordered his brigade to lie down. While lying on the ground the boys were subjected to some of the most horrible fire ever endured, but yet the boys stood it with a coolness of veterans. As the left came up, the command again was given to advance, and the brigade drove the Rebels out. The fight over for the 50th, the soldiers marched back behind the cover of the hill and bivouacked for the night. Captain Burket of Company C was wounded in the leg in this action.

## Lieutenant Samuel K. Schwenk

Company A, Field and Staff, Antietam, Maryland, September 17, 1862

> We left the battlefield of South Mountain and marched across the mountain, almost covered with dead and wounded Rebels on Monday afternoon. This was without a doubt one of the hardest blows the Rebels have been dealt since the beginning of the war. Gen. Garland from South Carolina was killed, and many other prominent officers were killed, wounded and taken prisoner. Devastation and carnage were soon broadcast through the woods and over the mountain; the dead lay in groups along the road which we traveled. On Tuesday Christ's Brigade was drawn up in battle array, and under artillery fire, but did not become engaged. On Wednesday Morning the fight commenced at daylight. We were under fire all forenoon; crossed the "Antietam" at 1 P.M. and advanced toward the right, under cover of the hill (there is high elevation on either side of the creek). Our brigade, commanded by Col. Christ, now held the extreme right of Burnside's army. After resting for a short time the whole line was ordered to advance. Col Christ, at the head of the brigade boldly carrying in his own hands the colors of "Virtue, Liberty and Independence," commanded his troops to forward and every man marched up that hill amidst the whistling of bullets and howling shells, with unflinching bravery. Reaching the top of the hill we had gained more ground than the left wing and the center, (Christ commanded the extreme right of Burnside's army) and had to halt and wait for them to come up. Christ ordered us to "Lie down" and here we lay in line flat upon the ground for about half and hour, under a horrible cross fire of shot, shell, grape and other missiles from the enemies batteries. Troops never passed through a more hazardous and ungracious ordeal with the same coolness that our men stood this awful fire. When the left came up we again drove the Rebels out of a cornfield and orchard completely routing them. We then marched back of the hill and bivouacked in line of battle for the night.
>
> On Thursday there was no engagement, but brisk skirmishing all day. Our companies were engaged in skirmishing with them from 7 A.M. to 6 P.M., firing rapidly all day. Every man behaved nobly, discharging up to two hundred rounds of cartridges. In the evening we were relieved by fresh troops and re-crossed the Antietam. On Friday the whole army advanced via Sharpsburg to the Iron

Works. The meritorious conduct of Acting General Christ, and the undaunted courage of Col. Brenholtz and brave actions of Major Overton shown on all occasions during battle, reflect honor upon our "Old Keystone State," and add another shinning wreath to the renowned garland already worn by the troops from Pennsylvania. And no troops have ever fought with more courageous determination, or displayed greater heroic valor, than the officers and men of the 50th Regiment, and yet the papers seem to pass them unnoticed.

## Corporal Charles E. Brown

**Antietam, Maryland, September 1862**

On September 17th we went into the battle of Antietam. We lost heavy in this battle and among the loss was our drummer boy Jere Helms. In this engagement Helms threw away his drum and took up a musket and charged with his comrades. He was shot through the head and died almost instantly. The Rebel army was almost knocked to pieces.

General Burnside told McClellan to give him five thousand fresh troops and he would drive the balance of Lee's army to the Potomac. McClellan refused to do so, and although he had thirty thousand troops on reserve they never fired a shot in the Battle of Antietam. McClellan stopped the battle and for two days we lay around and in the meantime Lee got his army over the Potomac and put them in good shape again.

## Private John Doudle

**Antietam, Maryland, September 1862**

Returning to the brigade during the morning we crossed the stone bridge and filed to the right, marching to the crest of a hill, where we formed ready for action.

Prostrated on the ground, at the crest of the hill we endured a severe fire from the enemy's artillery; in about an hour after forming, the command "Forward" was given. Though tired and exhausted having been on picket duty all night, we entered the battle with the greatest enthusiasm charging upon the enemy and driving them from their position. The engagement was short, but during that time our loss was killed Jeremiah Helms private, Augustus Berger private, Daniel McGlenn, private and Richard Fahl, private. The wounded in the Company were Jonathan Brennan, private, Jacob Helms, private John Graeff, private Frank Fenstermacher, private and Samuel Agley, private.

## First Sergeant William H. Mennig

September 20, 1862

> Editors, *Pottsville Miners' Journal:*
> My last letter you will remember was dated from Washington City, and was written a few days after the fight at Bull Run. Since then we have again done a little in the fighting line and I am happy to say we did better than we did at Bull Run, for the time we came off first beat and the Secesh party had to skedaddle. I will give you a list of the names of the killed and wounded of Company C in this regiment.
>
> Company C is commanded by Capt. Daniel Burket and was raised in Schuylkill Haven and vicinity. This Company was very lucky at South Mountain, as we did not lose a man. We however suffered severely in the late fight at Sharpsburg considering the time we were under fire. Our loss was 2 killed and 8 wounded. Killed was Richard Fahl, and Daniel McGlenn, Wounded was Augustus Berger who since has been reported as died, Jeremiah Helms shot in the head, Jonthan Branner, shot in the shoulder, Samuel Agley shot in the leg, John Graff shot in the face, Franklin Fenstermacher, shot in the shoulder and Jacob Hehn shot in the arm.

The $50^{th}$ remained in position until five o'clock on the afternoon of September 18, when the division was relieved and they fell back across the Antietam. The regiment recrossed the Antietam and marched toward the Potomac River and encamped within one mile of Shepherdstown.

## Corporal Charles E. Brown

Potomac River, September 1862

> We received orders to march. We marched down a road that crosses the Potomac River, when we got there we found the Rebels were well fortified on the other side. When we got to the river we found the rebels were fortified on the other side. When we came to the river front we found it was full of dead soldiers. The Philadelphia Exchange Regiment had attempted to cross the river. After they were in the river, they were fired upon by the Rebels From this event all the soldiers had their own opinion of McClellan.

The dead men referred to are members of the $118^{th}$ Regiment Pennsylvania Volunteers, also known as the Corn Exchange Regiment, who were raised in Philadelphia on July 27, 1862 by members of the Corn Exchange of Philadelphia. On September 12 the regiment was engaged in the Maryland Campaign. On the eighteenth it was sent forward as pickets at the Burnside Bridge, and on the evening of the nineteenth the Corn Exchange moved to the Potomac River. The following morning the regiment was ordered to cross the Potomac with orders to move to Shepherdstown. It was in the process of moving across the river when they were attacked by a heavy force of Rebels. Unsupported and receiving heavy fire from front and flank, the regiment was cut up severely. The loss in the regiment was 64 killed in action and 124 wounded, with 94 missing—a total of 282 men out of about 800 who were caught in the river on that day.

## Private John Doudle

Pleasant Valley, Maryland, September 1862

> On the 18th [we] assisted in burying the dead and caring for the wounded. On the 19th, we marched to the Antietam Iron Works, where we encamped for a short time. We then passed into Pleasant Valley, and then marched to the Point of Rocks, Maryland, where we did picket duty for about two weeks. During our stay at Point of Rocks we fished and feasted on fresh fish, which was caught in great abundance.
>
> General McClellan had decided to move his army across the Potomac, and either compel the enemy to give battle near Winchester, Va., or retreat towards Richmond.

## Corporal Charles E. Brown

Pleasant Valley, Maryland, September 1862

> On the 19th of September we were once again on the march leaving Antietam, we marched to Pleasant Valley, Maryland. At this time General McClellan was relieved of his command and General Burnside was given command of the Army of the Potomac. [Burnside officially succeeded McClellan in November 1862.] This was very welcome news to the soldiers. While we are here we get very many visitors. Our good old President, the man that saved our country, Abraham Lincoln, and some of his cabinet officers paid us a visit. We also had people from Schuylkill Haven down to see us, and people from different parts of the Northern States. Their visits were enjoyed very much by the soldiers.

This poem, written about the battle of Antietam, appeared in the *Pottsville Miners' Journal*, August 1, 1863.

*After the Battle of Antietam*

*The harvest moon oe'r the battle plain*
*Shines dim in the filmy eyes of the dead,*
*And the yellow wealth of the later grain,*
*Ground by the millstones of death and pain,*
*And wet with the life blood of the slain,*
*Is kneaded to horrible bread.*

*The dying by twos and threes, as Night*
*Kisses their brows with cooling breath,*
*Gather, with falling outward sight,*
*To tell of the inward visions bright*
*That rise like a tender morning light*
*Over the hills of death.*

*Two, who have stood up hand in hand—*
*Brothers to-day as in years gone by,*
*When, on the slopes of the Northern land,*
*Was braided closely each separate strand*
*Of their lives in perfect, golden band—*
*Close to each other lie.*

*"Tom," says the eldest, wiping slow*
*from his comrade's lips the crimson stain,*
*"Does the thirst torment you now?" "Oh, no,"*
*says the other, with broken voice and low:*
*"My wounds stopped bleeding an hour ago.*
*And now I am free from pain.*

*"Don't think of my trouble, Ben, for you*
*are wounded far worse, I know, than I;*
*I am only a little stiff and blue*
*With lying out in the evening dew,*
*But, Ben, you are shattered through and through:*
*Do you think you are going to die?"*

*"No, Tom; the bleeding is almost done:*
*I shall live this many and many a day;*

*And I felt all around to find my gun,*
*As I heard the firing just as the sun*
*Went down; the Rebels, I think, have run,*
*The noise was so far away.*

*"I shall live to fight as never before;*
*In the battle's front I shall bear my part;*
*And when it is over, on the floor*
*I shall play with my boy; and by the door*
*My wife shall sit, with the fear no more*
*Of war in gentle heart."*

*"Oh Ben I the days of battle appear*
*a great way off; I'll forget them soon,*
*I have been thinking, while lying here,*
*It was just a year ago-a year—*
*That I went a nutting with Nellie dear,*
*In the sunny afternoon.*

*"The hills were as bright as hills could be,*
*and Nellie, she wore a dress like down;*
*and under the green old chestnut tree,*
*pelted by dropping nuts, sat she,*
*looking up with half scared eyes at me*
*as I shook out the chestnuts brown.*

*"I came down safe, and she kissed me then,*
*with a face as glad as the happy sun,*
*and she gave me handful of brown nuts, Ben;*
*they lay so soft in her hand that when*
*I took them they slid and got back again,*
*Somehow; so I kept but one.*

*"I have that nut in my knapsack still;*
*I shall go for more with Nellie soon;*
*They are ripe by this time up on the hill.*
*Tomorrow, perhaps, I shall go—I am ill,*
*And its cloudy tonight but tomorrow will*
*Be fair in the afternoon.*

*"I am going a nutting with Nellie, and you*
*will sit with your wife and boy at home,*
*The day is bright as ever I knew,*
*And the chestnuts have ripen'd the summer through,*
*Still as the love in your eyes of blue*
*Nellie, dear Nellie, come."*

*Night on the battle plain stained with gore*
*Night in the eyes now closed for aye;*
*But a morning bathes a night-less shore,*
*Where a maiden watches and waits no more,*
*Nor a wife sits mute by a cottage door,*
*With a child that forgets to play.*

*From the Official Records*
*Reports of Colonel Benjamin C. Christ, 50th Pennsylvania Infantry, Commanding 1st Brigade*
*1st Division, 9th Army Corps*
*South Mountain and Antietam, Near Antietam Creek, Maryland*
*September 14, 1862*

*SIR: I respectfully submit the following report of the action of my command at the battle of South Mountain, on Sunday, September 14, 1862:*

*Leaving our encampment on the morning of the 14th, we proceeded along the Hagerstown road to a point near the base of the mountain, where we were considerably annoyed by the shot and shell of the enemy until we filed off on the road to the left that led us directly to the top of the mountain. Before reaching the summit, I was ordered to form in line of battle on the right of the road, but before this movement was completed the enemy opened a battery, which commanded this road. Cook's battery, which was just being placed in position at this time, received this fire directly in front, and from its great severity they were obliged to retire with their caissons, leaving two of their pieces in danger of being taken by the enemy. The Seventy-ninth New York Volunteers, Colonel Morrison, was immediately ordered to the front on the left of the road, and the Seventeenth Michigan, Colonel Worthington, on the right of the road, to protect these pieces.*

*The enemy held their position for some considerable time, and fired their shot and shell with terrible effect until about 2 o'clock, when I commenced the attack with infantry. From the previous disposition of my command, it was impossible for me to give my attention to the whole field. I therefore led forward the Seventeenth Michigan on the right of the road, while Colonel Welsh advanced on the left with the Forty-fifth Pennsylvania and Forty-sixth New York Volunteers. Supported by the Seventy-ninth New York, the Seventeenth Michigan moved steadily forward until they arrived within good range, and then opened a fire on the enemy with terrible effect, piling the road and field with his dead and wounded, and finally completely routing him, driving him in the utmost confusion across the field into the woods, and capturing a number of prisoners.*

*Under any circumstances the conduct of both officers and men of this regiment was worthy of the highest commendation, but especially so when taking into consideration that they were mustered into service as late as the 21st of August, 1862, and that this was their first engagement.*

*Later in the day the Seventy-ninth New York and Twenty-eighth Massachusetts Volunteers were ordered to the front, and assisted in repulsing the enemy in his second attempt to force our lines. The Fiftieth Pennsylvania and Eighth Michigan Volunteers were ordered in the early part of the afternoon to the position held by General Cox, where they contributed largely in maintaining that position, and twice assisted in repulsing the enemy.*

*With few exceptions, both officers and men discharged their whole duty. I append a list of casualties.*

*All of which is respectfully submitted.*
*B.C. CHRIST,*
*Colonel, Commanding First Brigade.*

Antietam Creek, Maryland, September 21, 1862

*Sir: I respectfully submit the following report of the part borne by my command in the engagement near Sharpsburg, on Wednesday, September 17, 1862:*

*About 10 o'clock a.m. I was ordered to support some batteries covering our advance near the stone bridge across Antietam Creek. During the afternoon I crossed the bridge and marched to the right, and parallel with the stream, for several hundred yards. I here deployed the Seventy-ninth New York Volunteers as skirmishers, supported by the Fiftieth Pennsylvania, Twenty-eighth Massachusetts, and Seventeenth Michigan Volunteers, and then moved forward in front of the enemy's battery (heavily supported by infantry), in the rear of a corn-field, on the right of the road. On reaching the crest of a hill, about 350 yards in front of the battery, I discovered that my support on my left had not come up. Deeming my force alone inadequate for the attack on both artillery and infantry, I was obliged to halt until supported on my left.*

*While halting under cover from the enemy directly in front, he opened a battery on my left which commanded my whole line from left to right, and for thirty minutes we were under a most severe fire of round shot, shell, grape, and canister, and suffered severely. It was impossible to move forward for the reason before stated—no place in the neighbor-hood that afforded any cover—and the alternative presented itself either to retire from a good and only position from which to advance on the enemy in front, or to wait patiently until some demonstration on the left would compel him to change the direction of his fire. Again, I could not get under cover without retiring at least 250 yards, in full view of the enemy, and if there would have been the least confusion the men might have retreated in disorder, and exposed a larger and more disordered front to his fire, which would have largely increased the list of casualties. I chose the former, and was gratified by having my expectations realized.*

*A demonstration on the left compelled the enemy to change the direction of his fire, and my supports coming, we moved to the front, where we engaged the enemy on his left and in about one hour succeeded in driving both his artillery and infantry from the position. I charged on the battery with the Seventeenth Michigan Regiment (this being the regiment immediately in front), supported by the Fiftieth Pennsylvania and Twenty-eighth Massachusetts Volunteers, but when within 100 yards of his guns (and while he was covered by a hill which prevented my advance column from shooting either his horses or their riders), he limbered up his pieces and retired. I did not deem it prudent to advance after his artillery had retired, for the reason that the woods were lined with his sharpshooters, and I would only have exposed my command to their fire without gaining anything. I retired with my charging party to my line of battle, and maintained my position until ordered to take another farther down and near the bridge, where the men slept on their arms for the night.*

*In this engagement it is impossible to particularize regiments, officers, or men, for, from the moment we were brought under fire until ordered to retire near the bridge, all displayed the utmost coolness and courage, ready and prompt to move forward at the word of command, and both officers and men vying with each other in the discharge of their duty. My especial acknowledgments are, however, due to my acting assistant adjutant-general, Capt. William F. Lusk, for the assistance rendered me not only during this but also during the engagement of the 14th.*

*All of which is respectfully submitted.*
*B.C. CHRIST,*
*Colonel, Commanding First Brigade.*

*Official Report*
*Orlando B. Willcox*
*Mouth of Antietam Creek, Maryland, September 21, 1862*

*Sir: I have the honor to submit my report for the 17th instant.*

*This division marched out of camp to the hills overlooking the Antietam, near the stone bridge, Sharpsburg road. My orders, received from General Burnside in person, were to cross over after Sturgis should have carried the bridge, and after Cox's and*

*Rodman's divisions should have crossed. My orders then were to take the right of the Corps in the attack on Sharpsburg.*

*After crossing the bridge, the road turns sharply to the right, runs up the stream about 200 yards, then to the left along an open hollow or ravine, which winds along to the village, overlooked by heights to the right and left. Once on the heights, the country is rolling and intersected with field fences, many of which are of stone. The enemy's sharpshooters were posted behind these fences as well as hay-stacks, which also, with orchards and corn-fields, served to conceal their lines. A battery of field guns also commanded the road and hollow down to the river, and the whole plateau above was swept by cross-fire of artillery.*

*Christ's brigade was filed across the hollow and drawn up along the crest on the right of the road, his left resting near the road, the Seventy-ninth New York (Highlanders), Lieutenant-Colonel Morrison commanding, deployed as skirmishers, and the other three regiments of the brigade in line of battle. These regiments were the Fiftieth Pennsylvania Major Overton; the Twenty-eighth Massachusetts, Captain Caraher, and Seventeenth Michigan, Colonel Worthington.*

*The Second Brigade, under Colonel Welsh, formed on the heights to the left of the road, deploying the One hundredth Pennsylvania, Lieutenant Colonel Leckey, as skirmishers, and forming his other three regiments in line of battle, viz: Forty-fifth Pennsylvania, Lieutenant-Colonel Curtin, on the right; Forty-sixth New York Lieutenant-Colonel Gerhardt, in the center; Eighth Michigan, Captain Ely, on the left. I brought with the division Cook's battery, Eighth Massachusetts, and left Benjamin's battery, Second U.S. Artillery, doing good work in a commanding position across the river in our rear, against the enemy's guns on the plateau and heights in front of us. My division now formed part of a line which Generals Burnside and Cox were commanding, and all moved forward about —— o'clock. We were under fire from the moment a man appeared at the crest of the plateau or crossed the hollow. Taking two pieces of Cook's battery, under Lieutenant Coffin, I moved up the road, while the two brigades gallantly advanced over the plateau toward Sharpsburg.*

*The rest of Cook's battery was posted on a hill near the bridge. Crook's brigade, of Cox's division, followed in support of my line. Christ's brigade attacked a force of the enemy's infantry along his front, and drove them steadily before him. In following them up, his brigade got in advance of the rest of the line; his supports were not up. While halting, the enemy turned their battery on him from their right (our left), and for a few moments his troops were exposed to the fire of their battery, a fire of infantry from a corn-field in his front protected by a stone fence, and from a battery farther up in front, beyond the corn-field. The left coming up soon attracted the attention of the flanking battery. Lieutenant Coffin directed his pieces on the battery beyond the corn-field, and at the same time Christ threw forward the Seventeenth Michigan, with supports, to charge the battery, seeing the guns were withdrawn.*

*Meantime Welsh conducted his brigade against the enemy in his front and drove them before him with the same success, his right following the crest of the hollow, gradually approaching Christ's left, so that by the time we entered Sharpsburg the quarter part of my division was on the right of the road and extended across the hollow, up the side hill, and on the plateau. On this side hill was an orchard, in which a large force of the enemy was posted and firing heavily at both Welsh and Christ.*

*In finding a position for Coffin's two guns at the head of a lane, which turned up at the first house we passed, I was now able both to see and assist my division at every part of the ground, and Coffin threw solid shot, shell, and canister with great precision and effect into the enemy's ranks. The force in the orchard were dislodged, and fled up the hill-side, followed by our fire of both infantry and artillery, and Welsh occupied the orchard.*

*Our musket ammunition was now exhausted. We had carried the heights of Sharpsburg, and rested partly in the town and partly on the hills. The enemy kept up a desultory fire along our line, but at a respectful distance, so that when Sturgis on the extreme left became heavily pressed, and I was ordered to withdraw to the place where my division formed near the river, every regiment marched back in perfect order. To assist the struggling left, I had already detached Coffin, with his two guns. He moved across the field to the left and rear, and opened upon the enemy within 300 yards. Here he remained, doing signal execution, until he also exhausted his ammunition and withdrew.*

*As Lieutenant Benjamin was detached from the division, I in-close* [sic] *a copy of his report separately. I have particularly to notice the good conduct of Cols. B.C. Christ and Thomas Welsh, commanding brigades, and all the officers and men under their commands. There is no officer or man among them who cannot feel proud of having been engaged in the battle of Sharpsburg, and I recommend that all the regiments of my division be allowed to inscribe "Sharpsburg" on their colors as well as "South Mountain." I would also commend the cool, skillful, and gallant conduct of Lieutenant Benjamin and his officers and men, and the efficiency of Lieut. John N. Coffin of Cook's battery, who, with his section, acted under my own eyes, moving up in the most dashing manner into the village, and striking with his shot on every side. He mentions his two chiefs of pieces, Sergts. William Davis and Newell B. Allen, and all his men. Of my personal staff, I have particularly to commend Capt. Robert A. Hutchins, assistant adjutant-general, and my aides, Lieutenant Brackett, Twenty-eighth Massachusetts Volunteers, and Lieut. James W. Romeyn, Fourth Michigan, for promptness and fearlessness in carrying orders, and Lieutenant* [Orrin M.] *Dearborn, aide de-camp, also in charge of the ammunition train, for following up the command with ammunition and delivering it to all the troops of the Corps at a critical time.*

*This report is with the supplementary battle reports.*

*Respectfully,*

*O.B. WILLCOX*

# 1862-1863

*"Fighting for Burnside, a brave and loyal man."*

On October 29, 1862, after spending weeks on picket duty, the 50th Regiment formed up and marched to the banks of the Potomac and forded the river at Point of Rocks, Maryland. The water was uncomfortably cold and caused some discomfort among the boys in Company C.

## Private John Doudle

Falmouth, Virginia, October 1862

On the 29th of October, 1862 the regiment forded the Potomac River at the Point of Rocks. Notwithstanding the water was about three feet deep and the weather was cold and disagreeable, we waded into the water and marched on to Waterford, Va. At Waterford we halted for a few days, then proceeded onto Gaskins Mills, where we made another halt. Owing to some trouble with the arrangements for transportation of the Commissary stores, provisions ran short; hence this place was called Camp Starvation.

After passing through Ricketstown, Salem, White Sulphur Springs, and Rappahannock Station the regiment was placed on duty as the rear guard of the army and in that position we stayed until the army arrived at Falmouth.

## Corporal Charles E. Brown

Falmouth, Virginia, October 1862

We marched down the valley and finally went into camp on the North side of the Rappahannock River, opposite Fredericksburg. At this place we took a good rest while General Burnside reorganized the army. He divided it into three grand divisions. General Hooker was given command of the right grand division, General Sumner was given command of the center grand division, and General Franklin was given command of the left grand division.

On November 7, 1862, President Lincoln, unhappy with General George McClellan, relieved him of command of the Army of the Potomac. In McClellan's place Lincoln appointed General Ambrose Burnside. President Lincoln had offered the job to Burnside twice before, but the general always refused, never feeling he had the qualities to command so great of an army. By November 19 the remainder of the Army of the Potomac arrived at Falmouth, Virginia. General Burnside was placed in command of the army and throughout the month of November and early December concentrated his forces opposite the city of Fredericksburg. During the battle of Fredericksburg, the 50th Regiment was deployed as skirmishers and pickets making a solid connection between the grand divisions of Sumner and Franklin.

While the men were fighting bravely on the battlefields, citizens at home were carrying out state elections. It was very difficult for the soldier to cast his vote in the field, and in some states a power of attorney was needed. The men of Company C conducted their own election at their camp. Lieutenant George W. Brumm wrote to the *Pottsville Miners' Journal*, providing the results of their mock election and expressing the soldiers' displeasure at being deprived the vote. He stated that the election was held under the eyes of the officers and "that is the way the soldiers vote everywhere, to sustain the policy of the President." Every state, according to Brumm, would have been swept by the Republicans if the soldiers had been allowed to vote. Angered, Brumm stated, "This is an account the Breckinridgers must settle with the soldiers when they return home."

## Lieutenant George W. Brumm

In Camp Near Waterloo, Virginia, November 12, 1862

Editors, *Miners' Journal:*

I herewith transmit to you the returns of an election held today by Company C, 50th Regiment, P.V. The aggregate number of the Company is eighty-two (82) men of which 23 voted. 29 are absent, wounded in the hospitals at Fredrick, Washington etc. 7 are non-residents of Schuylkill County, and 23 are under age.

Of the men who have not voted I would guarantee that at least nine-tenths would have voted for Campbell had they been home at the time of the election.

You can have no idea what an indignant feeling exists among the Pennsylvania Volunteers against the men who have deprived the soldiers of their vote.

One of the officers of Company E, in which quite a number of men are from Lebanon County, told me while we were holding the election, that it was no use to hold and election in their Company as all the men went one way, all being Union Republicans.

I must close as we have just received marching orders.

The vote of the Company is as follows:

Auditor General

| | |
|---|---|
| Cochran [Union Republican] | 21 |
| Slenker [Democrat] | 2 |

Congress

| | |
|---|---|
| Campbell [Union Republican] | 21 |
| Strouse [Democrat] | 2 |

Yours Respectfully,
Geo. W. Brumm
Lieut. Co. C, 50th Regt. P.V.

## Private John Doudle

**Opposite Fredericksburg, Virginia, December 1862**

General Ambrose E. Burnsides [*sic*], having been placed in command of the Army of the Potomac, concentrated his forces in front of Fredericksburg, preparatory to attacking the enemy at that point. Hence on the 13th of December we crossed the pontoon bridge immediately in front of Fredericksburg and was placed on the extreme left of the Centre division.

In our immediate front there was very little fighting done. The regiment however did good service as the connecting link between the left wing and the centre of the main army, and was always ready to execute any order that might be issued from her commander.

On the night of the 15th we were withdrawn to the opposite side of the river and went back to its former winter quarters. The only casualty reported was the wounding of Milo Spencer from Company D.

We remained in winter quarters opposite Fredericksburg doing a great deal of picket duty on the banks of the Rappahannock until the 13th February, 1863 when we were ordered to Newport News, via Aquia Creek.

## Corporal Charles E. Brown

Opposite Fredericksburg, Virginia, December 1862–February 1863

> On December 13th, 1862 we began preparations to cross the river. However, it was first necessary to drive the Rebels away from the riverbank, so that we would be enabled to lay our pontoons on the river.
>
> We were in the center grand division. Each division had its own pontoons. The three divisions were finally enabled to cross the river and went into battle. General Franklin and his division were down in the lowlands, where the Rebels did not have any advantage over our troops, and he was expected to drive their right wing back. I saw General Franklin's troops whip the Rebels at least half a dozen times that day, but he never followed them up. Then night came on and our generals had a council of war, and came to the conclusion that their position was impregnable, and ordered a retreat across the river without the Rebels finding out we [were] doing. We placed ground on the pontoons so the Rebels would not hear us crossing, because if they knew that we were retreating, they would open fire and it would have caused a panic ion our army. Finally we were enabled to get back to our camp without any trouble.
>
> We remained here all winter. We had plenty to eat and drink and had lots of fun. They then ordered Burnsides to make another attempt to go up the valley where he could ford the river. He made all the preparations for doing so, and we started up the valley, but we got stuck in the mud, we turned around and went back to our camp and remained there until spring time.

What Charles Brown describes in the last part of his narrative is the famous "Mud March." In January of 1863 General Ambrose Burnside initiated a new offensive. Unfortunately, it got bogged down in the dank and dreary weather of late January.

On January 20, 1863, General Burnside ordered his army to the march in an effort to try and outpace the Army of Northern Virginia. His army was very tired, having only been in camp for less than five weeks and drained from the disastrous battle of Fredericksburg. Burnside had hoped to cross the river above the Army of Northern Virginia's left flank. Taking all of their equipment with them—pontoon boats, artillery, supply wagons—the army moved out. By that afternoon it started raining and rained for the next several days. The heavy mule-driven wagons bogged down in the mud, sometimes up to the wheels hubs. The artillery sank deep in the mud. The infantry slipped and slid all over the wet roads. By the next day the army could not move and was completely stalled. Burnside had no choice but to end the movement and send his army back to camp.

## Private John Doudle

Newport News, Virginia, February 1863

> While at Newport News through the efforts of Lieut. Col Brenholtz each man was provided with a short jacket, light blue pantaloons and white gloves, and believe me at this time there was no finer looking or better drilled regiment in the Corps. Lieut. Col. Brenholtz felt proud of his regiment and took great pains to have it appear to good advantage on all public occasions.

The uniform that Doudle describes was called the state uniform. Many states supplied uniforms for their men and Pennsylvania had a short, distinctive shell jacket. It included a low cut collar, nine buttons on the front, three on the cuff with a straight cut to the skirt. The normal uniform worn in the field by the common soldier in the Union army was the four-button sack coat. Army regulations stated:

> *The uniform coat for all enlisted infantry men, shall be a single-breasted frock of dark blue cloth, made without plaits, with a skirt extending one-half the distance from the top of the hip to the bend of the knee; one row of nine buttons on the breast, placed at equal distances; stand up collar to rise no higher than to permit the chin to turn freely over it, to hook in front at the bottom and then to slope up and backward at an angle of thirty degrees on each side; cuffs pointed according to pattern, and to button with two small buttons at the under seam; collar and cuffs edged with a cord or welt of cloth as follows, to wit: Scarlet for Artillery, sky-blue for infantry, yellow for Engineers, crimson for Ordnance and Hospital stewards. On each shoulder a metallic scale according to pattern; narrow lining for skirt of the coat of the same color and material as the coat; pockets in the folds of the skirts with one button at each hip to range with the lowest buttons on the breast; no buttons at the ends of the pockets.*

Each infantry man of Company C was also issued a knapsack that held his personal equipment, shirt, drawers, sewing kit, letter writing items, religious tracts, socks, eating utensils, metal plate and tin cup, a rubber gum blanket, an extra blanket and one half of a shelter tent. The blanked was rolled and carried on the outside of the knapsack. He also carried a canteen and a haversack that contained his food or extra ammunition, and a model 1855 cartridge box that held forty rounds of ammunition in two separate tins. On the outside of the leather box was a brass oval metal plate with "U.S." inscribed on it. This box was carried by a shoulder belt that also had an oval brass plate containing an eagle. On his belt the soldier carried his bayonet in a leather scabbard and a small cap pouch lined in lambswool that held the percussion caps for his musket.

At this time the regiment was armed with an Austrian rifled musket. The Austrian was actually referred to as the model 1854, or more popularly known as the Lorenz. During the war this weapon was the second most imported weapon used. According to ordnance returns from the 50th Regiment, the boys used the .57-caliber minnie ball, firing an elongated cartridge. The Austrian Lorenz was used by the men until the regiment was issued 1863 Springfield rifle muskets in 1864.

## Anonymous, Company C

Newport News, Virginia, March 9, 1863

Editors, *Miners' Journal:*
Your invaluable paper reaches us regularly every week, and is always a very welcome visitor. We are at present encamped on the James River, two miles above the landing at Newport News and are very comfortably situated. Indeed it is a remarkable change from the "mud" at Fredericksburg, and the health of the men shows that a change was beneficial. Our regiment is (in the absence of Col Christ, who is commanding the 2nd Brigade, 1st Division) commanded by Lieut. Col Brenholtz, from Reading, a very efficient officer.

Our Schuylkill County companies have gone through an entire change as far as commissioned officers are concerned. The Promotions area as follows:

1st Lieut. Samuel Schwenk promoted to Captain of Company A; 2nd Lieut. Edward F. West promoted to 1st Lieut; Orderly Sgt. Henry J. Alspach to 2nd Lieut; 3rd Sgt. William H. Hiney to 2nd Lieut. Company C; 2nd Lieut Alfred J. Huntzinger, Company I promoted to Captain of Company K and detached as Aide de Camp on Col. Christ's staff. Orderly Sgt. Richard Rahn, promoted to 2nd Lieut. Company I, and in a few days I will be able to inform you of Lieut Rahn s promotion to Captainery of Company I, Captain Bossard having resigned and gone home.

We now number about four hundred and fifty effective men for duty, out of nine hundred and sixty four when we left Harrisburg.

Why do not some of our friends, who have the opportunity, (which will probably be the only one) visit the 48th and 50th? It's only a few days journey.

As far as we are concerned we know nothing of further movements. Our destination will probably be to some southern port. You who are at home have far more facilities for gaining knowledge of war matters than us soldiers. We know nothing but to obey orders.

Today for the first time we ascertained who was to be our commander. Our old commander, our especially favorite, Burnside, who knows how to command an army and hereafter must not be interfered with by politicians at home.

When we again are marched forth to meet the enemy under the command of our able leader, we are sure of victory. Hereafter there are to be impediments. No "copperheads" will be permitted by our friends at home to stand in our way.

The 48th is laying about two miles below us. I visited their camp this morning. The officers and men are all in excellent health and spirits.

The reception of the Hon. James H. Campbell by his friends at home was satisfactorily received by his many friends here. The soldiers are the friends of those who stand by the administration.

We have nearly all of our time taken up with drills. I will give you a routine of our duty as follows:

Reveille at 6 A.M.
Sick call at 7 A.M.
Breakfast at 7 A.M.
Guard mounting at 8 A.M.
Company drill 8:30 A.M. to 9:30 A.M.
Battalion Drill 10 A.M. to 11 A.M.
Dinner at 12 noon
Company drill (skirmish) from 1 to 2 P.M.
Battalion drill 3 to 4 P.M.
Dress parade at 5 P.M.
Supper at 6 P.M.
Tattoo 8:30 P.M.
Taps at 9.P.M.
On Tuesday and Fridays Brigade drills from 1 to 4 P.M.
On Sunday a general inspection of arms, accoutrements and clothing.

The weather has been very cold for the past week, the health of the regiment continues excellent.

P.S. The Copperheads have no show in this part of the country.

"VETERAN"

# 1863

*Victory belongs to the most persevering.*

—*Napoleon Bonaparte, Campaigning in Mississippi, Tennessee & Kentucky*

After Fredericksburg, General Burnside was assigned to the command of the Department of Ohio. This department included Kentucky and east Tennessee. In March the 9th Corps was transferred to the field of operations in the west. The 9th was stationed in Kentucky during the months of April and May 1863, performing light duty in good quarters. In mid-June the corps was ordered to support General Grant, who was besieging the city of Vicksburg, Mississippi. The 9th Corps was not actively engaged during this period. After the surrender of Vicksburg, two divisions under General John Parke moved toward Jackson, Mississippi, and engaged the Rebels at this location. Vicksburg did not cost the corps many casualties but the conditions in Mississippi caused many in the ranks to succumb to malaria. Corporal Benjamin Brown of Company C, brother to Corporal Charles E. Brown, died from malaria while in the Vicksburg area. He is buried in the Vicksburg National Cemetery.

## Private John Doudle

Movement to Kentucky, March 1863

> During the month spent at Newport News the time was almost constantly employed in drilling, during which the regiment attracted much attention by the precision and uniformity in executing the commands. March 22nd, 1863 we were put on board the steamboat *Coroner,* preparatory to a new scene of action.
>
> On the 22nd of March 1863 we were sent with the Ninth Corps to the Department of the Ohio via Baltimore, Md. and Parkersburg, Va. arriving at Covington, Ky. on the 27th. The trip from Newport News to Baltimore [was] by boat, thence to Parkersburg by rail, then down the Ohio River by boat to Cincinnati.

All along the route the troops were treated kindly. Hot coffee and fresh bread were issued to the regiment at Cumberland, Md. and Grafton Va. After taking our dinner at Cincinnati, on the 27th we proceeded to Nicholasville, Ky. where we arrived the next morning. We marched to Camp Dick Robinson where we encamped until April 12th when we moved to Stanford. Here we remained until the 30th, when we moved to Ustanville: On May 5th we crossed the mountains and encamped at Somerset.

One remarkable fact was greatly appreciated by the Company. The vendors of butter, eggs, pies etc. were either honest or had not learned how to trick the soldiers into paying extra prices for everything. In comparison to customs in other cities, we bought butter for ten cents per pound and eggs for six cents per dozen, and a good-sized pie for five cents. As it seemed lard was scarce. They must have put the shortening edgeways as they were very tough.

June 4th we broke camp at Somerset, and marched back to Nicholasville, where we took cars and proceeded to Cincinnati, Ohio, where we arrived on the 8th and were then sent to Vicksburg, Mississippi. The route taken, by rail from Cincinnati to Cairo, then by boat down the Mississippi River to the Yazoo, then up the Yazoo to Haines Bluff.

## Corporal Charles E. Brown

**Vicksburg, Mississippi, June 1863**

General Hooker was now given command of the Army and our Ninth Corps received orders to go to Vicksburg, Mississippi. We got started and moved down the Mississippi. When we got on the Mississippi River, we had a lot of trouble with the Rebels. Every now and then they would hide behind the levees and fire on us. Our captain would run the boat right onto the levee and then the Rebels would mount their horses and ride into the country, and before long they would appear at another place. This went on until we finally reached the mouth of the Yazoo River in the rear of Vicksburg.

We landed at the mouth of the Yazoo River, we were sent here to prevent the Rebels from attacking General Grant in the rear. He had General Pemberton penned up in Vicksburg and the Rebels were gathering an army at Jackson, the capital of Mississippi, to attack General Grant in the rear and make him raise the siege of Vicksburg. Our arrival spoiled the plans of the Rebels, and on the night of July 3rd 1863 General Pemberton sent a flag of truce and a note asking General Grant on what terms he would allow him to surrender. General Grant wrote one of these messages which have become memorable and historical for their briefness. He turned the note over and on the other side wrote.

"Unconditional" and sent it back. Next morning General Pemberton sent a new message with the announcement that he would surrender. This he did. Thirty three thousand men with full equipment were surrendered to General Grant on the fourth of July 1863. This was a big day for the Northern Army.

## Private John Doudle

Vicksburg, Mississippi, June 1863

While going down the river a squad of Rebels opened fire on our steamer, but fortunately for us no one was hurt. Landing at Haines Bluff, the regiment encamped about two miles above the wharf.

The Ninth Corps was sent to Vicksburg to reinforce General U.S. Grant who had surrounded the Rebel General Pemberton and cut of all his communications, as Grant was in dread of General Joseph E. Johnston, who was assigned by the Rebel authorities to the work of raising the siege of Vicksburg by an attack on Grant's rear. To prevent this [the] Ninth Corps and other troops were stationed at Haines Bluff. Our duty was more of observation than of direct contact with the enemy; hence our forces had a fortnight of quiet.

On July 4th, 1863 General Pemberton surrendered to General Grant, Vicksburg and his whole army, but as to how many men I never ascertained.

## Corporal Charles E. Brown

Vicksburg, Mississippi, June 1863

At Vicksburg the Rebels had eaten most of their mules and horses, so Grant had to feed them, and it took all the food he had. We received orders to march on the Capitol of Jackson Mississippi. When we were issued our rations we were given all the codfish we wanted. That is the kind of food we had to live on, on the long march during the long hot month of July. In a very warm climate the earth does not hold any water. The people live on cistern water and the Rebels had them all dry…We had to cross two rivers the Big Black and the Yazoo Rivers. Of these two rivers the water was bad and would kill any man who drank any quantity of it. We lived by eating fish.

We arrived near Jackson and moved up to the breastworks as close to the confederates as we can get. They were well fortified and have a good position. We fought them for eight days and could not whip them. Then our General made a flank movement at night. In the morning we discovered the Rebels had left and in a great hurry too. Large quantities of their equipment was left behind. We marched into the city and had a great time for several hours. Then we had to get ready and go back to Vicksburg and go north, so we started to march that day. Our Lieut. Col. Brenholtz was wounded and we had to carry him on a stretcher to the river, and send him home, but he died on the way. He was a good officer, and had he lived he surely would have made his mark. He was a young man from Reading and a lawyer by profession.

We lost lots of our men from the disease called spotted fever. I have a brother in the National Cemetery at Vicksburg who died from this fever.

## Private John Doudle

Mississippi, July 1863

On the following day after the surrender of Vicksburg General Sherman, with the Ninth Corps and other troops, started in pursuit of Johnson. The regiment moved with the rest of the troops toward Big Black River.

On the 10th the Corps came in contact with the enemy near Jackson the capital of Mississippi. The 50th and 46th New York occupied a position on the Canton road.

The enemy's defenses consisted of a line of breast works enabling them to make a decided resistance to any attempt, which we made to dislodge them. General Sherman seeing the enemy so strongly posted decided to wait the arrival of the heavy artillery and supplies of ammunition.

On the 11th the two armies were watching each other, and as the weather was excessively warm we suffered a great deal.

On the 16th a reconnaissance was ordered for the purpose of developing the enemy's position and its forces. A gallant advance was made while the Rebels made a free use of their batteries, but in a very short time the enemy fled, which resulted in a victory for the Union Army.

It was here where our gallant commander Lieut. Col Brenholtz fell mortally wounded, leading his men on to victory. The esteem in which he was held by the regiment was feelingly manifested in what subsequently took place.

General Sherman destroyed a great amount of railroad and other property. Lieut. Col. Brenholtz's wound was of such a serious nature that he could not be placed in an ambulance, but might survive if carefully carried on a stretcher upon the shoulders of four men. Volunteers were called for and he was carried that way more than 40 miles to the rear of Vicksburg. He subsequently died at Evansville, Ind. while going up the Ohio River.

History seldom records incidents of greater love for a superior officer than was exhibited by the volunteer party who carried and attended Lieut. Col. Brenholtz from Jackson to the rear of Vicksburg, to a place called Mill Dale.

On the death of Lieutenant Colonel Brenholtz, the officers of the 50th Regiment put together a committee of three officers to put forth a preamble and resolution concerning their beloved late leader. Lieutenant George Brumm, one of the officers assigned the duty, sent this notice to the *Pottsville Miners' Journal*:

> *Action of the Fiftieth Regt. P.V. on the Death of Lieut. Col. Thos. S. Brenholtz*
> *At a special meeting of the officers of the 50th Regt., P.V. held 23d inst., the following preamble and resolutions were presented and unanimously adopted;*
>
> *It having pleased Almighty God in the dispensation of his Providence to place a fatal termination to the wound received at Jackson Mississippi, July 13th, 1863, and thus remove from our midst in the prime of his manhood, our late commander and friend, Lieut. Col. Thomas S. Brenholtz, of Reading, Berks County, Pa. We deem it proper to give some slight expression to our feelings on this sad occasion, moved as we are by the many lessons such as providence has designed to teach, by the character and the sorrow we feel at his loss.*
>
> *WHEREAS: In his devotion to his country, in his desire to excel in the knowledge and performance of the duties of the soldier in which his life became a sacrifice. In his strength of character and his warmth of heart we had a bright example, and we shall ever cherish it as such in our memories and hearts; therefore,*
>
> *Resolved, That by the death of our lamented commander and friend, we have sustained an irreparable loss, having found him in those characteristics which ever adorn the character of the true soldier, and fitted him for the quiet intercourse of camp, and the arduous duties of the field combat.*
>
> *Resolved, That true to the noble impulses which induced him to exchange comforts of home and the peaceful walks of civil life, for the onerous duties of a soldier's life, he ever stood bravely at his post in the hour of danger, and sealed his devotion to free principles with his blood.*
>
> *Resolved, That while we sincerely regret and condole with the bereaved family and friends of the deceased, we earnestly hope that they may in this hour of trouble find in that God in whom they have trusted, that consolation which the world cannot give and be resigned to this most severe dispensation.*
>
> *Resolved, That we wear the usual badge of mourning for thirty days, and that a copy of the above be forwarded to his family, and to the press for publication.*
>
> *Lieut. G.W. Brumm*
> *Lieut. Horatio N. Adams*
> *Lieut. Richard Kahn.*

Another anonymous member of Company C, this time writing under the pen name "Nailer," wrote this letter to the *Pottsville Miners' Journal* from their camp near Mill Dale, Mississippi:

## Anonymous, Company C

At Camp Near Mill Dale, Mississippi, July 26, 1863

> Editors, *Miners' Journal:*
> We are now in our old camp at Snyder's Bluff, after being absent for a space of three weeks, during the time we have been engaged in digging entrenchments, hard marching, and doing considerable skirmishing. We left camp at Snyder's Bluff on the 30th of June; marched about eight miles toward big black, where we halted and threw up rifle pits for the defense of General Grant's rear. We laid there snuggly until the 4th of July, when orders were received to have three days rations in our haversacks and be ready to march immediately. We marched about six miles, when we encamped for the night. We started bright and early the next morning, and marched within two miles of the river, where we laid until 3 o'clock of the 7th of July, when we again took the road and crossed the river, and marched until about 1 o'clock the next morning, through one of the severest rain storms we have ever experienced. We halted for the remainder of the day, until 5 o'clock in the evening when we again took to our line of march towards Jackson, at which Joe Johnston's army was strongly fortified. We proceeded on for two days in which time we arrived within three miles of Jackson, where we formed in line of battle to protect our flanks. We remained in this position until evening when we proceeded to within a mile of the city, at which place there is an Insane Asylum, which was well crowded, and the lunatics kept chattering and cursing the Yanks so much that the boys were unable to sleep any that night. The next morning bright an early, we were ordered into line, in the meantime the Rebels presenting us with a few bunches of grape, which did not digest very well with the boys. We were shoved about for eight days, skirmishing and supporting skirmishers under fire the whole time, during which our gallant Lieutenant Colonel, Thos S. Brenholtz, received a wound; the ball has not been extracted yet. Private Christian Gulliver of our Company C was slightly wounded in the arm.
>
> On the morning of the 17th, our army entered the city of Jackson. Col Christ's Brigade (of which we form the right) was the first that entered Jackson. We stacked arms in one of the principle streets. As soon as the command "Rest" was given, the men made a rush for the tobacco, grub (we having kept on half

rations during the time we were around Jackson) and other valuable articles. We laid in the city about two hours, and in that time the boys were well supplied.

Jackson is a neat little place. It is composed of wealthy planters' residences, stores, one newspaper office, an armory, consisting of about 7,000 stands of small arms, a State Prison, Court House, Capitol building and State House, three fire engines, four railroads running through the town. We captured about 1,000 prisoners, a great many being deserters. After stopping in the city for about two hours, we were ordered back to our old camping grounds, near the asylum. While we were in the city, private George Reed, of Co. C captured a Rebel flag from one of the buildings. We laid to Camp Lunatic, as some of the boys name it, until the 20th when we were ordered to march back to where we are quartered now. Our Corps commander, Major General Parke, marched us very hard. Water was scarce, and the heat being excessive, and the dust six inches deep, a great many of our Corps died along the road, and since we have been in camp we have buried no less than 100 men, the effects of hard marching. Private William Herb of Co. H was buried this morning, and we have 80 men of our regiment that are unfit for duty. From the effects of the march.

"Nailer"

## Captain Daniel F. Burket

Mill Dale, Mississippi, July 28, 1863

*[From the editor, Pottsville Miners' Journal, August 20, 1863]*
***The Fiftieth Regt. P.V....We take pleasure in laying before our readers the following interesting and patriotic letter from Capt. Burket of the Fiftieth Regiment. Although a private letter and its publication not contemplated by the writer, yet it sentiments and facts should be laid before a community which feels pride in the career of the gallant Captain's regiment.***

Mill Dale, Miss. July 28th 1863

This is my first opportunity to write to you since our return from Jackson. It was a horrible march back, the distance being 45 miles. The troops suffered a great deal from the heat and bad water. All the water in this State is cistern, and a few days we were left without any. But it seems to me as if providence was with us. When the rumor prevailed among the troops that the water had given out, a heavy black cloud rose and the rain commenced to pour down so that every brook and stream was filled. On the 23rd last General Grant relieved us from his army and we are now waiting transportation I suppose for the east. General Grant complimented the 9th Corps highly for its bravery in battle. We came out with very little loss. Col Brenholtz was dangerously wounded and private G. Gulliver of my company, slightly in the arm. Our regiment behaved nobly. Private G. Reed of my company captured a splendid Rebel flag. I never saw the army so cheerful but on the other hand the men feel sorry to hear the news from New York. They swear vengeance on all traitors and never will they be ashamed, traitors must be driven out of the land. To do this 90% of the army will volunteer. Traitors must feel the strong arm of liberty loving men. We are willing to serve ten years longer that traitors may be driven from the land. This is our motto in the army. How can we be friends with men at home who are stabbing us in the back! No Never! They have planned to destroy the country. Let the contest come; the sooner the better. If they refuse to come out into the army and fight, send for some old troops. They will bring them. I suppose the people are satisfied with the black troops. I assure you that they are a great service to us. They do any amount of labor and fight well. No back down in them. They are easy to handle. I wish we had more of them. This is what we want, and every man in the army wishes the same. I must close my letter. Please give my respects to all loyal persons, but no traitors.

Capt. Burket
Co. C, 50th Regt. P.V. 9th Army Corps.

## Private John Doudle

Mill Dale, Mississippi, August 1863

Our regiment arrived at its old campground, at Mill Dale, on the 23rd of July where it remained until August 10th. On the 10th we marched to Haines Bluff and embarked on the steamer, South Wester, bound for Cairo, Illinois, where we arrived on the 16th. Taking Cairo, we proceeded to Crab Orchard Kentucky, via Cincinnati, Ohio and Nicholasville Kentucky.

The campaign in Mississippi was especially severe in its effects upon officers and men, the excessive heat, the malaria that settled like a pall of death around the camps upon the Yazoo River, the scarcity of water and its bad quality, and the forced marches told fearfully upon all.

The hardships which all were obliged to endure were excessive. The water which the horses refused to drink we were obliged to use in making coffee. Fevers, chills, congestion, diarrhea and other diseases attacked the troops. Many sank down by the roadside and died from sunstroke and sheer exhaustion. William H. Minnig [*sic*], of our Company was sent to Mound City, Illinois, and died in the hospital.

The regiment remained in Mississippi until August 10. After a short rest period the 50th Regiment, along with the 9th Corps, moved into Kentucky. By the time the corps entered Kentucky, General Burnside had started a movement into east Tennessee. By the middle of August the regiment had only eighty men fit for duty. Some men were in the hospital for wounds received in action, but the majority of the men were sick from malaria that they contracted in Mississippi. According to the official history of the regiment, the eighty men who were fit for duty all suffered from chills and fevers.

The regiment remained in camp at Knoxville for several weeks. While in camp the health of the men improved greatly.

## Corporal Charles E. Brown

Knoxville, Tennessee, August 1863

After staying in Kentucky for a while, we were sent back to Knoxville, Tennessee. We marched over the Cumberland Mountains, and [it] took us fourteen days to reach Knoxville again. We rested in camp for a few days then proceeded to march to Louden, some twenty miles below Knoxville. The Rebels were on the other side of the Tennessee River, and they had destroyed almost everything of use and value. They destroyed all the bridges and even ran their engines into the river.

General Longstreet was sent here to capture us. He had the best Corps in the Rebel army and we retreated to Knoxville fighting all the way. We reached Knoxville and found out that General Burnside had fortified it really well. We then turned right around and commenced to fight the Rebels. They had us penned in Knoxville for twenty-two days, this took place during the latter part of November and December of the year 1863.

## Anonymous, Company C

Crab Orchard, Tennessee, September 6, 1863

Editors, *Miners' Journal:*

Since my last we have changed our base from Mill Dale, Miss. to our old place, the Department of Kentucky, Major Gen. Burnside commanding. We had quite a nice time coming up the river. We left Mill Dale on board the steamboat Southwester, on the 10th of August, and proceeded up the Mississippi River to Cairo, Ill. landing several times for wood and coal. We stopped over night at Cairo, when we embarked on board of freight cars, and went on our way rejoicing. We changed cars at Sandoval, Ill. when we again proceeded through Illinois, Indiana, Ohio, to Cincinnati, where we were entertained by the citizens. We partook of a hearty breakfast, and left sadly thinking of old times. We proceeded to the ferry where we crossed to Covington, Ky. and marched back about a mile and a half where we encamped on the Licking River, in a nice position. We received two months pay there and the boys were pretty flush. We sported around Cincinnati and Covington at a great rate. On the 24th of August we were ordered to have two days rations in our grub bags, and to go to Hickman's Bridge, Ky. We started in the evening, and those who slept that night found themselves in Lexington when we waked up. We laid in town until three o'clock, running around and meeting our old friends in the 48th Pa. Vols. They have a nice place, not much to do but eat drink and be merry. The train left at three o'clock, leaving many of its passengers behind. We went on to Nicholasville, where we laid over night. We marched three 3½ miles the next morning, to Camp Nelson where we laid 9 or 10 days, living high and paying high for it. On the 1st we started for this place which the Kentuckians boast as being the Saratoga of the South. While we were at Mill Dale, Miss. Corporal Ben Brown of Schuylkill Haven, and a member of Company C died. He was beloved by all who knew him, and the Company deeply regrets his loss. Our Lieut Col. Thomas Brenholtz died on the 19th of August, at Evansville Ind. while on his way up the river. The officers and men feel irreparable loss of so noble and brave a man. The officers are wearing crape for 30 days in honor of the deceased. Brigadier General Welsh, late Colonel of the 45 Regt., P.V. died in Cincinnati.

We are encamped on a widow lady's ground, she having lost her husband and two sons hung by Morgan's men. The eldest son was 16, and the other 14 years old. The only son left lies at the point of death. Her husband was a captain in the Union Army, and was home on sick furlough. He was taken and hung when he was trying to get to his regiment. All three were hung on one tree, and left hanging until the citizens took them down and buried them. I will write again when anything turns up that will interest you.

"Nailer"

## Private John Doudle

### Knoxville, Tennessee, September 1863

September 10th, 1863 the regiment, with the Ninth Corps took up the line of march for Knoxville, via Cumberland Gap. Less than a hundred men and officers were fit for duty.

Arriving at Knoxville on the 26th, we all thought we would have a resting spell, but we were all disappointed, for we had been here scarcely a week when we were ordered to Blue Springs as a supporting force to a portion of the 23rd Army Corps.

The enemy had taken a strong position. About 4,000 of the 23rd Corps, under Colonel Carter, tried to drive them for about eight hours and finally reported to General Burnside that they could not dislodge them. The General ordered them to make way for our division (numbering less than 3,000 men). We went at them with a will, and drove them right under their batteries and could we have had a hour more daylight we could have captured half their force. The division won quite a reputation in the affair and was highly complimented.

The regiment had only two wounded in this engagement: Patrick McCollough from Company C and George Devinney a musician from Company H. The latter died from the effects of his wounds.

Returning from Blue Springs, we proceeded to London, and falling back to Lenoir Station, we erected winter quarters and expected to have a comfortable time, but as the old saying goes, "There is no rest for the weary."

## Anonymous, Company C

### Knoxville, Tennessee, October 17, 1863

Editors, *Miners' Journal:*

We left Crab Orchard, Ky. on the 10th of September and started for this city. We left with 8 days rations, 5 in the knapsack, and three in the haversacks. We marched to Mount Vernon, 14 miles from Crab Orchard, where we encamped for the night. We left camp at three o'clock next morning and marched 11 miles where we laid over night again. Then we received two months pay, up to the 1st of September. We marched off the next morning, some pretty flush, and more with empty pocket books, on account of having to pay for clothing overdrawn, and marched 8 miles to London, (a place noted for apple jacks) where we laid Saturday afternoon and Sunday morning. On Monday we took the road again and marched to Jones Creek, where we stopped for the night. The next day we marched 14 miles to a town called Barboursville. We laid near the town all night. We again started off the next day, and got 8 miles where we had to lay two days on account of the rain and bad roads. On the 17th we crossed the Cumberland River and marched within nine miles of the celebrated Cumberland Gap. The next day we marched through the gap and went into camp. At 1½ o'clock on the next morning we marched back to the Gap, and turned in our Austrian rifles and received Springfield rifles in their place. These arms were captured in the surrender of the Rebels under General Frazier at the Gap. We marched 20 miles through a town called Cassville, which has been nearly destroyed by the Rebels. The next day we reached Morristown, 21 miles distant from where we camped. Morristown is a nice place situated on the East Tennessee and Virginia

Railroad. We laid 1½ days there and then started and marched to Mosey Creek, another railroad station 1¼ miles from Morristown. We left early in the morning and marched 20 miles to Ellwoods Farm where we stopped for the night. Next day we arrived at Knoxville. We laid comfortably near Knoxville until the 8th of October, when we left with sorrowful thoughts and five days rations. We marched to town, and got aboard cars and proceeded as far as Bulls Gap, where we disembarked and slung our knapsacks on our backs and marched three miles, when we found a poor looking camp. We stopped till the morning of the 10th, when we got orders to advance on the enemy. Well, off we went, and got within a mile of Blue Springs, where we formed line of battle. We kept changing position until about three o'clock, when we marched to the front and formed our line in a hollow; threw out part of the 45th P.V. as skirmishers. Then we advanced through a corn field, where we met with a heavy enemy fire. We rushed on, yelling and running. But the Rebs had no loads to carry and beat us running, one thing they deserve special credit for. We went on till we got near their batteries. Then we were ordered to lie down. Well, we lied down and the next mourning we got up and they were gone. So we packed up and put out after them. We marched 21 miles after them but could not catch them. We passed through Greensville and Rheastown. Next day we about faced and marched back leaving the mounted men [to] go on after them. Well, we marched back to Blue Springs. When the men were skirmishing in the morning, the Rebels told them to bring on their bald headed Burnside and his 9th Army Corps. He did so, but they did not feel inclined to receive us, so they made a hasty retreat, leaving their cartridges behind them. We marched within four miles of Blue Springs where we were [to] take the cars, but there were no cars to take us, so we marched to Bulls Gap. They played the same game on us there so we marched to Morristown, where we got the cars and rode into Knoxville, and marched to camp where we now are.

Patrick McCullough of Co. C, was slightly wounded, George Deveny, drummer of Company H, was also wounded.

In the Ninth Corps there were 10 killed, 42 wounded and seven missing.

Nailer

On October 10 the division had a small fight at Blue Springs, Tennessee and on November 16 the whole 9th Corps was engaged at Campbell's Station. According to Samuel P. Bates's *History of the Pennsylvania Volunteers*, the regiment arrived upon the field on October 10 and was immediately brought into position on the left of the front line. A charge was ordered, and the enemy was driven back in confusion, and pursued to a point near the Virginia line. It was estimated that the enemy's force in this battle was double that of our own. The loss of the regiment was inconsiderable.

Returning to Lenoir Station the regiment was ordered to build winter quarters and hold off anything approaching from the southwest. The company was in camp but just two weeks when General James Longstreet attacked the regiment with a large force and almost routed the 23rd Army Corps. The 9th Corps was sent in support and pushed Longstreet back toward the river.

In early November General Longstreet was ordered to attack General Burnside's troops at Knoxville. Running along parallel routes, Longstreet and Burnside raced for Campbell Station. Burnside hoped to arrive first and continue onto Knoxville, and Longstreet hoped to cut off Burnside and force him to fight outside his earthworks. On November 16, 1863, Burnside reached Campbell Station—first. His main force arrived about noon and just a short time later, Longstreet arrived. Longstreet tried a double envelopment, striking both flanks at the same time. The fight on the right was fierce but the Union soldiers held and he was unable to turn the left. Burnside ordered his two divisions to withdraw slowly to a ridge in their rear. Longstreet suspended his attack leaving Burnside free to fall back toward Knoxville. The 50th was on the right of line and directly in the front and held for four hours.

## Private John Doudle

Campbell Station, Tennessee, November 1863

> On the 14th of November the Rebel General Longstreet, with a force crossed the Tennessee River at Hough's Ferry. We hurried to the front on the extreme right with orders to push at once to the ferry on the supposition that the enemy had re-crossed the river. After pushing our advance 100 yards, we threw out skirmishers to cover our front, and then deployed in line of battle. The skirmishers were ordered to move forward cautiously, and if challenged or fired upon, not to reply, but seek cover and if possible, hold their position. We had not moved over 100 yards, this whole line was challenged, and, of course, we came to a halt. Orders had been received not to attack, but hold our position until daylight, which we did. Our skirmishers and the enemy's were not over 40 rods apart.
>
> During the night it rained and stormed and, notwithstanding, the weather was very cold. The regiment was ordered to charge at daylight, but before that time the whole program was changed for wise and prudential purposes; hence we fell back to Lenoir Station and assisted in holding the enemy in check during which time we were obliged too burn large quantities of stores, etc. among which were the books and papers of the regiment. It now became a matter of some consequence as to who should reach Campbell Station first, a point where the Kingston Road intersects the London Road. The race was an exciting one: Col. Hartranft with his division was only a few minutes in advance of the enemy.

> Here the decisive battle of the campaign was fought. The enemy more than doubled Burnside's forces and yet we held them in check for several hours. The 50th was in the front on the right. For four hours we sustained heavy artillery fire and at short ranges for over half and hour.
>
> A portion of the 23rd Corps broke on our left, but rallied again nearly in the former line. As the 50th regiment did not waver, although the regiment was obliged to change its position several times in order to prevent a flank movement on part of the enemy.
>
> When we finally retired it was under a combined Infantry and artillery fire over an open plain for about 400 yards before we could get cover.
>
> The conduct of the officers and men of the Ninth Corps was beyond all praise, and the Battle of Campbell Station will be remembered proudly by those who were fortunate enough to participate in it. We arrived at Knoxville after a tedious night march at three o'clock in the morning of the 17th, having been marching and fighting, and without sleep since the 14th. We took a rest until towards 12 o'clock when we again went into position and commenced digging rifle pits. For the first few days work could be done by daylight, but after that everything had to be done at night, as the enemy were almost in speaking distance and it was unsafe for any man to show his head above the rifle pits.

The 50th occupied the central position on the left wing in rifle pits they made. On November 29, at the crack of dawn, the enemy charged Fort Sanders, a high point just northwest of the city of Knoxville.

## Corporal Charles E. Brown

Knoxville, Tennessee, November 1863

> We had all the wire entanglements and a ditch about twelve feet wide and about ten or twelve feet deep. This was the place where most of the fighting took place, and where an attack was made almost every night. At last this ditch was more than full, and piled high above the ground with dead bodies of soldiers. This gave the Rebels an advantage, for they came right over the top of the dead. We did not move our cannon any more, but loaded them as fast as we could, and fired right into the port holes and over on top of the fort. A Rebel Colonel got on top of the fort and with a Rebel flag in his hands waved it and shouted to his boys following him to come on, that they had us. Our General Faurara [Ferrero], our division commander, ran up and pulled him down, with his Rebel flag. It then turned out that they were classmates at West Point. During this day we whipped

the Rebels and slaughtered them unmercifully. The next morning they asked us to Parley, in order to bury their dead. It was granted them.

They began the work of burying their dead and it took them a full two days to do so. The scenes here were very frightful. I saw many of the dead soldiers who fell in the ditch first, they had their bayonets on their guns. Some of the guns with the bayonets on them stood straight up and I saw as many as two, three or four strings of men on one gun. They were so dreadfully tangled up in the guns. There was about four or five feet of water in the ditch and about half of this was blood and the other half water.

For four or five days after this when daylight came there were no Rebels to be found. We made a feeble attempt to follow them, but we had no shoes or clothing, and hardly anything to eat, and were therefore handicapped and were unable to do much.

General Grant sent his cavalry up and made plans to capture Longstreet and his army, but he got away on them. The fighting was over in Tennessee and we marched to Blaine's Crossroads and went into camp getting ready to re enlist.

## Private John Doudle

Knoxville, Tennessee, December 1863

While in the rifle pits, the greater the danger the more reckless everyone seemed to grow. Thus for 13 days the troops patiently and heroically endured the privations of the siege. Our rations were cut down so low that we used the sweepings of the mills.

On the 29th of November at early dawn the enemy made charge on Fort Sanders. The 50th held a position to the right of the fort. A small detail of the regiment was sent to assist the garrison in repelling the enemy.

The attack was made with great impetuosity and sustained with great unflinching valor, but was repulsed with terrible slaughter. The anxiety attending the siege was keenly visible on all countenances, but one could discern the determination to hold out to the bitter end. This feeling all possessed. Not a man in the trenches thought we would hold our position. All seemed to share our noble commander's idea. Longstreet, finding it unsafe for him to remain longer, withdrew during the night of the 4th of December.

The casualties of the regiment during the campaign from Houghe's Ferry to the raising of the Siege of Knoxville December 5, are: four killed in action and seven wounded in action.

Immediately after the siege was raised the regiment with the Ninth Corps followed the enemy as far as Rutledge, then encamped at Blairs Crossroads, as the troops suffered a great deal, having been on short rations since the siege of Knoxville, laying out night after night in the rain, destitute of clothing, and two hundred miles from our base of supplies, many were barefooted and the winter set in with snow upon the ground The sufferings we endured while on this campaign and marching over the mountains, 200 miles back to Nicholasville, Ky. were equally as great as those endured by our forefathers at Valley Forge.

*From the Official Records:*
*Col. B.C. Christ*
*Report.*
*The report of the action that took place during the Knoxville, Tenn. Campaign. November 4th through. December 23rd 1863.*

*On the same evening, in compliance with orders from division headquarters, I temporarily detached from the brigade and took from their position in the rifle-pits the Twenty-ninth Regiment Massachusetts Volunteers, and sent them to re-enforce that part of the command occupying Fort Sanders and its immediate surroundings. About midnight five companies of this regiment were detached, and, under the command of a Thomas W. Clark, were ordered to the support of Colonel Morrison, commanding First Brigade, in the rifle pits on our left, the right wing of this regiment, under command Major Chipman, still occupying their position on the hill in rear of the fort, but were subsequently ordered into the rifle pits on the left and near the fort, and both detachments were thus situated when the attack on Fort Sanders on the morning of the 29th began. The detachment under command of Major Chipman were first ordered into the fort, and the one under Captain Clark, pursuant to orders, soon followed, the first arriving during the hottest of the fight, and the last before the battle was over, and both contributing largely to the successful results on that occasion, each detachment capturing a battle-flag from the enemy as a part of the spoils of the victory.*

*Detaching the Twenty-ninth Regiment Massachusetts Volunteers from my command left me a long line of front to picket and protect with three small regiments. My men were obliged to go on picket every other day, and when off such duty were obliged, from necessity, to be in a cramped position in the rifle-pits during the day to avoid the balls of the enemy's sharpshooters, and at night, in pursuance of orders, one-third of them were kept constantly awake to guard against surprise. Add to this one-fourth rations of coffee and one-half rations of coarse, heavy corn bread, and the fact that they were poorly shod (some even barefooted) and poorly clothed, without overcoats, and many of them without blankets, and it will be seen that their privations and sufferings were equal to, if not in excess of, any other portion of the Union forces since the commencement of the war. Yet, notwithstanding all these sufferings—and it should be recorded to their credit—there was neither murmur nor complaint. All promptly and cheerfully performed their duty, and expressed themselves ready and willing to endure even greater hardships if it would contribute to the success of our arms and drive the enemy out of East Tennessee.*

*As a further evidence of their patriotism and loyalty and their determination to assist to the last in crushing out this hell-born and hell-bound Rebellion, I would state that two of these regiments, the Twenty-ninth Massachusetts and Fiftieth Pennsylvania, have already re-enlisted as veteran volunteers. The Forty-sixth New York have nearly if not quite the required number, while the Twenty-seventh Michigan regret that they have not been in the service long enough to avail themselves of the provisions of General Orders, No.—.*

*About 3 o'clock on the morning of the 5th of December, Captain Schwenk, of the Fiftieth Pennsylvania, in command of the picket, brought in a prisoner, with the information that the enemy had raised the siege and under cover of the night had retreated. This prisoner I immediately sent to division headquarters.*

*At 10 a.m. (5th), in pursuance of orders, I proceeded with the Twenty-seventh Michigan, Twenty-ninth Massachusetts, and Fiftieth Pennsylvania to a paper-mill about 4 miles below Knoxville, between the London and Clinton roads, in search of a Georgia regiment of Rebels reported to have been cut off and unable to join their command. I scoured the country from the river to the Clinton road.*

*To Captain Schwenk, Company A, Fiftieth Pennsylvania Volunteers, I am much indebted for the manner in which he handled his skirmishers on the evening we reached Huff's Ferry, and for the effort he made to penetrate the enemy's line in order to ascertain what he was doing. I am satisfied that in these attempts he failed only because success was impossible.*

*All of which is respectfully submitted.*
*B.C. Christ*

# Re-enlistment and Return Home

*Keep your fears to yourself, but share your courage with others.*

—*Robert Louis Stevenson*

On January 1, 1864, nearly the entire regiment re-enlisted at the camp at Blaine's Crossroads. As of this date the regiment fielded about three hundred officers and men. Back in September 1861, ninety-five men had enlisted at Schuylkill Haven into the original Company C. Forty-six of the original men re-enlisted as veteran volunteers; twelve men had either been killed in action or died from other causes; one man resigned; seventeen men were discharged under Surgeons' Certificate or for wounds received in action; six men were listed as deserters and six men were listed as not on the M.O. register. Seven men would muster out on September 29, 1864, on expiration of term.

By January 1, 1864, Company C had spent 845 days on active duty. The regiment was in dire need of clothing, shoes and equipment. They had not drawn an item of clothing from September up to January. Before the men were reissued new clothing and shoes they had to march over two hundred miles to Nicholasville, Kentucky. This march was performed in 10 days. Many of the men were barefoot and, to make matters worse, the snow was covering the ground. Before they began the march the regiment drew thirty raw hides that the men made into moccasins. But during the march the wetness and muddy roads made the moccasins stretch and the men could not keep them on their feet.

In late December 1863, Colonel Christ wrote in a letter to his son Harry, "I assure you we have been roughing it of late, lying night after night in the rain on the wet ground, sometimes without fire, when it was so cold that it was impossible to sleep. The sufferings endured while at Blaine's Cross Roads and on the march over the mountains back to Nicholasville, Kentucky, were equally as great as those endured by our forefathers at Valley Forge."

They passed over mountains, making the march almost unbearable, but they still continued on, finally arriving at Nicholasville. During the march, half the men were without underclothing and shoes. Almost every man was without socks, eighty-five men had no pants and forty-seven men had no jackets. While at Nicholasville the men finally drew new clothing and shoes. The regiment of veteran volunteers was granted a veteran furlough of thirty days and they arrived back at Harrisburg at Camp Curtain on February 6, 1864. The boys of Company C took the train for Pottsville and Schuylkill Haven and went on a well-deserved furlough.

## Private John Doudle

Blaine's Crossroads, Kentucky, January 1863–1864

On the 1[st] of January the regiment re-enlisted at Blaine's Cross Roads for three more years during the war, and [with the] circumstances we were in at the present time as we were all young men, we thought it would be a shame to disband such a noble and brave organization as the Ninth Corps and such gallant officers. Even the name mentioned along the time of General A.E. Burnside would fill the soldier's heart with such patriotism that they would risk life and limb for his sake if necessary, and which we often did, and as we were participants in so many battles and endured so many privations that we determined to wipe secession from the land.

After our re-enlistment the great question was, how are we going to march 200 miles with about six inches of snow on the ground, and the weather extremely cold. To protect the feet of the shoeless, on the homeward march, shoes were made of rawhide. Many of them had to be abandoned during our first day's march. The heat from within and the melting snow made them stretch as to be almost useless, and a great many threw them away and wrapped their feet in such clothing as could be spared. To add to our distress we were nearly perished and starved with hunger. After our arrival at Camp Dick Robinson, Nicholasville, Ky. the regiment was supplied with new clothing, blankets, provisions shoes, etc. When it was drawn up in line preparatory to taking the cars for Cincinnati. Its appearance had improved wonderfully, each man having donned his new suit.

After arriving at Cincinnati the regiment was quartered in the fifth St. Market House, waiting our pay, after which we proceeded to Harrisburg, Pa. where we arrived February 6[th]. In a few days after at Harrisburg each man was given a 30 day's furlough, sent home to relate to our loved ones the many incidents of camp life and the fortunes and misfortunes of war. Co. C of which I was a member arrived at Schuylkill Haven and met with a hearty reception and was presented with a beautiful silk flag by the ladies of town and an elegant address by the Honorable H.N. Coxe. Our respected Captain D.F. Burket, while on furlough, opened a recruiting office for the purpose of filling our ranks as Company C and in fact the regiment was now very small in number owing to our service done since 1861. He soon had Company C's ranks full and our furlough expired.

Camp Dick Robinson was a Federal recruiting camp started in August of 1861. It was located south of the Ohio River and was named in honor of a Mr. Richard Robinson who was a staunch Union supporter who offered his home and farm to Federal service.

*From the Official Records*
*Report of Colonel Benjamin C. Christ*
*Actions in Kentucky*
*HDQRS. SECOND BRIG., FIRST Div., NINTH ARMY CORPS,*
*Blaine's Cross-Roads, Tenn., January 1, 1864.*
*SIR: In compliance with circular from division headquarters, I have the honor to submit the following report of the operations of my command from the time of breaking camp at Lenoir's Station until its arrival at this point:*

*The brigade left their quarters about noon on Saturday, November 14, and marched to Huff's Ferry, where it arrived after dark. I was ordered to the front with instructions, if possible, to push to the river. Arriving at the outer picket line of General White's division of the Twenty-third Corps, I deployed a line of skirmishers, under command of Capt. Samuel K. Schwenk, Fiftieth Pennsylvania Volunteers, and pushed them at first about 75 to 100 yards in advance of General White's. After forming in line of battle with Third Regiment (holding one in reserve), I sent a heavy support to Captain Schwenk, and ordered him to cautiously advance his line. They did not, however, advance 50 yards before they were challenged by the enemy's picket. Captain Schwenk halted his men, sought cover, and maintained that position during the night. The woods were so dark and the enemy so constantly vigilant, that all idea of pushing to the river during the night had to be abandoned.*

*At 4 a.m. of the 15th, we left our position and marched to Lenoir's Station, where we arrived at 12 p.m. and remained, keeping the enemy in check until daylight the next morning (16th). When we marched to Campbell's Station, where we arrived at 10 a.m., and took up a position on the left of the road in support of some batteries.*

*About 12 o'clock I was ordered to take a position on the right of the road in rear of and as support of the Third Brigade (Colonel Humphrey's). A short time after taking this latter position I threw forward the Twenty-ninth Massachusetts Volunteers (Colonel Peirce commanding) on Colonel Humphrey's right, to protect his flank against a movement of the enemy in that direction. Subsequently I relieved Colonel Humphrey altogether, and took a position on our extreme right and in front. I held this position for about three hours under both artillery and infantry fire of the enemy.*

*At 3.30 p.m. I was ordered to retire, leaving my skirmishers to cover my line as much as possible. I moved to the rear about 200 yards under a severe fire of artillery*

1. Canal boatmen gather on Dock Street in Schuylkill Haven, near the place where many men first enlisted. Ca. 1860s. *Courtesy of the Historical Society of Schuylkill County.*

2. Many of the boys of Company C were boatmen who worked the Schuylkill Canal. *Courtesy of the Historical Society of Schuylkill County.*

3. Canal boats of the type the boys of Company C worked on. These boats are docked at the Dock Street Basin, Schuylkill Haven. Boys of Company C drilled nearby. *Courtesy of the Historical Society of Schuylkill County.*

4. Officers of the 50th PVVI at the Ceremony for the National Cemetery at Gettysburg, 1865. *Courtesy of the Library of Congress.*

5. The men of Company C marched down the Port Royal Road during their time at Port Royal. *Courtesy of the Library of Congress.*

6. One of the first places the 50th served was the Coosaw River, Port Royal, South Carolina. *Courtesy of the Library of Congress.*

7. General Ambrose Burnside and the staff of the 9th Corps at Warrenton, Virginia, 1862. *Courtesy of the Library of Congress.*

8. Officers of the 50th PVVI posing with the famous John Burns at Gettysburg, 1865. Captain Charles E. Brown stands second from the left in the back row, wearing his Medal of Honor. *Courtesy of the Library of Congress.*

9. Burnside Bridge, Antietam Creek, Maryland. The 50th marched across this bridge and filed off to the right into battle. *Courtesy of the Library of Congress.*

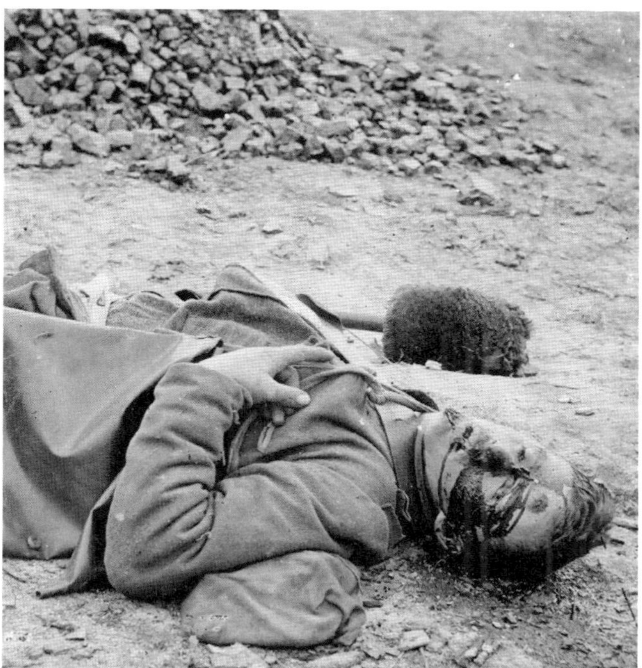

10. The horror of war. A dead Union Soldier near Petersburg, Virginia—a sight seen many times by the men of Company C. *Courtesy of the Library of Congress.*

11. A dead Confederate soldier inside fortifications near where the 50$^{th}$ fought. *Courtesy of the Library of Congress.*

12. The entrance to the mine dug under a Rebel fort by fellow Schuylkill Countians of the 48$^{th}$ PVI. The boys of Company C played an important part in this engagement. *Courtesy of the Library of Congress.*

13. Statue of Brigadier General Benjamin C. Christ, Antietam Battlefield, Maryland, marking the high-water mark of the company's advance.

14. The open field that Company C advanced during the Battle of Antietam on September 17, 1862.

15. The Sherrick Farm, Antietam, Maryland. Young Jere Helms was cared for and died in this stone barn.

16. Members of the 47th Virginia Living History Regiment holding a reproduction of the flag captured by Charles Brown. Gettysburg, Pennsylvania, 2005.

17. Tombstone and Medal of Honor plaque of Captain Charles E. Brown, in the First Union Cemetery, Schuylkill Haven.

18. Captain Charles E. Brown, ca. 1880. *Courtesy of the Historical Society of Schuylkill County.*

19. Medal of Honor marker for Henry Hill in the First Union Cemetery, Schuylkill Haven.

20. Henry Hill, ca. 1880.
*Courtesy of the Historical Society of Schuylkill County.*

21. A simple marker for a brave man. Captain D.F. Burket, the man who raised Company C, is buried in the First Union Cemetery, Schuylkill Haven.

22. GAR marker of William Tyson, who was wounded in the right hand during the Wilderness Campaign. First Union Cemetery, Schuylkill Haven.

23. Tombstone of Irving W. Tyson, a boatman, who was wounded in the battle of the Wilderness and was the last surviving member of Company C.

24. Many men of the 50th PVVI are buried in the GAR plot at the First Union Cemetery, Schuylkill Haven.

25. GAR marker of Lafayette Baker, who served with Company C from 1861 to 1865.

26. Tombstone of Corporal William Wildermuth, one of the last surviving members of the old Company C.

27. The author in front of the 50th PVVI monument, Antietam Battlefield, Maryland. The field behind is where the 50th advanced into battle.

*in my front (now my rear) and from the enemy's infantry and sharpshooters on our right (now my left). I now halted my column, faced to the enemy, and called in my skirmishers, and then moved to the rear over an open plain for near one-half mile under a heavy fire from one of the enemy's batteries. Arriving at our new position, I formed in rear of our batteries until 5 p.m., when, according to orders, I marched to Knoxville, where I arrived at 3 o'clock on the morning of the 17th, and was assigned a position in rear of Fort Sanders until 9 a.m., when I was ordered to take a position near the railroad, with my right resting on Creek, and my left extending toward Fort Sanders and connecting with Colonel Humphrey's right.*

*Although the men were worn down with fighting, marching, amid loss of sleep for the last three days and nights, yet they immediately, and under the circumstances with great alacrity, commenced digging rifle-pits, throwing up earth-works, constructing abatis, amid otherwise strengthening their position. At first this work was done during the day, but after the advance of the enemy's lines it was done under cover of the night.*

*From the 17th until the 5th of December my command, in common with the rest of the troops, were nearly surrounded by a superior force of the enemy, by which all outward communication was nearly cut off.*

*On the evenings of the 18th, 19th, and 20th, a number of buildings were by my order burned on my front, for the reason that they afforded shelter to the enemy.*

*On the night of the 28th, from information received from division headquarters and from indications and movements of the enemy, I had every reason to expect an attack on my position, and consequently had taken every precaution to render it unsuccessful. About 10 o'clock a charge was made, but by setting fire to some combustible materials previously prepared in the large round-house and other railroad buildings, as well as a number of private houses, making a complete wall of fire along my entire front, together with the determined resistance of a strong line of skirmishers advantageously posted in small pits and lunettes, the enemy were checked and soon after retired.*

## Corporal Charles E. Brown

Schuylkill Haven, Pennsylvania, January 1864

On the 13th of January, 1864 we have already re-enlisted and are starting for Sinsintia Court House. Before we started they gave us raw hides to make shoes. We cut a piece sufficiently large enough to wrap our feet in, and then cut a piece to tie them around our legs. We began to march with six inches of snow on the ground, and our raw hide moccasins only lasted five or six miles. The snow had melted and then froze. We could see blood stains all a ong the road, from the feet of the soldiers who preceded us. In a few days we met a train of pack mules, they were sent to meet us and had everything we needed but not

> in sufficient quantity. At last we reached Sinsintia Court House and we received some pay due us. We went to the Market House and had a fine time for several hours. We then left for Harrisburg and was [*sic*] given a month's furlough. We came back to Schuylkill Haven and remained here for thirty days.

While home on leave Captain Daniel F. Burket actively recruited thirty-one recruits during the month of February. During the early part of March, prior to departing Schuylkill Haven on March 8, three additional men enlisted in the ranks. After the company departed Schuylkill Haven, ten more men would find their way to the company campgrounds and enlist, giving a grand total of forty-four new men for 1864 and bringing the company almost to full strength.

## Private William H. Tyson

In the Field, Virginia

> Let me tell you, I was only 14 years old when the war broke out. The years of "61," "62" and "63" passed too slowly for me. But in 1864 I became 18 years of age and on February 22nd of that year I enlisted in Company C, of the 50th P.V.I. My brother Irving W. Tyson was in the same company as were many of the boys from Schuylkill Haven.

On March 20 the regiment rendezvoused at Annapolis, Maryland, where they spent time setting up camp, getting reorganized militarily, drilling and equipping the new recruits and preparing for the upcoming campaign season. The 50th was assigned to the 2nd Brigade, 1st Division of the 9th Army Corps.

## Private John Doudle,

Back in the Field, Virginia, March–April 1864

> We left Schuylkill Haven on the 8th of March, 1864 and proceeded to Camp Curtin, where we remained till the 20th. We then were sent to Annapolis, Md. and camped on the same grounds that we camped on in 1861. The regiment being recruited to the minimum standard and was fully organized and drilled. We were assigned to the Second brigade, Third Division of the Ninth Army Corps, with Col. B.C. Christ in command of the Second Brigade. On the 23rd of April, the Ninth Corps moved from Annapolis and on the 25th we were received by President Lincoln and marched to Alexandria, Va. and encamped. On the 27th the line of march was again taken up and on the 28th we passed over the Bull Run battle ground, resting at Warrington Junction until the 30th of April.

# 1864
# The Wilderness

*I heard the bullets whistle, and believe me, there is something charming in the sound.*
—*George Washington*

The battle of the Wilderness was fought between May 5 and 7, 1864. On the morning of May 5 the battle opened when the Union V Corps attacked Confederate General Richard Ewell's corps near the Orange Turnpike. During the afternoon General W.S. Hancock's II Corps, along with General George W. Getty's VI Corps, attacked Confederate General A.P. Hill's corps on the Plank Road. Both armies were trying to maneuver in dense woods and the fighting was inconclusive. Both sides settled in for the night, calling for reinforcements.

At dawn on May 6, General Hancock once again opened the battle and drove Hill's corps backward in total confusion. Later in the day General James Longstreet arrived with his corps and prevented the collapse of the Confederate right flank. The battle was actually a tactical draw, but this time General Grant did not withdraw like other Union generals had done in the past. On May 7 the Union army advanced by the left flank toward Spotsylvania Court House. During this engagement there were over 101,000 Union forces and 61,000 plus Confederate forces involved. Total combined casualties included 29,800, Federal 18,400, and Confederate 11,400.

On May 5 the 50$^{th}$ and the boys of Company C arrived at the banks of the Rapidan River and crossed at Germania Ford. Early the next morning the regiment formed line in a line of battle at the Wilderness Tavern, and by three o'clock the next afternoon the company found itself heavily engaged in the battle of the Wilderness. For the new recruits this would bring home the horror of war and battle in a very short time. These new recruits would "see the elephant" for the first time. Most of the new men had been in uniform for only a little over two months.

Company C lost First Sergeant William Hill, a veteran killed in action; Private Peter Fritz, a new recruit with less than three months service who died from the wounds he received in the battle; and Sam Martz, Levan Warner, Daniel Ebert and veteran Mike Reiley.

## Sergeant Charles E. Brown

Marching in Virginia, May 1864

After our short furlough we moved into Virginia, we marched down into Virginia when we arrived at the Wilderness, and on the 6th of May the battle began. We were standing in the woods awaiting the orders to charge on the Rebels, when 1st Sgt. William Hill gave the command, "Attention Company!" As he gave the command this black snake stood right up in front of him. Myself and Henry Hill struck it with our guns and knocked it down, but the snake came up again, then we killed it.

## Corporal John Doudle

On the March, Virginia, May 1864

On May 5th we crossed the Rapidan River at Germanna [*sic*] Ford, passing on to the front near the Wilderness Tavern, where we formed in line of battle, a little before three o'clock, and on the 6th the regiment was heavily engaged and at one time the Rebels were around us in the form of a horse shoe. Then we double quicked to a part of the field where our forces were stampeding. Our presence had the effect of infusing new energy into the disordered and broken ranks.

Our ammunition was nearly exhausted. When Lieut. Col. Overton sent word to the Brigade Commander B.C. Christ asking for a fresh supply of ammunition, but there was none to be had; the request was made the second time, when word was sent back, "Hold your ground at the point of a bayonet." Col. Overton did hold his ground, but at the cost of 70 men killed and wounded in the regiment.

The killed in our Company was 1st. Sgt. William Hill, Private Samuel Mertz, Private Michael Riley, Private Levan J. Warner.

The wounded included, Private David Berger, Private Adam Lloyd, Private William Eckert, Private George W. Lloyd, Private Irving Tyson, Private Josiah Wright, Private Peter Fritz, Private William Hoffman, Private Charles Shappel and Private Jonathan McHargue. Peter Fritz died from his wounds.

## Sergeant. Charles E. Brown

Wilderness, Virginia, May 1864

Now we are charging the Rebels, we are losing large numbers of our Company, they are being killed and wounded. Sergeant Hill was one of the first to get wounded, that was

> about ten minutes after the snake stood in front of him. In thirty minutes he was dead. After the battle I hunted up his diary and in it found he had written what we should do with him and for his family if he were killed in battle. In this battle Captain Burket was wounded very severe and Company C lost more men in the battle than the rest of the regiment lost. Myself and Henry Hill got so close to the Rebels that we could almost reach one another with our guns. Our regiment then retreated and that put myself and Hill in a bad fix. The Rebels kept shouting, "Surrender you Yankee son's of bitches." We were behind two big trees and they shot lots of the bark off these trees. I said, "Hill we must run or they will come out and capture us." So we began to run, and believe me the bullets came after us like hail. Running back we saw the dead and wounded lying all over the woods, but we got back safe. Soon it got dark, and the battle was almost over. About 10 o'clock myself and Peter Garret went over the battlefield to see what we could find; however we did not find anything of good account.

Corporal Henry Hill was awarded the Medal of Honor for his actions on this day. The citation for Corporal Hill reads: "This soldier, with one companion, would not retire when his regiment fell back in confusion after an unsuccessful charge, but instead advanced and continued firing upon the enemy until the regiment re-formed and regained its position" The medal was awarded to him on September 23, 1897. Charles Brown, the companion who would not retreat, would earn the Medal of Honor for himself in a little over three months.

Captain Samuel K. Schwenk in charge of Company A wrote to the *Pottsville Miners' Journal* and praised the actions of the men of the 50th Regiment on May 6: "The Regiment was engaged in the hottest of the fight at the Wilderness, and drove the enemy in good style to his rifle pits, which he was compelled to leave during the night."

Immediately following the Wilderness campaign General Grant and General Meade attempted to advance on Richmond by a left flank movement. On May 8 the move was stalled at Spotsylvania Court House. During the two weeks there was a series of battles fought. Over 152, 000 men fought in the battle, with the Federal army having over 100,000 men and Confederate forces numbering in excess of 52,000. Over 30,000 men were listed as casualties during the engagement, 18,000 Federal and 12,000 Confederate.

The most famous of the battles was the Union attack at the Bloody Angle on May 12–13. General Lee's forces were almost cut in two and Union forces captured nearly a whole division of Confederate forces. In what was one of the bloodiest battles fought during the war, the Confederate forces counterattacked and sealed the gap made by Grant's Federals. For over twenty hours the battle raged. On May 19 Confederate forces tried to turn the right flank of the Federal forces but failed at the Harris farm and were beaten with a heavy loss. On May 21, 1864, General Grant disengaged and continued his march toward Richmond.

General George Meade ordered General Burnside to select two of the best regiments in his corps to protect the rear of the army while moving from the field. The 50th Pennsylvania was chosen as one of the two regiments and was closely pursued by the enemy's cavalry forces.

On May 9, while moving along the Fredericksburg Road, the 50th had come in contact with enemy forces at the Nye River and was hotly engaged. Ordered to cross the river, the regiment was placed on a small rise in the land about a quarter of a mile from the river. The brigade was attacked by a considerable force. The 50th made a charge up a steep incline and routed the enemy, even though they were outnumbered. In the battle of Spotsylvania Court House on May 12, the 50th suffered a heavy loss and the regiment was cut in two. Part of the regiment went with Captain Schwenk and was thought lost but the men fought their way out and were fighting desperately on the right of the line. Captain Schwenk, along with men of the 20th Michigan, 51st Pennsylvania, 1st, 20th and 27th Michigan and 109th New York, made a valiant bayonet charge and drove the Rebels back into their rifle pits.

## Private William H. Tyson

Spotsylvania Court House, May 1864

I got my first real taste of fighting during the terrible Wilderness Campaign. And when I say it was terrible, I mean just that. You could hardly see in the dense gloomy thickets and it was hand to hand fighting most of the time. During this series of battles, I had an experience I'll never forget. It was late in the afternoon. We were lying on our stomachs. There was a soldier close beside me. He was dying. I gave him what little water that remained in my canteen. Not many minutes later he died. Strapped to my side was my haversack bag containing hard tack and sugar. After a time I became hungry and reached back for the bag. It was wet. As I held it up to my eyes, I saw that the bag was drenched in blood. The dead man beside me had suffered a gaping wound in his side. It was his blood that was on my haversack of food.

The night before we got out of the woods, a fire started. You read of this in history books but one had to be there to really appreciate how frightful it was. The blood curdling cries of the dying men as flames slowly roasted their bodies almost set us mad. There was nothing we could do.

Then came the Ny River battle and that was plenty bad. On May 12th at Spotsylvania. It was the worst battle of my life.

## Sergeant Charles E. Brown

Spotsylvania Court House, May 1864

On the 7th of May General Grant made a flank movement upon General Lee. We were getting close to Spotsylvania Court House. Here we were fighting for a good many days. It is in history as the 12th day of May 1864. That was the hardest day of fighting. However we did fight hard battles before and after the twelfth. We had many killed, wounded and taken prisoner. Our Company lost fourteen men by being taken prisoner. A good many of Company C were also killed and wounded. Among the wounded were Captain Burket, August Mellon and William Wildermuth, three good and brave soldiers, and many others.

## Private William H. Tyson

Spotsylvania Court House, Virginia, May 1864

On May 12th at Spotsylvania I was in the worst battle of my life. This was at the Bloody Angle. We had to club the Johnnies with our musket butts. It was a case of keeping eyes ahead, and no matter who fell beside you keep going. The dead were pulled one on top of another. I got out of that lucky enough.

## Sergeant Charles E. Brown

Spotsylvania Court House, Virginia, May 1864

On the 18th day of May we were some miles below Spotsylvania Court House, the fighting was very hard here. On this day Henry Hill and another good soldier were wounded. We fought at the river and we fought at the same river at another place. We fought here from the 23rd to the 27th. We then arrived at Bethesda Church, on June 1st. Here William Henry was wounded and died a month or so later. At this time I was given command of the Company. I was the fourth Sergeant. All the commissioned officers and sergeants above and below me in rank were killed, wounded or taken prisoners. This left me in command of my Company.

## Sergeant James H. Levan

In the rifle pits, May 21, 1864

[A letter to his brother, as it appeared in the *Pottsville Miners' Journal*]
Dear Editors:
We have plenty to do, fighting everyday and working every night like bees. I can't say what the Corps (9th) has done, for the woods are so thick, that I can only

see our Brigade. We were in the fight on the 6th, we lost our orderly that day, and the loss in our regiment was heavy. On the 9th we met the enemy again. Our Brigade led the advance and engaged the Rebels. We laid them out handsomely that day. Captain Burket was wounded in the charge on this day. Our loss was not so heavy in the regiment. We had skirmishing and some small fighting until the twelfth, when two brigades of our Division charged into the woods, at the same time the Johnnies came charging on us: they discovered us first and got on our flanks and rear. It was terrible; such a shower of grape, canister, spherical case and shells, to say nothing of the musketry. But we pressed on and got up to their works, and the sight we saw there: it was every man for himself. The bayonet and the butt of the musket were brought into play, for there was no time to load. They came around us like bees, but every man was a hero there, and we soon advanced again. I pray that I may never see such a slaughter again.

I was taken prisoner twice before I got out of the woods. The first I knew of our being surrounded was when I heard someone say, "Surrender you Dammed Yankee, its all up with you." I looked up and saw a terrible big officer swinging his sword over my head. My blood ran cold. I thought of the horrors of Libby Prison, and then I thought of home. The last thought gave me courage and strength. So I jumped for him and took him in the pit of his stomach. I then gave a yell and started on the run. I thought I was free, when another greasy Johnny presented his gun in my front, which caused me to halt. "Drop that gun, its all up with you," he said, when all of a sudden some one took him along side of the head, which caused him to drop mighty sudden, and away went I and if I did not do some tall running there is no snakes. When I got [to] a clearing I laid down to rest for a few minutes. I then started to hunt up the regiment. I soon found the Captain of Company B. We got eight men together, when the Lieut. Colonel came along; we formed a line and rallied the stragglers. Gen. Burnside came up and said, "Boys don't go back, but go and support those guns," meaning a battery that had no support, which the Rebels attempted to take, "And hold it any cost." We had just taken our position when Lieutenant Brumm came to us with both our flags. It infused new life into us. Brumm derives the greatest credit. He took the new flag out of the Rebel's hands. Our Color Sergeants were shot.

We were then ordered to the front, to hold the enemy in check who were advancing. There we lay, a handful of men sharp-shooting the enemy pickets. General Wilcox saw us there, and said, "Boys, you have done nobly," and proposed three cheers for us.

In the fighting up to the 21st, our Company (C) lost 42 men killed and wounded, besides eleven whom we can't account for. They went into the charge in the woods on the 13th with us, but never came out.

I am the only Sergeant out of five left. The whole eight corporals are killed or wounded. The regiment is very small. Our loss is 333. The greater part are from the first five companies. We have left but five commissioned officers left for duty in the regiment. On the 12th, one captain was killed, 2 wounded and missing. One 1st Lieut., one 2nd Lieut. and our Adjutant are missing.

*From the Official Records*
*Report on the Wilderness, Ny River and Spotsylvania Campaigns*
*Lieutenant Colonel Byron M. Cutcheon*
*CAPTAIN: In accordance with instructions from headquarters First Division, Ninth Army Corps, I have the honor to submit the following report of the part taken in the several actions of this campaign up to the 30th July, 1864, by the several regiments in this brigade:*

*Preliminary Remarks*
*At the beginning of this campaign this brigade (then the Second Brigade, Third Division, Ninth Army Corps) consisted of the following regiments, viz: Seventy-ninth New York Volunteers, the Fiftieth Pennsylvania Veteran Volunteers, Twentieth Michigan Volunteer infantry, the First Michigan Sharpshooters, and the Sixtieth Ohio Volunteer Infantry. On the 4th of May the brigade marched from Warrenton Junction, but the Seventy-ninth New York and the Sixtieth Ohio were left as garrison and did not rejoin until after the battle of the Wilderness. We crossed the Rapidan at noon of May 5, and took post on the right of the army to cover the ford, but did not become engaged on that day.*

## The Battle of the Wilderness

*At 3 o'clock of the morning of 6th May the brigade, Col. B. C. Christ commanding, was put in motion and marched up the plank road until it arrived at the Wilderness Run…The Twentieth Michigan and Fiftieth Pennsylvania were formed in line along the right of the open field before mentioned, when the enemy opened upon them a brisk fire of artillery from a battery upon a ridge to the left (south) of the field and across the run. By order of Colonel Christ the Twentieth Michigan and Fiftieth Pennsylvania Volunteers now moved back to the left and formed—the Fiftieth to the left and the Twentieth to the right of the road by which we had advanced at its debouchments upon the open field. The First Sharpshooters remained upon the skirmish line covering the front of the brigade and connecting with the Fifth Corps on the right and with the Second Division, Ninth Army Corps, upon the left. The*

*Twentieth Michigan and Fiftieth Pennsylvania Volunteers now threw up an abatis in their front and remained quiet until the middle of the afternoon, when, in accordance with orders from the general commanding, they were hastily withdrawn without waiting for the withdrawal of the First Michigan Sharpshooters. These latter were ordered to withdraw, the reserve companies immediately, and the skirmishers as quickly and as quietly as possible…*

*Meanwhile, the Twentieth Michigan and Fiftieth Pennsylvania, marching almost at the double-quick, came up in rear of the position, where the Second Division of the Corps and the First Brigade of this division were then actively engaged. These regiments immediately formed in line, and advanced to support the troops just mentioned…All things being in readiness, at 5 p.m. the order was given to advance, which was done in fine style, driving in the enemy's skirmishers rapidly, and we soon attacked their main line, which was also forced back…In advancing, however, the left of the Fiftieth Pennsylvania retired somewhat, leaving my right exposed, and at the same time I discovered that I was receiving some part of the fire of our own line farther to the right. I therefore retired sufficiently to restore my connection with the Fiftieth Pennsylvania. At this juncture a Rebel column, apparently of one brigade, was discovered moving around our left at a distance of not more than 200 yards, protected by a line of flankers. I immediately strengthened and extended my skirmish line, and ordered them to pitch into this column as it was moving by the flank. This they did vigorously, and at the same time, by my request, the Eleventh New Hampshire was moved up on my left, and the result was that the Rebel column became dissatisfied with its position and retired without attacking. So ended our active participation in the battle of the Wilderness…*

## March to Spotsylvania

*Before daylight of May 8 we withdrew from the Wilderness and halted near the Old Tavern. This brigade was detailed as rear Guard of the army, and the Twentieth Michigan and Fiftieth Pennsylvania were rear guard to the brigade. These two regiments moved abreast, the former left in front on the right of the road, and the latter right in front on the left of the road, with a section of artillery between.*

*Each regiment kept a Company of skirmishers to the rear, and thus we moved, ready to form line of battle at any moment by filing right and left, with the artillery in the center. The enemy followed at a short distance, but did not press us at all. That night we bivouacked on the plank road 3 miles southeast of Chancellorsville. Next morning took to the road in the following order: Sixtieth Ohio, Twentieth Michigan, Fiftieth Pennsylvania, First Michigan Sharpshooters, Seventy-ninth New York.*

# The Battle of the Ny River

*At about 9 a.m. we came in sight of Ny River, and a part of the Sixtieth Ohio was sent forward as skirmishers, with the remaining companies of that regiment as reserve...we crossed the river and advanced almost to the crest of the hill, with but little opposition...The Fiftieth Pennsylvania was thrown into position on the right of the Twentieth, and the First Sharpshooters on the left, while the Seventy-ninth New York took position near the Gayle house. The First Sharpshooters were now thrown quickly forward to the position occupied by Lieutenant Lounsberry, who now formed on their left, while the Fiftieth was in like manner advanced to the position where I had posted Company D, of the Twentieth. The fight now became quite sharp. When the enemy charged the First Sharpshooters, through some misapprehension or other cause, broke and fell back in much confusion, and was rallied with difficulty.*

*Lieutenant Lounsberry, however, with his Company of the Twentieth, still maintained the position which the First Sharpshooters had left, and did not leave it until the Seventy-ninth New York charged in gallant style, driving back the enemy, and the First Sharpshooters had been rallied and returned to their position. He then reported to his regiment with a loss of 4 men, at about the same moment that the First Sharpshooters fell back, the Sixtieth Ohio fell back also, after a stubborn fight, and thus the whole weight of the attack on the right of the road fell upon the Fiftieth Pennsylvania. This regiment held its ground for a few minutes) but finally the whole left wing, with Lieutenant-Colonel Overton, fell back under the crest. The Twentieth still lay in reserve, but was becoming engaged. At this moment reverse seemed imminent. The First Sharpshooters and Sixtieth Ohio had been broken and were a good deal scattered (though Colonel McElroy had rallied a few of his men upon the left of the Twentieth), and the left of the Fiftieth was forced back. It was here that the bravery of one man was most conspicuous and did much to avert disaster. Capt. Samuel K. Schwenk, Fiftieth Pennsylvania Volunteers, took command of the four right companies of that regiment, and charging with the bayonet, he drove back the enemy just as the Twentieth Michigan came up on the "double-quick" to his support, and the right was restored on the crest. At the same moment the Seventeenth Michigan dashed up the road, and the Seventy-ninth New York, Colonel Morrison commanding, charged in front of the Gayle house, and the enemy was repulsed all along the line. We occupied the crest, and during the afternoon fortified it as best we could. Thus this division gained a foothold nearer Spotsylvania Court-House than any other part of the line.*

# The Battle of Spotsylvania Court House May 10–12

*May 10, 1864, our brigade remained in the position taken on the previous day, the Twentieth Michigan and Fiftieth Pennsylvania on the right of the road, and the Seventy-ninth New York, First Michigan Sharpshooters, and Sixtieth Ohio on the left of the same. The day was chiefly occupied in strengthening our position…Having constructed breast-works during the night of the 10th, the troops remained quiet behind them until near night of the 11th, when they were withdrawn behind the Ny to re-establish the line, but before morning of the 12th they again occupied the south bank of the river, preparatory to the general assault of that day. During the morning the brigade bore no active part, except as a supporting column…About the middle of the afternoon the brigade was moved into position to take part in the assault. The brigade was posted in the second line, supporting the First Brigade, General Hartranft commanding, and in the following order from right to left First Michigan Sharpshooters, Twentieth Michigan, Fiftieth Pennsylvania…All things being in readiness, the charge was ordered. On the right, in front of the First Sharpshooters, the ground was covered with a bushy, small growth of trees, which concealed the movements of the line. On the left, in front of the Fiftieth Pennsylvania, was a dense growth of pine timber difficult to pass in line of battle…The advance was gallantly made, the line advancing about 200 yards under the most terrific fire of shells, canister, and musketry. Under the fire the first line was soon checked and melted away. The second line, however, with such of the first as joined it in the advance, pushed forward rapidly and steadily until within a short distance of the enemy's works…The Fiftieth Pennsylvania, on account of the thickness of the woods, were unable to keep up with the Twentieth, except one Company on the right, under Captain Schwenk, who again behaved with the most conspicuous gallantry. During the few minutes that the brigade lay in this position, a brigade of the enemy had passed around our left, and charged with the purpose of capturing the batteries supported by the Second Michigan…The advance of the enemy was checked and after a short and severe contest, the first column was repulsed with considerable loss to the enemy. The guns were then turned on the column approaching from the left, and that too was quickly repulsed… It was this assaulting column of the enemy that in returning from the attack struck this division in the flank. They first came in contact with the Seventeenth Michigan, a large portion of which they captured. They next struck the Fiftieth Pennsylvania Volunteers on the left of this brigade, and doubling then up in the thick pine woods, succeeded in making prisoners of about 100 of them also. A small portion of them, however, rallying around their colors, gallantly fought their way out, contending hand-to-hand in many instances with bayonets and butts of guns. Captain Schwenk with his Company joined the troops on his right and maintained his position to the last. All this transpired in less time than it can be written…*

*The regiment at large did all that men could do under the circumstances, and most of them were, at some stage of the fight, prisoners, and some were captured and recaptured several times...The lines were drawn back and re-established, and after this most bloody day the troops rested in the mud upon their arms. After the battle of the 12th the troops enjoyed a period of comparative rest, and were engaged in strengthening their works, changing position occasionally, until the 21st of May, when they took up the line of march for the North Anna River...*

*The Fiftieth Pennsylvania occupied an island in the river, acting as an advanced post. The march to the Totopotomoy was without incident worthy of especial note. On the 29th of May the Fiftieth Pennsylvania was engaged in some skirmishing, without serious loss, near Shady Grove Church.*

## Corporal John Doudle

Captured, May 1864

When Captain D.F. Burket was wounded at the Nye River, on May 9th, 1864 the company lost a brave officer, as he was always at the head of his command and was ever ready to rush upon the enemy. First Lieut. George W. Brumm from Minersville, Schuylkill Co, was next in command and took charge of Company C, as Capt. Burket was obliged to go to the hospital, being wounded in the shoulder. I must give Lieut. George Brumm praise, as he was every inch a soldier and a gentleman; from the date of our organization and the muster of the company. Comrade Brumm was in every way very kind, obliging and generous, and took great pains with the company in the line of drill. Many of the Company officers thought themselves above the privates, but not so with officer Brumm, as he would sit around the old camp fire and joke with the boys, singing war songs and telling stories which were a delight to listen to.

The 50th Regiment with the Ninth Army Corps, on May 12, encountered the enemy at Spotsylvania Court House. The Ninth Corps occupied a position on the right of the Fredericksburg Road. In our front was a thick wood, and as the bullets so thick, we were ordered to lie down, and when the enemy ceased firing part of our forces advanced to the right, and what was left of us on the left wing advanced upon the enemy's breast works and captured quite a number of prisoners. General Lee, sending a brigade in our rear, overpowered us and we were obliged to surrender. And I was made a prisoner.

Early in the war, a soldier, if captured, had the chance he would be exchanged. Union and Confederate forces had signed a cartel containing a section that required both sides to parole all prisoners within ten days of capture. The captives were allowed to return to their respective sides if they vowed not to take up arms again. The system was a complete failure. By 1864 General Grant ended the exchange system, as he did not feel it was logical to send captured soldiers back to their lines to fight the same men over again. "If we commence a system of exchanges which liberates all prisoners taken, we will have to fight until the whole south is exterminated."

## Corporal John Doudle

Captured, May 1864

The enemy captured over a hundred of the regiment. The names of those that were captured from Company C are: David Raudenbush, Sergt. Levi Eckert, wounded and captured, Elias Berger, Samuel Agly, John Eckert, William Guertler, Jacob Helm, Henry Heim, William Hain, William Williams, Peter Dunkle, Garret Kerrigan and myself. We were then taken to the rear of Lee's Army to commence a life of misery.

Since the war I have been informed that Lieut. Brumm and Sergt. James H. Levan, also a member of Company C, saved the regimental flag from falling into enemy hands at Spotsylvania Court House, on the 12th day of May 1864, the day of our capture. They must have had a great struggle for life, as it was a hand to hand fight where we were. The butt end of the musket was freely used, while they were forced to surrender. General Robert E. Lee, sending a brigade in our rear and overpowered and surrounded us and we were taken prisoner.

We were encamped in a field in the rear of the Court House, surrounded by guards, and as the day was wet they let us make fires to dry our clothing as best we could. In the evening the boys amused themselves by singing patriotic songs. I knew some very good ones myself, and some of my comrades requested me to sing, forgetting that we were in Rebel dom, the song runs thus, "Jeff Davis, you thief, if I had you but here, Your beautiful plans I'd be ruining, Faith, I'd give you a taste of my bayonet, be dad, Actually for trying to burst our Union." The Rebels could not listen to this, and Comrade Berger espied a Rebel Lieutenant and several guards approaching to where we were, and told me to cease singing, which I did. The darkness of the night saved me, as they said to some of the men, "If we find out who was singing, he will never see daylight." That ended my singing while a prisoner of war.

On the 13th of May we were ordered to fall into line to be taken away, as the Rebels thought we might be recaptured by our forces. We marched along, but as to where we were going we could not imagine. One thing we did know, however, that we were getting very hungry, as the rations we received from Uncle Sam, while in our lines, were all gone, with poor prospects of receiving more.

For Corporal John Doudle and his comrades captured on May 12, 1864, General Grant's cancellation of the exchange agreement sent the men into the hell of prison life where they become victims of Rebel cruelty.

## Corporal John Doudle

Captured, May 1864

While we were marching into Rebel held territory I know of one occasion when we were almost starved. We halted for a little while and cooked some clover, but as we had no salt we could not eat it, it having no taste whatever. On the following day we received two crackers, but these did not satisfy our appetite, as we were ready to lie down and die. We thought the end might soon come, and that the enemy would become tired of this business.

When we were all searched and the enemy had taken everything they could from us, we were put on board freight cars and received orders to move. They told us that we were going to a beautiful place down in Georgia, where there was an abundance of everything, owing to the riches of the state, with plenty of good water and a healthy country where we would be treated well. They informed us that the reason we fared so ill here in Virginia was because it had been the battle ground since the Rebellion first started, and that they did not have it for themselves: we could believe that or leave it alone.

We left Lynchburg about the 23rd of May. The guards seemed very sociable on our journey, and when the train would stop they would allow us to go out and get some water.

An incident occurred at Augusta, Ga. which I will relate. Upon our arrival at that place we were sidetracked for what cause we could not say, and remained there several hours. Comrade Berger of my Company was in possession of a penny, and was in the act of getting water which was close by when he met a colored man who was selling eatables to the prisoners. Berger presented his penny, making the colored man believe it was a two and one half gold piece, and in return he had quite a quantity of food and a great amount of change. When the colored man found out his mistake, Berger was already on top of the freight car, and could not be found. As he was passing our car we heard him make the remark, "Dem Yanks am up to all debilment."

Here we also saw a Schuylkill Haven man, Samuel Byerly, who was a spy for our government and was no doubt sent to see where we were to be stationed, but we had the presence of mind not to recognize him (for we knew it would be instant death for old Sam)...

Orders having come for our train to move, we left Augusta and proceeded to Macon, where we remained for a few hours. Leaving Macon on the evening of the 27th of May and on the morning of the 28th we arrived at Andersonville, Ga. which was the place intended for us.

# 1864
# Andersonville, Georgia

*The name Andersonville will be a dark spot to American civilization for time to come.*

—*Corporal John Doudle*

Andersonville Prison was located in Sumter County, Georgia, about sixty miles southeast of Macon. It was constructed in February 1864 to receive excess Union prisoners held in overcrowded prisons in Richmond, North Carolina and South Carolina. The prisoners lived in an open field without the benefit of proper shelter, sleeping in homemade shebangs or under a blanket thrown upon the ground. The miserable prisoners were exposed to the hot sun, pouring rain and were poorly fed. Almost all inmates suffered from disease and malnutrition.

## Corporal John Doudle

Prisoner, Andersonville, Georgia, May–June 1864

Upon our arrival at Andersonville, Georgia on Saturday May 28th 1864, we were ordered from the cars for the purpose of marching to the prison which was about a mile from the station. We looked around us anxiously to see and we were surprised to find that it was a small way station, with a few houses in sight. The day was warm, and we were marching toward the prison, then we saw it and looked in and saw a mass of prisoners on the inside of the stockace.

Our hearts sank within us. We saw no shelter of any kind to keep the scorching sun from the prisoners. As we came near the gate of the prison we noticed that a regiment of Rebels was drawn up in line and was held in that position until we were in the prison. We were then informed that they did this every time a large crowd of prisoners would arrive for fear of an outbreak.

Andersonville Prison, where the greatest Rebel atrocity was reached, is located in Sumter County, Georgia, about one mile from Andersonville. A small station on the Georgia Central R.R. 62 miles southeast of Macon, Ga. and about 50 or 60 miles from the Alabama state line. Andersonville was put there because it is a wild, swampy place, the ground was low and thinly settled, and was well calculated for the purpose it was intended for. The land for a considerable distance around it was almost entirely covered with forest and consisted principally of oak and pine, and large quantities of it were destroyed for the purpose of clearing away the land. It can be seen dear reader, how easily the Rebel government could have furnished the shelter for their prisoners.

Some differ in opinion as to the stockade. Some say it had an area of 25 acres, while others claim 27. But I cannot really say. It could not be all occupied, however, on account of the low, swampy marsh. A creek five or six inches deep and several feet wide entered the east side of the prison and ran through it. This stream had, we were told, its origin a short distance from the camp, and was impure and warm. To add to its natural filthiness, the Rebels built a cook house across the stream on the side where it entered the prison, and the water was often covered with filth and grease. The Rebels would often wash their dirty, lousy clothes in the stream, and almost everyday we could see dozens along the bank for that purpose, and this was the water the prisoners were obliged to drink.

The entire stockade was built of pine logs, 16 feet high, and after some of the prisoners had succeeded in tunneling out, they built a second stockade, a short distance from the first, and in intervening space they had fires to prevent the prisoners escaping.

Sentinel boxes were built on top of the stockade, about 50 or 60 feet apart, and were reached by means of a ladder. About thirty feet from the stockade was a small railing fastened on posts about four feet high, and was called the dead line. Woe to the poor prisoner, whether ignorant or not, who crossed or even touched it, as it was sudden death.

The Rebels, in building this terrible prison, cut down all the trees inside except two which stood in the Northeast corner of the prison and gave no shelter whatever. The earth, with exception of the swamp, was a hard clay with a slight covering of sand.

Lying starving upon this unmerciful earth, dying from exposure, hunger and thirst, the sun beating upon us, with no blankets and no shelter. In many cases the prisoners' hands and faces were burned to blisters. What would those suffering prisoners not give, who were dying if they could only [have] had some shade to soothe their fevered brows; but the Rebels had cut it away.

Since the war some of the Rebels have endeavored to prove that the Union Prisoners were treated well. What plea can they make for the fact that thousands of men died in this pen. After the Rebels purposely cut down the entire shade trees which would have been welcome, and in some manner ease their sufferings. I have since been informed that 13,000 and some hundred Union Soldiers perished, averaging more than a 1,000 deaths to every month that the prison existed. There is no spot upon earth where man's inhumanity to man was more fully demonstrated than this terrible place, and the name Andersonville will be a dark spot to American civilization for time to come.

By May 28, 1864, a thousand men a day were arriving at Andersonville, adding to the wretchedness of all those already being held there. Some men would give up all hope and die quickly while others would last only weeks; the more stalwart ones would survive many months.

## Corporal John Doudle

Prisoner, Andersonville, Georgia, Summer 1864

As we marched through the gate I could hardily believe that this horrible place was to contain so many of us, even for a few days.

My blood ran cold with the horror as I looked around and saw men, who but a short time ago enjoyed health and strength, so worn down by long suffering and disease, that they hardily looked like human beings. Some of them were almost naked and covered with filth and vermin, presenting an appearance that made our hearts sink within us. As we looked upon them the thought came into my mind. "How can I live in this horrid place?"

After the gates were closed upon us, we looked around us dumbfounded, and did not know what to do or think about it. Around us we saw a huge wall of pine logs shutting us out from the outside world, and on the top of this wall was a line of guards who with rifles in hand were ready and only to willing to end our mortal career by sending a ball through us for the least violation imposed upon us.

Toward evening their came into camp a large army wagon, drawn by four mules, which contained rations for the prisoners. We received one pint of corn meal. And when we asked how long we were to live on such rations, we were informed by other prisoners 24 hours, and we soon found out that such was the case. Salt must have been scarce for the Rebels because we seldom received any. We managed to cook our corn meal as the Rebels gave us a small piece of wood, about a foot long and about three inches thick, and we were pretty hungry and we soon made short work of it.

Our minds wandered back to Uncle Sam's lines and the good coffee and hardtack, and plenty of it, and to think that we were shut up in a Rebel stockade to starve and die away from home and friends, and no way to escape. Night was fast approaching and the air was chilly; besides we had no shelter or blankets and we said to ourselves can this be hell on earth?

We laid down spoon fashion, and when we were tired of lying on one side, we would all turn around and lie on the other side. During the night we had a "right smart" shower of rain, as the Rebels would call it, and we were drenched to the skin and our sleep for that night was gone. In the morning we looked like drowned rats, but the sun came out very hot, and our clothing dried upon us. The mud was almost ankle deep.

The members who were captured of Company C, 50th regiment, P.V., were as follows; Elias Berger, Jacob Helm, Henry Helm, William Hain, David Raudenbush, William Williams, Peter Dunkle, Garrett Kerrigan, Samuel Agley, William Guertler, Levi Eckert, John Eckert and myself, and we came to the conclusion that we would stick to each other, and do all we could for one and another. But what could we do in a place like Andersonville but look at each other's misery and do nothing to alleviate our sufferings?

Myself and Elias Berger thought we would explore the encampment to see how things looked. We saw one of the poor prisoners getting a tin cup full of water, and was not thinking about the dead line, and a guard waiting for such an opportunity aimed his musket and sent a bullet through his skull without one word of warning. We thought nobody but a coward would do such an act. We were informed that the guard would receive a furlough for shooting the "Damned Yankee."

We occupied a small place near the creek on the southeast side of the pen, and named it Duck Island. Elias Berger and I bought a tin cup for one dollar, all the money we had. So one or the other would be obliged to cook our corn meal in it. I got out of the prison a few days before him [Berger] and left it behind [the cup], thinking that he would bring it home and keep it as a relic, but he failed to do so.

While trying to survive the horrors of Andersonville prison most men shared their suffering with each other. Soldiers remained in the close-knit communities from which they came. The men of Company C stayed together and helped one and another get through the ordeal. They shared their meager rations and took care of each other when one became ill. Almost all of the men were ill, suffering from scurvy, diarrhea and fevers.

## Corporal John Doudle

Prisoner, Andersonville, Georgia, June 1864

The 1st of June brought rain, and the prison pen was in horrible condition, where there were so many men, and the mud was ankle deep. We were compelled to lie down like cattle, and in spite of ourselves we would fall asleep; in the morning the prints of our bodies could be seen in the mud. Rain was the order of the day. It rained every day, more or less, for 21 days in June. The sun would come out, perhaps long enough to dry our clothes, while hundreds of men were dying from exposure, thirst, disease and starvation.

### June–July 1864

That dreadful disease, scurvy, set in amongst us, one-half of the prisoners were more or less afflicted with it. More than one-half of the men afflicted with the disease died from its effects. Scurvy is the result of impure air, bad water, and improper food. The first indication of this dreaded disease was at the mouth or gums, as they became soft or ulcerated and in a short time, if not checked, the teeth became loose and in many cases would just drop out. In some cases the body would be covered with scaly yellowish spots, which soon developed into running sores and would soon leave the body of the victim in horrible condition, the face and body would swell up and the skin would burst. I had scurvy in the gums, but I managed to get a sweet potato, which helped take it away.

A most painful diarrhea, or discharge from the bowels, largely composed of blood, almost always accompanied the disease, and added to the sufferings of its victims. Perhaps it will be a strange history dear friend. You can meditate a while and think how things were going in Andersonville Prison Pen.

The dead house was only a short distance from the prison, and was constructed of pine limbs and brush which formed a screen or cover to keep off the sun. To this horrid spot more than 13,000 dead soldiers, prisoners of war, were carried during the history of this one southern prison. After the death of a prisoner his comrades would pin on his bosom or clothing his name, Company and regiment, and those who had no friends or comrades would have on their clothes "Unknown." They were then carried to the dead house and laid side by side on the ground. A considerable number of men were employed to move the Corpses from the dead house to the place of burial.

One of the prisoners managed to escape by playing a clever trick on the Rebels. He feigned death, and several of his comrades carried him to the dead house and placed him in line with the dead. In the morning the burying party found his place vacant. He no doubt struck a bee line for the Union lines, and we all hoped the poor fellow did. After that the Rebels placed a guard over the dead men, for the purpose of preventing any more Yankee tricks.

When they built a new stockade on the outer side, the prisoners made a grand rush for the inner one and carried it away for fuel, as wood was scarce on the inside, and at this time we received our rations of raw or half raw. Wood was almost valueless, and we did not get enough to cook our scanty food. Captain Wirz issued an order if we did not bring back the wood he would stop our rations entirely. Our rations at this time consisted mainly of corn meal, and for quite some time beans were our only food. Sometimes they were raw and sometimes they were cooked, they were full of holes and in a filthy condition not fit to eat.

There was a Rebel sutler at the place, and he would furnish produce to any one who had money, at a good round sum, so as to get every dollar that they did not steal when they captured us. One dollar of Uncle Sam's money would buy ten dollars worth of Confederate scrip, and then they would charge seven dollars for a bushel of potatoes or they would trade sweet potatoes for New York State buttons, which the Rebels prized most highly.

Scurvy was a disease that affected almost all Andersonville prisoners. Though Doudle believed that scurvy came from bad water, improper air and bad food, the actual cause of scurvy was a deficiency of vitamin C in the diet of the soldiers, characterized by weakness, anemia and spongy gums.

## Corporal John Doudle

Prisoner, Andersonville, Georgia, July–August 1864

In July of 1864 about this time the hanging of six of our comrades in suffering took place. They were prisoners of war who seeing no other way but to starve, they formed themselves into a band of marauders, or Mosby's Raiders, as the camp called them, and had things pretty near their own way. They robbed the prisoners, and at least one poor fellow's death was traced to these hands. Many others were badly beaten because they would not submit to their demands.

The prison at this time was in a filthy condition. It was before the Stockade was enlarged, and we were crowded in the pen like cattle. Sickness was increasing at a fearful rate and the deaths were averaging at the rate of six per day. The poor prisoners, who were starving and dying, Lying upon the bare ground exposed to the weather, were in no mood to endure tyranny from those who should be their friends. So they organized a Company of regulators to enforce law and order, having for their leader a man named Key, from Illinois. A fresh lot of troops would give those robbers a fresh opportunity to continue their work, as they would rob and murder. At last they were caught in the act and it was reported to Captain Wirz. They were taken out and a jury of twelve fresh prisoners selected out of the camp, or rather the prison, and gave them a fair and impartial trial, and brought a verdict of "Robbery and murder in the first degree."

Captain Wirz retained them outside for awhile thinking that things would change, but they didn't. On the 11th of July a gallows was erected on the south side of the pen, and the six who were sentenced to death were hung. When the drop fell the rope broke away from around the neck of one of the men. He then ran through the prison. He was soon recaptured, however, and brought back and was launched into eternity. While they were on the scaffold, they were asked if they had anything to say. One of them spoke up and told one of his comrades of his regiment, but not a participant in robbery and murder, to tell his friends if he ever got that far, to tell them how he met his fate. A Catholic Priest visited them quite often and prayed that their lives might be saved. But his pleadings were in vain, as the prisoners were determined to set and example of them. And they were hung.

Like any society there were nefarious prisoners who preyed on people. Andersonville had its share of thieves, traitors and murderers who would do anything to ensure their own survival. Groups of prisoners, known as "the Raiders," banded together to beat and murder the helpless for their meager rations or personal items. They did whatever they pleased and were the feared by every prisoner in the pen. It is said the majority of the Raiders were bounty jumpers, deserters and cowards. They lived a better form of life than most of the prisoners, as they traded with the Rebel guards and lived very well off the bounty of their vicious deeds. There were hundreds of Raiders within the confines of the prison.

After enduring months of attacks, atrocities and murders perpetrated by the Raiders, the prisoners at Andersonville formed a police force within the prison to look out for the helpless and dying prisoners. They called the police force the "Regulators," and they were led by a Sergeant Leroy Key from an Illinois regiment. The Regulators were made up from men of the western states of Illinois, Indiana, Iowa and Ohio.

With the help of the prison commanding officer, the hated and dreaded Captain Henry Wirz, the Regulators set out on a campaign to arrest and confine as many of the Raiders as they could. Wirz allowed the Regulators to have their captives held outside the prison until the time of a trial was set. The guards helped the Regulators to arrest the Raiders and in doing so they took back from the Raiders the shebangs and tents that belonged to the prisoners.

On July 10, 1864, within the confines of Andersonville prison the Raiders were put on trial. The jury consisted of "Fresh Fish," or new men who just arrived at the prison and did not know of the dirty deeds of the Raiders. Most of the Raiders were found guilty and were sent through a gantlet of men who stoned them and hit them with clubs or just plain punched them. Six of the ringleaders were sentenced to death. Private Patrick Delaney, Company E, 83rd PVI; Private Charles F. Curtis, Company A, 5th Rhode Island Artillery; Corporal William Collins, Company D, 88th PVI; Private James Sarsfield, Company C, 140th New York Infantry; Private John Sullivan, Company C, 140th New York Infantry; and Seaman A. Munn (Muir) United States Navy.

On the afternoon of July 11, all six mounted a gallows erected inside the prison. Meal sacks were placed over their heads and the trap was sprung. Five of the Raiders dropped to their deaths. Collins, being the heaviest of the group, fell to the ground after his rope broke. He pleaded for his life but was dragged back up to the gallows and thrown off. Today, six graves stand by themselves at Andersonville prison cemetery. They are never decorated with American flags during Memorial Day. The six were dishonorably discharged for their foul deeds against their fellow prisoners.

## Corporal John Doudle.

Prisoner, Andersonville, Georgia, June–November 1864

> I cannot say whether Wirz had a spy in prison or not, to take note of what the prisoner's plans were, as he was in possession of all the facts. On some occasion, when a tunnel would be in operation, some of our men would inform for a plug of tobacco or an extra meal. As soon as Wirz heard that the prisoners were planning an attempt to force the stockade, he stationed a double guard around the prison, and was determined to hold on to us as long as he could. Then he would see a large crowd collecting inside, he would discharge a cannon over the prison, and as he was so tyrannical we did not know how soon he would blow us to atoms. There were men dying all around us, who would not be able to go even if they could. Wirz posted a notice on the inside of the gate, which read as follows:
>
> NOTICE
>
> *Not wishing to shed the blood of hundreds not connected with those who concocted a plan to force the stockade, and in this way make their escape, I hereby warn the leaders and those who formed themselves into a band to carry this out, that I am in full possession of all the facts, and have made my dispositions accordingly, so as to frustrate*

*it. No choice would be left me but to open with grape and canister on the stockade, and what effect this would have in this densely crowded place need not be told.*

H. Wirz

*June 25th, 1864*

Before the hanging of the raiders, Elias Berger, William Heim, William Williams and myself had the pleasure of seeing and breathing the pure air outside of the pen on a very sad occasion. It was when we carried Harry Heim to his last resting place, as he could only hold out about a month.

He died on July 2nd 1864 and when we were out we got an idea of how they buried him. They dug a trench several feet deep and placed the Corpse down in this trench and filled it up. By so doing there was always a grave. In the early history of the prison, the Rebels found coffins, but during the hot weather the deaths were to great, so they buried them like hogs.

Large amounts of soldiers came into the camp every few days and would bring word into camp that our army was advancing on Richmond. But we would often say, "It does not look as if our Army was doing anything towards victory, judging from the way the Union soldiers are coming into this hell hole." Then a rumor would be circulated in prison that Col. Ould was at Macon or Charleston, preparing for the exchange of prisoners, but we became so used to it that we paid no attention to it whatever.

There were so many prisoners arriving in the prison every day that we came to the conclusion that we would en masse ourselves and force the stockade, and in this way make our escape. We imagined ourselves attacking the guards and seizing the artillery, turning it upon the Rebels, then making for our lines as best we could.

The 4th of July came, and Captain Wirz thought he would punish us a little by not giving us any rations on that day. We had a good shower of rain which drenched us completely. Our clothes commenced to look shabby, and we had no change, lying in mud, exposed to the rain, and we had no shelter.

August was the warmest month of all we experienced. The rains had not been sufficient to wash most of the filth away, and the prison was in terrible condition, infested by maggots, which spread over the whole prison. We could hardly look upon the poor prisoners covered with vermin, some who were too feeble in strength to help them. It was a sickening site [*sic*] to behold.

On the afternoon of August 9th a great rainstorm, accompanied by thunder and lightning came upon us. The large dark clouds approaching form the west, constant flashes of lightning and sharp quick claps of thunder reminded us of a heavy cannonade. All indicated that a fearful storm was approaching, and we watched it approach with a great deal of anxiety, as it was not pleasant in our unsheltered condition to be exposed to such a terrible storm. The lightning struck the trees outside the prison in such rapid succession, so that we thought the heavens were falling down, consequently we did not notice that a small stream through the prison had become a raging torrent. The sound of a cannon from one of the forts announced the fact that the Rebels were very excited. A break in the wall of the stockade happened. The greatest excitement existed among the Rebels, who falling into line and marching to the place where the break in the stockade had occurred for the purpose of preventing the prisoners making their escape. Although the storm was ragging with great fury, and the rain pouring down in torrents, we commenced to crowd toward the stream, thinking some chance of escape would prevent itself, but we failed, as the Rebels had formed a strong guard to prevent this.

After the storm subsided some of the prisoners jumped into the stream and caught some of the floating timber, but Capt. Wirz, with a "devil in him as big as a goat" ordered the soldiers not to use the wood, threatening that if we did not stop that our rations would be stopped for several days. No rations were issued on this day, and, hungry [and] wet, we passed a most miserable night. Whether Wirz did this from a desire to show us that he was earnest about stopping our rations for several days, if we used the wood, or from the desire to take spite out of us for the trouble that the elements had made for him, we could not tell, but one or the other must have been the cause of it, for the captain was in a terrible rage until the break was fixed. The Rebels worked hard all night, and replaced the stockade into its former position.

The next day after the flood it was very warm until the afternoon when it rained again for a few hours and made the mud ankle deep. It was a sight to see those poor prisoners who were on the brink of the grave. It washed all the maggots out of the prison and hastened a great many of the sickest prisoners to their last resting place, but it also bettered the condition of the camp for those who were living.

I had always supposed it to be the privilege of a prisoner of war to make his escape if he could, but there it was considered a crime, and a man was tracked like a felon or an outlaw, or shot down like a dog, or devoured by furious blood hounds.

Tunneling came into the prisoners' minds, and so as to effect an escape we would dig down a few feet, making believe we were digging a well, but as the old saying is, "There was a traitor in camp." When a tunnel was nearly completed, some one would inform Capt. Wirz for the sake of a plug of tobacco or an extra pint of corn meal.

I knew of one occasion where a tunnel was nearly completed, and perhaps a great number might have escaped, only for this traitor in camp. But dear friend that man did not fare well. The men caught him and shaved the one side of his hair off and branded a "T" on his forehead and he was shunned by all. In a few weeks he was carried out to his place of rest.

Thus day by day, we saw our brave men dying all around us, and we could not see, or help, but only feel, that if some deliverance did not soon come, it would only be a short time before we would all perish. Our rations often consisted of only one pint of meal, a few raw beans, and no salt. Friend, you can imagine how it was.

September 1st brought us quite a change in the weather The days were very warm and the nights so cold that we shivered in agony.

Comrade Wagner and I tried to be admitted to the hospital, but I heard that anyone who entered into it never came out alive, so we came to the conclusion that if we were to die we would die in the prison surrounded by our friends, as the treatment in the hospital was no better than in the stockade. The poor fellows were compelled to lie on the bare ground and very little shelter was furnished, this with the want of medicine brought on certain death. These poor wretched fellows, with trembling limbs and pain racked bodies had been so reduced by the terrible agony they endured, that they were beyond semblance of human beings covered with filth and vermin, and were the ones who begged of their destroyers for a bone or a drink of pure water, but their pleadings were in vain.

## Corporal John Doudle

Prisoner, Andersonville, Georgia, The Andersonville Hospital

My Thoughts:

Thousands throughout the country have a personal interest in this ill fated spot, for thither husbands, sons and brothers were carried to finish their earthly course, their career as patriots and soldiers, and there within a short distance their bones lie. It may seem to some a lost contribution to national honor, but to many otherwise. Though no monument or granite ever marked the place where those heroes lie, telling of the mighty sacrifices that was made there, countless homes in every part of our land, who shall imitate the power and the extent of the influence shall go forth from there to awaken the fires of patriotism in other hearts, bidding them go and do likewise if need be. Indignation too, will fan the flame, for the sad conviction is forced upon the minds of the people that were it not for utter neglect and inhumanity, thousands of valuable lives might have been spared that are now lost forever.

Lost to friends and a country by this one cause. It is a tearful history, a sad record, and many will shrink from this revolting tale here given.

It is confidently asserted that there are none of these statements but will be corroborated by every one who had the misfortune to be a prisoner of war in that unhappy locality. The condition of things was horrible in the extreme. A single glimpse of things within was enough to make a man sick for the rest of his life, he could but turn away in loathing and disgust from the sight of so much wretchedness and misery, so much filth and pollution. Most of the prisoners at that time were from Belle Island, who had endured all the hardships of the previous winter and were worn and wasted by exposure and its consequent diseases. There were comparatively few of them then: scarcely over 300. A circumstance accounted for in two days. In the first place a man never went in and came out alive, for usually he was so low upon his admission that there was nothing to hope for. In the second place, if a soldier had a friend or comrade to help him he would not go in at all, for he preferred to die in the comparative quiet of the stockade, surrounded by such comforts as friendly sympathy could procure, rather than end his days where so much wretchedness was congregated. This was the last resort, and to see a poor fellow brought upon a blanket was to conclude that his race was well nigh run and there remained nothing for him to do but to breathe his life away. In the midst of such misery as was inconceivable to any but those who watched the melancholy around themselves.

The utter want of cleanliness, the pestilential air, the improper and miserable food, and the scanty medicines all combined to render a swift coming of death for sure.

One could not expect anything else when he entered. If by any possibility one survived the shock, and was forth among his fellows a living man. It was looked upon something as well nigh miraculous, and was rarely if ever known. It was a general expectation when any went into the hospital that it was the last of earth for them, for how could it be otherwise? Where was the single condition that tended in the least degree to restoration? Where was the slightest thing favorable to anything like invigoration?

The excellent condition of our northern hospitals, their comfortable benches, tender nursing, abundant remedies.

Before the plan of marking and numbering was observed those who died while waiting to be carried to the hospital were buried with the single word, "Unknown." There many of them who had been reared in luxury, and who had friends whose hearts would well nigh break if they knew half the truth respecting their sufferings. I thought it ignorance for them, but melancholy for the poor soldier. I have shed many a tear at their sad fate, as I did not know how soon my own turn would come. We could be compared to nothing but living skeletons, which fact a great many can vouch for when I came home.

Every morning a large army wagon would be driven to the dead house and 20 or 30 bodies would be loaded in like so many logs of wood, one on top of the other, some with an arm hanging out at the side, and others with their limbs protruding, for there was no covering at all.

The Rebels finally became ashamed of themselves for want of decency, and provided a covered wagon. The place of burial was about a half of mile from the stockade and was situated on the high ground, was level and surrounded with pine forests, which made it very pleasant. It is emphatically a soldier's cemetery and a fearful comment upon southern cruelty. But for their wretched system of treatment the earth would not hold in its embrace so many of our brave boys, but for this so many of the survivors would not carry with them broken constitutions and maimed bodies as they now do. The recitals of these tales of horror touch the deepest springs of sympathy, and kindles the fires of indignation to a fervid glow. But it is not for us to strike a blow which justice demands.

Vengeance is mine, I will repay, saith the Lord. The cry of the martyred thousands has gone up to high heaven, not heedlessly, but to the means of a visitation to the oppressors which they will be ill prepared to meet. Fearful wrongs may not always exist. There comes a time when right will assert its inherent dignity and show itself triumphant. But meantime the friends of the soldier in the North should be awake to their duty and their trust. We have seen the misery of hope deferred, written on many a countenance as we have passed the patient creatures on their lowly couch of earth. We have seen their gaunt faces and protruding bones make their silent and wistful appeal week by week and wondered that there were none to remember us in our sorrow. We have witnessed among all there want and woe, their firm devotion to the Union cause, and known their intense longing for victory and success to crown the Federal arms. No statement I have made but will be confirmed by every prisoner at Andersonville, who knew anything about the interior of the hospital or prison pen.

It beggars all description, as the whole truth cannot be told. It is to be hoped that the time past will suffice, and that like experiences will not have to be wrought out by the Company of soldiers in the future. The Georgia cemetery should be a mighty trumpet to proclaim against it.

Those men were no exiles for crimes. They had left their homes with the intention of helping save the life and honor of our nation. Many of them were reared tenderly, and had fond mothers in Northern homes, who had given them to the service of their country with a patriotic devotion, praying for their safe return. Others had fond wives and loving children in peaceful homes.

> Oh! Who can tell the utter misery and despair of these dying men when they remembered their awful condition? How they must have wished and prayed to be at home. Such was the cause of those who endured the prison life. It is hard in death to part with loved ones at home, when surrounded by their many friends and with all that love and kindness could do to smooth the way over the dark water; but to die an outcast, yea, like a dog was bitter indeed.

According to records, 49,485 Union prisoners suffered within the walls of Andersonville. The death rate there was the highest of any prison during the Civil War. In a thirteen-month period over 13,700 men perished from disease or were murdered by Rebel guards or suffered just plain general neglect. The prison operated until April 1865.

## Corporal John Doudle

Andersonville Prison, Charleston Race Course Prison
Departure, September–October 1864

> About the 4th of the month (September) quite a number of prisoners came in and brought news that the exchange of prisoners would commence in a few days. Some believed it and others did not, as we were fooled so often about the exchange prisoners that we took little stock in it. On the 6th, rumors commenced to take a more definite effect, and an order came into camp that a number of detachments were to be ready to leave the prison at a moments warning. On the following morning six detachments or about 2,000, left, as we believed, for our lines, and on the 9th 10th, 11th, 12th and on the 13th our detachment was ordered to fall into line. We soon had ourselves in readiness, as we did not have anything with us when we entered the prison, so it did not take us long to get ready. We bade farewell to those whom we left behind, and marched to the south side gate.
>
> They marched us to the station and away we went, thinking we would soon be in Union lines. It was a sad sight to those who were sick, and were not able to go along with us, but we cheered them by telling them they would soon follow, as soon as the Rebels could get transportation for them. Such dear friend, was the terrible treatment the Union soldiers received while prisoners of war at Andersonville Prison, Georgia. Under a tyrannical Prussian named Capt. H. Wirz.
>
> As we marched to the depot, or station, we could not help but thinking of the terrible misery we had endured, the horrible sights we had seen since we entered that terrible place, and remembered with sorrow the many comrades who so miserably perished there.

We arrived at Macon during the night, remained there a few hours, and then started for Savannah, Georgia; but we did not remain there long, when we again resumed our journey. The Rebels informed us that we were going to Charleston, S.C. to be paroled, as transportation was waiting for us there.

We arrived at the above place in the morning. It had rained during the night, which made it very uncomfortable, for our clothes were almost worn to a thread, having received none since our capture. We were barefooted and were a sight to behold. We were ordered out of the cars and falling into line were marched to the Race course, in the rear of Charleston.

At this place there was a stockade around the prison. The Rebels stationed guards around us, and, with a team and plow, ran a furrow around the prisoners which served as our dead line, and to anyone crossing over the furrow it meant instant death. One poor fellow, who had been a prisoner so long that he became insane, stepped over this furrow, and the Rebel guard put a bullet through his head and ended his misery.

There was nothing left standing of the buildings that we could see, except the Judge's stand and one building which the officers occupiec and they were pretty well rotted away. At this place the Rebels thought variety was the spice of life, for one single day they issued corn meal, flour, beans, hominy, molasses, beef and a little salt. It sounds very large but in reality it was small, for it consisted of one spoon full of each. Some of the men had nothing to put it in, and not much wood to cook it with.

Here it was that the Sisters Of Charity, accompanied by a priest, would come up from Charleston every day almost, and bring food and little necessaries of life, and would come right in among us dirty, filthy and half starved creatures; but the Rebel authorities soon put a stop to this.

At this place we could see our gunboats bombarding Charleston. We were "So near yet so far," and still no sign of exchange. There [we] were, so near our own lines, and we would often ask ourselves, "Can this be a humbug or are they building another stockade?" If they were, we kept ignorant of the fact. Night was fast approaching and the rain was falling down upon us. Barefooted, shelter less, half-naked, half starved, and our health broken down by exposure and long suffering, we were indeed miserable, and did not know yet where it would all end. We thought to ourselves, "They are trying to kill us, but we still will try and live as long as we can.

At the Charleston Race Course prison I will describe an incident. I never saw but one instance of disobedience of orders by a Rebel soldier, and that was at Charleston, when the prisoners had crowded rather too close up on the dead line, or furrow when the settlers had come up from the city with sweet potatoes

> and other produce, which could be bought at a good fair price. On one occasion the men got too close to the crowd. Col Daniels of the Fifth Georgia Regt. seeing this stepped up to one of the guards and ordered him to fire into the crowd. He replied, "I cannot do it, Colonel." "I order you to fire into those men," repeated the Colonel sternly. "I cannot do it." The Colonel said no more, but walked away. Whether the sentinel was punished or not I could not say.
>
> I was eyewitness to a very laughable affair the night before we left Charleston. Two prisoners had got into an old well, thinking they might escape when the prisoners were all gone. They were detected by the Rebel officers and brought forth, looking very dirty and evidently feeling rather cheap, to be made subjects for laughter, by their own men as well as the Rebels. They searched around thinking to find some more, but as there were none to be found they loaded us into freight cars and away we went to another stockade.

While at Andersonville, Doudle and the other prisoners were told by Captain Wirz that they were going to be paroled. Wirz lied and used psychology to keep the large number of prisoners in line, fearing a large breakout. Some of the prisoners were sent to Savannah and others to Charleston. Those who could not walk or were sick were left at Andersonville.

Doudle was fortunate in that he went to Charleston, and not Savannah, because most of the prisoners who went to Savannah were sent back to Andersonville.

# 1864–1865
## Cold Harbor

*We make war that we may live in peace.*

—*Aristotle*

Between May 31 and June 12, 1864, the battle of Cold Harbor was fought, with over 170,000 Federal and Confederate troops fighting in this campaign. There were an estimated 15,500 plus casualties recorded. On May 31, 1864, General Phil Sheridan's cavalry forces occupied the crossroads of Old Cold Harbor. Confederate forces attacked the cavalry forces, but General Sheridan's forces pushed back the attack. Through the night and into June 1, Confederate reinforcements arrived from Richmond and from the Totopotomoy Creek lines. Later that evening Federal forces, including the VI and XVII Corps, arrived on the field and attacked the Confederate forces and gained some ground.

On June 2, there was a seven-mile-long front that extended from Bethesda Church to the Chickahominy River. At sunrise on the third, the II and XVII Corps, and later on the IX Corps, made an assault on the line and were nearly destroyed. General Grant would later state that this attack was the only one he wished he had never ordered. The battle raged on until the night of June 12, when General Grant decided to move by the left flank.

At Cold Harbor, the 50$^{th}$ Pennsylvania and the boys of Company C were in the thickest of the fight under the command of Captain Schwenk. Schwenk was severely wounded during the fighting while bravely walking up and down their lines giving orders for the men to stay down and be wary of the enfilading cannon fire.

During the flank movement away from Cold Harbor on June 12, the 50$^{th}$ was selected to perform the rear guard action. They secured a position midway between the first position and the enemy's line. Under murderous fire, the 50$^{th}$ held the rear but suffered heavy casualties.

## Private William Tyson

In the Rifle Pits Near Richmond, June 1864

> At Weldon Station, Va. I got a flesh wound but kept on fighting because I didn't want to get separated from my comrades. Our Company had six killed and fourteen wounded in the Wilderness.
>
> Cold Harbor was a bad scrap and the 50th was in the thick of it. Reed's Station was another bloody fight I remember.

## Sergeant Charles E. Brown

Cold Harbor, Virginia, June 1864

> From June 1st to the 12th of 1864 we were at Cold Harbor and there was hard fighting everyday. We could see the steeples and house tops in the city of Richmond, but they would not let us in. We were soon ready to cross the James River on pontoons. We crossed the river and were proceeding to Petersburg.

By June 15 the Federal army had crossed the James River. Seeing that Richmond was well protected, General Grant decided to move south of the river and attack Petersburg, Virginia. After marching from Cold Harbor, General Meade's army arrived in front of Petersburg and attacked the Confederate defenses.

Petersburg was defended by General P.T. Beauregard with a force of 5,400 men well entrenched. A large, elaborately built line of defenses ran around the city in a semicircle. Starting near the marshy ground near the Appomattox River roughly two miles from the city, heading south, the defenses made the shape of a large horseshoe coming back to the river on the western end of town. On June 15 and 16, Federal forces attacked along the line and made significant gains driving back the Confederate forces from their first line of entrenchments. On June 17 General Beauregard fell back to the city, waiting for reinforcements from General Lee. On June 18 the II, XI and V Corps attacked but were driven back with heavy casualties. Confederate forces arrived and the city was laid to siege.

From June 21 to July 25 the 50th performed picket duty in front of Petersburg. By July 29 the men were relieved by a colored regiment and moved to the extreme left of the line.

## Sergeant Charles E. Brown

In the Rifle Pits Near Petersburg, Virginia, June 1864

> We reached Petersburg on the evening of the 15th of June. On the 16th of June we began fighting. We fought hard all day and drove the Rebels toward Petersburg.

On the seventeenth they made their last stand outside of their main breastworks. We charged up a hill on a Rebel battery in the morning. During this fight we had to retreat almost a half a dozen times. While we were charging up this hill the dust and smoke became so thick that we lost ourselves and actually fought amongst our own soldiers. In the evening of the 17th I had eight men in the Company beside my self and while we were getting ready to make another charge, and it to be the last charge, Jake Guertler cooked some coffee and gave me a cupful and said, "Brown, we will have a good drink of coffee before we get killed."

The order was given to charge. When we were halfway up the hill a shot came through and went right through Guertler's neck and under his chin and tore half of his neck away. Myself and seven other soldiers continued on toward the breast works. Of the seven that I can recall to memory are Peter Garrett, George Schwenk, William Tyson and Patrick O'Donnell.

Now it was getting dark, and we lay on our guns against the breast works. Then the Rebels laid their guns against the inside of the breast works. The bayonets were laid across on one another. They fired from all directions on us and we had to lay flat on the ground. It was all sand and we had ourselves dug into it. We took our bayonets and dug a deeper hole. Schwenk got out of the hole to do something and when he came back an officer had crept up the hill on hands and knees and got into this hole. This made George cross and he took firm hold upon him, pulled him out, and kicked him down the hill and said, "You darn coward, you wouldn't come up with us, now you won't get in my hole."

Now, we went and lifted one of our men up to look over the breast works to see if the Rebels had gone. We found that the Rebels had crept out of their position and left their guns behind them. This was one of the hardest days fighting I have ever seen.

At daylight on the eighteenth of June, the Rebels have retreated to their main breast works. Now we would start the Siege of Petersburg. We fight during the day light hours and build breast works at night. Our fortifications are fourteen miles long, and we are also building a railroad the same length. We are digging the railroad down in the earth, and we shovel and throw the ground towards the Rebel side. We have two engines on this road. They were called General Grant and General Meade. The railroad was within reach of the cannon fire of the Rebels. The reb's frequently fired their cannons at our engines but they could never reach them

In mid-June 1864 word would reach the residents of Schuylkill Haven that many of the boys from the local Company C were killed and wounded in the desperate fighting of May 1864. This news was devastating to the people of Schuylkill Haven.

George Heebner, a twenty-year-old veteran was the first to relay this grim news to the *Pottsville Miners' Journal*.

## Private George Heebner

In the Rifle Pits Near Richmond, Virginia, June 1864

Dear Editors:
As I looked over the column in the newspaper and observed a copy of the casualties of our Company, which was partly incorrect, I concluded to give you a correct statement of our loses which you will please publish. On the following you will find the names of those killed, wounded and missing while gallantly defending the shattered remnants of our old standard in the different engagements we took a grand part in.

In the Battle of the Wilderness, May 6th
Killed: Orderly Sgt. William Hill, Privates, Mike Reiley Levan J. Warner, Sam Martz
Wounded: Privates William Eckert, Peter Fritz, Christian Gulliver, William Hoffman, John Mehargue, Charles Schappel, Adam Lehwab, Irvin Tyson, Josiah Wright

In the Battle of the Ny River, May 9th
Killed: Private Dan Evert
Wounded: Corporal D.T. Burket, Sergt. Augustus Mellon, Charles Oswald, William Wildermuth, Henry M. Deibler and Christian Gulliver

In the Battle of Spotsylvania Court House, May 12th
Killed: Privates, Jacob Benedict, Thomas Lloyd, Franklin Sharer
Wounded and Missing: Corporal Levi Eckert, Privates, John Eckert, Jacob Hehn
Wounded: Privates, Josiah D. Lehman, Gottlieb Burket
Missing: Sergt. David Raudenbush, Corp. John Doudle, Privates, Samuel Agley, Elias Berger, Peter Dankle, William Guertler, Henry Hehn, William Hains, Garrett Kerrigan, Dan Sullivan and William Williams.

May 18th Wounded: Corp. Henry Hill
May 23rd Killed: Private John Reed
June 1st Wounded: lieut. William H. Hiney, Private George Cake.
June 3rd Killed: Emanuel Eckert, Albert Bartolet, Wounded William Koch, Lafayette Baker.

Please publish the above in your valuable paper. I remain respectfully
Geo. Heebner
Company C, 50th Regiment.

## Private George Heebner

**In Rifle Pits Near Petersburg, Virginia, July 1, 1864**

Dear Editors:

It may interest you to give a narrative of our march from Cold Harbor. On the night of the 12th of June, we received orders to strike tents and be ready to move at a moment's notice, which order was promptly executed. It took but a few moments delay, and the column was in the ready to march. Our destination was a mystery to us. The boys were constantly passing different remarks. Some said we were going to the White House, others thought to Harrison's landing, and some to the south side of the James. The latter surmises were correct. While the boys were arguing this subject the bugle sounded to move forward, when we commenced our march. It was a rather fatiguing one. We would move on perhaps a few rods, and then there would be another halt. In that manner we continued on during the remainder of the night. When daylight came we were but four miles distant from the place we started from in the evening. Shortly after daylight we halted and lit our fires and cooked breakfasts, which was rather scanty, comprising hard tack and coffee. Before our breakfast was completed the bugle again sounded "Forward." It took but a few moments until the column was in line, and proceeding on the march. We continued our march all day and we again halted in the evening and encamped for the night. Before daylight appeared we were again on the march, and on the evening of the 14th we arrived on the North side of the James, where we remained until the night of the 15th. The cause of our not crossing sooner was the delay in receiving pontoons. But the Engineers did very well considering the difficulties with which they had to contend. As soon as the pontoons were ready we crossed to the opposite side, but we had hardly crossed over when orders were received for a forced march. We again marched, part of the time at the double quick, when we arrived within ten miles of Petersburg where we halted and cooked our breakfast. We had but a few minutes to do it in. We proceeded on which brought us within two miles of the Cockade City. The 9th Corps was then formed in three columns. The Second Corps was also formed in the same order. In that position we remained until the next morning, when we were ordered about a half a mile to the right, to the same position the Second Corps had occupied previously. We had not been in that position long before we advanced in three columns, our Corps forming the left, the 2nd Corps at the center, and the 18th at the right. Our Division, which is under the command of General Wilcox, was formed in three lines. The Rebels seeing us advance commenced shelling us very rapidly, which caused some delaying advancing. However at 12 o'clock we advanced through shot and shell, when we arrived within two hundred yards of the Rebel breast works. We then charged on their pits which were very formidable. The 46th New York volunteers, also the 24th dismounted Cavalry of the same state, together with our regiment, formed the third line. We had not advanced far before the first and second line wavered and gave way to the right and left. The first thing we knew we were the first line, but we advanced with unerring aim until some of our boys were on the Rebel works, but we looked around and we saw nothing but the 46th New York together with our regiment. Our regiment being reduced down considerably by an enfolding fire from the enemy's battery, after holding the pits for a few minutes, we were compelled to fall back into the pits which the skirmishers had occupied. Our Brigade Commander then sent an order for the 46th New York to fall back, and our regiment to hold the pits at all hazards, which order was promptly carried out. During this engagement our Gallant Brigade Commander Colonel Christ, received a severe wound in the head while gallantly urging his men on, in the hottest of the contest.

I will give a list of the casualties of our Company since June 17th;
Killed: James Golles
Wounded: Edward Reiges, Samuel Hoffman. Sergt. James Levan, Jessie Wright, William Sirles.

A *New York Herald* newspaper correspondent reported the wounding of Colonel Benjamin Christ during the fight on June 17.

> *I cannot help paying a passing compliment to the gallantry and coolness of Col. Christ, who handled his men in the most admirable manner. His quick eye scoured the battle field, and where the enemy seemed the most determined, and where our men needed assistance, he quickly dispatched his regiments. He amply redeemed the fortunes of the 3rd Division, and it is regretted that his success was purchased at the price of a painful wound. A bullet struck him in the side of the head, just behind the left ear, and traversed about three inches of his skull.*

After heavy fighting during May and June 1864, General Ulysses S. Grant and his army was stalemated in front of the heavy fortifications surrounding Petersburg. Petersburg was the focal point for the Confederate supply line leading to Richmond.

Running north and south in front of Petersburg, the Federal entrenchments looked directly at the Confederate line.

## Sergeant Charles E. Brown

In the Rifle Pits Near Richmond
In Front of Petersburg, Virginia, July 1864

> While we were lying about the Petersburg line we got up everything we could eat that is suitable and good for our health. Vegetables, onions and fresh bread and two drinks of liquor fixed up as medicine to keep us healthy, was what we were allowed. There were thousands of dead soldiers lying between the lines that did not get buried till after the war. The stench was so terrible that we could hardily stand it. In our rear for miles and miles there were thousands of our soldiers and Rebel soldiers buried. After a big battle they plowed the ground six feet wide and then shoveled it out or rather made troughs in the earth, and then lay the soldier dead in them. Caps or some other part of clothing was placed over the face and then the ground was thrown on top of them. You could look for miles and miles in our rear and you would think it was a field of corn stubbles. Sometimes when a heavy wagon or the artillery would be hauled over these graves, the wheels would sometimes be drawn over the neck of one of the dead soldiers. This would cause the head to roll out from under the loose earth. Sometimes a wheel would roll over and arm or leg and this limb would then be uncovered and stand upright.

In the center of the Federal line was the 48th PVVI, a regiment consisting of many Pennsylvania coal miners—miners who all hailed from Schuylkill County. Organized in Pottsville in 1861, the 48th Regiment was very familiar to the boys of Company C; the men knew one another personally.

One day in early June the commanding officer of the 48th, Colonel Henry Pleasants, overheard a comment made by one of his soldiers who was watching the Rebels in their fortifications. The soldier confidently stated to one of his companions, "We could blow that damn fort up if we could run a mine shaft under it." Colonel Pleasants, a mining engineer who had worked the coalfields of Schuylkill County, understood fully what the soldier meant. Pleasants surveyed the terrain and drew up a map of the fortifications and gave this information to his commanding officer, Brigadier General Robert Porter, who, after considering the plan for a few days, took Colonel Pleasants to see General Burnside at the 9th Corps headquarters.

Pleasants explained his plan of digging a tunnel starting about fifty yards behind the Federal trench line and extending over five hundred feet. Sheltered from the Rebels' view, the tunnel would be dug like a drift mine in the anthracite region, sloping in an upward direction, alleviating any problems with water drainage within the mine. Burnside liked the idea and sent it along to General Meade, who was unsure of the feasibility of the plan but felt it would keep the men busy during this time of idleness.

The 48th immediately began digging the mine, at first with only their bayonets then by improvising tools. After three weeks of hard digging, the main tunnel was under the Rebel works. Pleasants once again surveyed the area and had the men dig a cross shaft, making the operation look like a long *T*, with the cross portion of the *T* running directly under the Rebel fortifications.

The whole time the 48th was digging the mine the Rebels were sinking counter mines trying to discover were the Federal mine was located, but with no success. With the mine completed, Pleasants ordered the men to place 320 kegs of powder in the gallery—each keg held twenty-five pounds of powder—running the fuses into the mine to a point, where they were spliced together. From this point a short run of fuse was sent to a wooden trough that held open powder close to the main explosives. The charge was set.

Burnside's plan was to rush troops into the open area created by the explosion in an attempt to force the Rebels to retreat from Petersburg and fall back to Richmond, where the war would surely come to a quick close.

At three o'clock in the morning of July 30, a soldier in the 48th lit the fuse leading to the charge. After thirty minutes nothing happened. General Grant, becoming impatient, ordered General Meade to have Burnside make the charge anyway. Pleasants ordered Sergeant Harry Reese, the mine foreman, to enter the mine and check the fuses. He found that the fuse had died out. Rushing out to get another splice, Reese came upon Lieutenant Jacob Douty crawling into the mine with a new fuse and splices. Both men crawled forward and replaced the connection. They relit the splice and rapidly exited the mine.

At 4:45 in the morning the mine exploded.

## Sergeant Charles E. Brown

In the Rifle Pits Near Richmond
In Front of Petersburg, Virginia, July 1864

> The 48th regiment was a Pottsville regiment, and they were undermining a Rebel fort. Colonel Henry Pleasants is doing the engineering. When they were nearly ready to blow up the fort, the Ninth Army Corps was getting ready. The fort was blown up on the morning of July 30th, 1864. The Fiftieth regiment is to charge on the left of the fort as soon as it is blown up. Once

the fort was blown up we started to charge. The fort was blown possibly forty feet in the air and it came down and broke in the middle and it turned up side down when it landed. One Rebel was frying crackers in a pan and it blew him about fifty or sixty feet in the air and he landed right in front of our Company. I placed my hand on his shoulder and asked him if were hurt. He looked at me and smiled and did not say a word. He was sitting up and had his pan and crackers in his lap. Our Company then received orders to go forward and that was the last I seen or heard of the Rebel.

We had a brigade of colored troops in our division, and they charged over the crater and up a hill called Spring Hill. At the top of the hill the Rebels were waiting for them and they fairly slaughtered them. What was left of them retreated and that ended the battle.

At the battle of Petersburg, I remember the narrow escape I.W. Tyson, brother of William Tyson of Schuylkill Haven, had from being blown to pieces. Tyson and John Fritz, commonly known as Jack Fritz, from our Company, was standing in the front line. Fritz was in the act of loading his gun. He had some difficulty in doing so and I helped him get his cartridges out. We had muzzle loaders. Fritz rammed down a cartridge and just as he was withdrawing the ram rod there came a thirty-two pound shell and took Fritz right out between Tyson and myself, in a space of not more than two feet wide. The blood and flesh was in my face and in Tyson's face. As I was removing the blood from my eyes Irwin Tyson said, "Look here Brown," we then looked upon the ground and seen Fritz's heart leaping there. Tyson called again to me to look at his heart as it bounded ten feet or more before it quieted down. It put me in mind of a chicken with its head cut off. This was the worst thing I ever saw in my life.

## Private William Tyson

### In the Rifle Pits Near Richmond
### In Front of Petersburg, Virginia, July 1864

In July of 1864 the Petersburg mine explosion occurred. I had been in front of Petersburg, during the siege for months. When the mine went up we were in rifle pits. The orders came to charge. Up and over we went. The confusion was almost beyond description. Our regiment had plenty of fighting for a few minutes but lack of support forced us to retreat. We couldn't get near the bodies for over two days and the air was foul.

During my war experience I saw terrible sights. It was nothing for us to rob a dead soldier of his shoes if yours were worn through. We stole food and ammunition from dead bodies on the field many times.

## Sergeant Charles E. Brown

In the Rifle Pits Near Richmond
Petersburg, Virginia, July 1864

> We went back to our works after the crater. We were now stationed right in front of the crater, and it is night. They are digging out their dead that were killed in the blow up. The lines here are only about one hundred feet apart. Now they agreed upon a truce so as to bury their dead. The most of our dead are colored men. After the dead were all buried went and rested.

On the morning of August 18, 1864, at Weldon Railroad, Union General Warren's corps and elements of the II and IX Corps advanced in good order and drove back Rebel pickets to Globe Tavern and began to rip up the railroad, fearing the Rebels were going to make an attack. Rebel General Henry Heth attacked the Federal forces, but was stopped by fresh Federal troops who, unknown to Heth, were in greater strength than anticipated.

On the afternoon of August 19, Rebel Generals Heth and Mahone made a well-timed attack against the well-fortified position of the federal troops. They attacked from the north and east simultaneously. Mahone actually hit a section of the Federal line and rolled up their flank, taking many prisoners. The Federal force counterattacked and by the evening had regained almost all of the ground lost in the day.

Sergeant Charles E. Brown of Company C was awarded the Medal of Honor for his actions at Weldon Railroad and for the capture of the flag of 47th Virginia Infantry.

## Sergeant Charles E. Brown

In the Rifle Pits Near Richmond
Near Weldon Railroad, Virginia, August 1864

> On August 18th 1864 we have orders to get ready to move in the evening with light marching equipment. It was during the night that we marched out and the colored troops took our place. The Rebels thought we were making some kind of a move so they opened all their artillery and mortars on us. A large mortar shell exploded over our Company. A lot of the scrap of this shell struck one man in the Company and [I] believe he bleed from over fifteen wounds in his body. We moved out on the road and marched south, but we don't know where we are going. All night we marched rapidly and now it was getting daylight. We turned off the road and here were army wagons all loaded with barrels of raw mackerel. The soldiers were throwing them out at us, we marched for a half a mile into the woods then we cooked our breakfast.

General Grant must have known all about the proposed charge of the Rebel General Mahone because he knew when and where he was going to break through our lines. The second Corps was in the breastworks where General Mahone was going to break through. They had orders as soon as the Rebels would charge on them, that they should retreat.

The Rebels charged us on the 19th, we could hear them shouting as they came on. The Second Corps soldiers were retreating. This battle was fought in an open field with a large woods on the right of the field and the artillery is on the left. Both were concealed in the woods. Our troops were pushing them back by hand. At least fifty cannon all, doubled with, charged with grape and canister are firing on the Rebels. The artillery has killed at least half of them. Then we received orders to charge on the balance of the Rebels. As soon as we began to charge they took to their heels and retreated as fast as possible. We took great numbers of prisoners.

We charged up to their breastworks and continued charging. Then we took the Rebel breastworks. There was not more than one out of every ten that escaped. While at the breastworks I heard a peculiar noise coming from the other side of the breast works: I crawled to the top of the works and looking around I saw Charles Oswald and Joseph Long fighting hand to hand with two Rebels. Oswald and Long had the best of the Rebels. Looking ahead about fifty yards, I saw a Rebel Sergeant and two color guards working their way through the woods. I was only wearing a sword and I had no gun, but I jumped down and picked up a Belgian rifle. I thought she was loaded and ran after the Sergeant and the two guards. When I got close to them I held my gun on them and commanded that they surrender. One of the guards attempted to raise his gun, and I said, "Drop that." And they both dropped their guns. I then made them turn around and marched them back to the breastworks. I then threw down my gun and took the flag from the sergeant and got on top of the breastworks and waved it. Our whole regiment was cheering me. But my waving of the flag drew the entire Rebel fire at me. The soles of my shoes were shot off as was also the rim of my hat. Many shots went through my clothing and it got too hot and I jumped back off the breast works. In shooting at me the Rebels killed Charles Burket, Adam Burket and William Wagner.

After the firing was somewhat lessened, we examined the flag and found that it was that of the 47th Virginia and found that it had been presented by the Ladies of the City of Richmond. It had the marks of many battles on it that were fought in Virginia. The sergeant and the color guards sitting nearby cried bitterly that the flag which they had prized so highly had been taken from them. I then struck the staff in the ground and lay down beside it and went to sleep.

> General Wilcox then came by and awakened me and said, Lieutenant Brown, while you were asleep I heard all about the capture of this flag, and the color sergeant and two color guards. Now the law of our government requires me to send this flag to Washington for safe keeping and there it will be labeled by whom and how it was captured, so that future generations can view it. General Wilcox also remarked that my capture of this flag was one of the bravest and daring acts that he had heard of during the war. He added that he would see that I was properly rewarded. I later examined the Belgian rifle and found that it was empty, so that I really made the capture of the flag, the sergeant and the two color guards with an empty gun.

The flag that Brown captured belonged to the 47th Virginia. It was the second flag of the regiment and of the third wool issue type. It was 47 inches by 47 inches, and the field was red, and a 5-inch blue wool cross with white fimbriation stretched from corner to corner. The border was of white cotton on the hoist edge, white on the three sides, with three whipped eyelets on the hoist edge. Ten of the Confederacy's thirteen five-point stars remained after capture. The unit designation was in yellow paint, and the battle honors were blue or black ink or paint. The flag listed the following battle honors: Seven Pines, Mechanicsville, Gains Mill, Frazier's Farms, Cedar Run, Manassas No. 2, Ox Hill, Harpers Ferry, Sharpsburg, Shepherdstown, Fredericksburg, Chancellorsville, and Gettysburg.

On February 24, 1905, Congress passed a bill authorizing the War Department to return its stockpile of captured Confederate battle flags to their original owners. Although the issue was hotly contested before the final decision was reached, many Union veterans urged the return of the flags.

Charles Brown stated: "Theodore Roosevelt sent the flag back to the Rebels before one generation had seen it."

## Sergeant Charles E. Brown

Petersburg, Virginia, August 1864

> On the twenty first day of August 1864 we marched back to Petersburg. We were always under fire when around Petersburg. General Hancock was fighting a battle near Reams Station, and we were ordered to hurry to his assistance.
>
> We marched on to the battlefield and the Rebels were retreating. It was a hard fought battle before we got there. The next day we went back to Petersburg. Now we are in Fort McGilvery, close to the river and very close to

> Petersburg. While in the fort the Rebel forces made it hot for us. Located there with us was the best battery in the army, it was called the Benjamin Battery. Our guns were always aimed at the port holes of the Rebel forts. One of the gunmen stood with the cord in his hand and another member of the battery used a pair of field glasses. As soon as the Rebels would push their guns to the port holes our gunners would fire on them. We would then have to run for the bomb proofs, as we could not stand their fire in the fort and we would have to crawl into the bomb proofs.

The 50th Regiment would remain at Fort McGilvery, on the banks of the Appomattox River. It was garrisoned there for the remainder of the winter months.

## Lieutenant Charles E. Brown

**In the Field Near Petersburg, Virginia, October–December 1864**

> In October 1864 I received orders to come to army headquarters with my company. I marched to headquarters with my company. There are a large number of Generals here and a large number of troops. All the generals made addresses, and then one of the generals came over to me and presented me with a medal of honor and a commission as a first lieutenant from congress for meritorious conduct. I was then mustered in as a first Lieutenant on the first day of November 1864. The first day of December 1864 I was mustered in as a Captain.
>
> We went back to our breastworks again having been taken from the fort and the fighting here and there. On December 31st 1864 Joseph Long got shot through the stomach and I never witnessed a man suffering like he did. They removed him to the hospital and there he died.

While the men of Company C continued on in the battlefield, many of their comrades were suffering a different kind of persecution from the Rebels. After being transferred from Charleston, Corporal John Doudle was sent to the Florence prison stockade, officially known as Camp Florence. This prison pen was in operation from September 1864 through February 1865. Over seventeen thousand Union soldiers were confined in Florence, and twenty-eight hundred died while being held there.

After General Sherman captured Atlanta, Confederates feared that he would soon liberate the Federal prisoners being held in Andersonville and other prison camps in Georgia. Rebel authorities decided they must move these prisoners out of the way of the advancing Sherman, and Florence was chosen as the destination site because of the accessibility of three railroads that entered the town, making the movement of prisoners easy.

## Corporal John Doudle

Prisoner, Florence Prison, South Carolina, October–December 1864

> While at Charleston we remained in this miserable condition until the 1st of October, when we received orders to fall inline, which did not take us long to do, and marched over to the railroad, which was not far from where we were camped, ignorant as too our destination. We were put on board freight cars and started off, but to where, no one could tell but those who held us in charge.
>
> We went on, and that evening about dark our train came to a stop, and we [were] ordered to get off the cars. We marched into a corn field close by the railroad, and remained there for that night, lying down upon the cold ground, taking a furrow for a bed and a ridge for a pillow. As the night was intensely cold, we suffered great agony and pain. Our teeth chattered and our knees knocked together.
>
> As I said to comrade Burger, "They have fooled us again, and no exchange." But exchange did come to some of the poor fellows that night, as quite a number died. When daylight approached, to our surprise our eyes rested upon another stockade. After our arrival in this prison, where we were informed that its name was Florence Prison, we, as usual, first located our ground, and then made a survey of our new quarters. The prison was constructed on the same principle as Andersonville, and resembled it in a great many ways. A stockade built of logs closed us from the outside world, and a small stream of water, with a swamp on either side, ran through the prison. The ground enclosed contained about 15 acres, of which four or five, bordering the stream, were so swampy that they could not be used or occupied.
>
> The dead line at this place was marked by a small, narrow ditch, with the same deadly significance attached to it. As in the other prison pens, it being certain death to cross it. Unlike the other prison pens, no sentry boxes were erected on top of the stockade. The sentinel stood on a lot of ground which had been thrown against the stockade form the outside.
>
> No shelter was furnished the prisoners, but as a considerable lot of offal from the trees, that had been cut down to build the stockade, was left on the inside, it furnished us with the material to build a shelter. It was good enough when it did not rain, but when it rained it felt very uncomfortable.
>
> It would be impossible for me to describe our feelings when we marched into this prison. We were broken down in body, almost in spirits. The thought would come into our minds continually, "How can we ever expect to live over the winter in this terrible place?"

Quite a number of men, to escape the horrors of prison life, were enlisting in the Rebel army; not with the hopes of doing any good service, but for the purpose of saving themselves by receiving shelter and rations, or rather enough to eat, and the hope of making their escape and getting back to Union lines. There were quite a number enlisted and remained away for some time, but they all came back again and had a suit of gray clothes on.

The food that we received was the worst description, and was barely enough to keep anyone alive. It consisted of one pint of corn meal or wheat flour, and sometimes a few raw beans. Sometimes we received salt, and as often none at all. It must have been very scarce. We received but very little meat, and what we did receive was covered with maggots and was not fit to eat.

The hospital department was connected with the prison, but as the sick fared no better in there than in the prison, very few were admitted. The officer in charge of the prison was named Barrett. He was a cowardly rascal, a fit companion for Capt. Wirz, or, as the prisoners would call him, a brutal Dutchman. Lieut. Barrett would frequently come into camp and discharge a revolver over the heads of the men.

On the 11th of December the Rebel doctors came into camp for the purpose of examining the worst cases to be paroled, and examined about 100 men. Jacob Heim and William Guertler, both of our Company were among the lucky ones, as Comrade Heim was suffering with rheumatism, and they thought they would be of no further service to the government. A few bribed themselves out by giving the doctors rings.

The hospital was situated in the northeastern part of the prison. It was under shelter, but was in a horrible condition. The men were lying upon the bare ground, with light covering, and were filthy and lousy, and the sight they presented was horrible to see.

The United States Sanitary Commission had sent a considerable amount of clothing to be distributed to the prisoners, but they did not receive one half of them. When the clothing came into camp, we were drawn into line. There were one or two suits to be distributed among thirty men. Each man's name and number was put on a small piece of paper, and then one man had to turn his back and pick them out: and the lucky number drew a shirt or a pair of drawers. But what they did with the balance of them I cannot say. It was said that the sheets were traded for sweet potatoes for those that were in the hospital as I never seen any distributed among the prisoners in the camp.

At Florence on each corner of the prison was a raised platform and from these pieces of artillery frowned upon the helpless inmates. At all hours, by day and by night, a man stood by these guns, ready for action in case any attempted out break on our part.

The ladies in that vicinity would pay us a visit to our prison, accompanied by the officers in command, and would stand on these platforms and throw in perhaps a few loafs of bread, just to see the poor prisoners crowd each other, and then they would laugh at the misery of the poor fellows. No true lady would have stood there and looked with such spirit at the sights before them; but they seemed to enjoy it.

As the Presidential election drew nigh the Rebels became excited and eager to know the result. McClellan was their favorite, and they had high hopes upon his success of being the next president. "If McClellan is elected," they would say, "we will soon have peace." On the day of the election a quantity of white and black beans were brought into the prison, with the understanding that they were to be used as ballots, whereby the political opinion of the prisoners might be ascertained, the white beans representing McClellan and the black ones President Lincoln. Two empty bags were hung on the inside of the prison. We were told we could go and deposit our vote as we pleased and a few men stood by to see that no fraud was committed, but the result was not gratifying to those who commenced it. I do not know the exact figures, but found out that Lincoln had two to one over McClellan. This was an expression of feeling and the opinion of the men who were half famished and ragged, yet were not in favor of a peace gained by any disgraceful compromise. In about a week the result was known, and the Rebels were blue indeed. Such a number of sour gloomy looking fellows was never seen.

I saw a man hanging by the thumbs outside the prison one day, and found out afterwards that it was one of the prisoners who was trying to escape, and it was the penalty he received. It was pretty hard to escape, as they were continually on the alert, and also had bloodhounds to put on our track. At Andersonville they had several and we could hear them yelping almost every hour.

The Rebel soldiers, belonging to the different battalions, were granted passes occasionally, which allowed them to come into the prison and trade for gold pens, rings, pocket knives, pocketbooks, buttons, or anything they could get, giving in return sweet potatoes or Confederate money.

A Rebel came in one day with a great desire to obtain some New York State buttons which the Rebels prized so highly, and they, being very showy, were in great demand and a high price. It was plain that he had traded for them before, as he had a full row on the coat he wore, and four of them on his back. While he was bargaining with two or three of the prisoners one of the boys stepped softly behind him and with a sharp knife cut off the four buttons of his coat tail, and then, presenting himself in front of the Rebel, he said: "I have a few New York

State buttons that perhaps I might sell you." "Have you?" said he, and then paying a good round sum for his own buttons, he left well pleased. A group of mud sills had a good laugh when he was out of sight.

On the north side of the stockade was a camp occupiec by slaves, under command of the Lieutenant and Engineer officer DeLoyle. This officer had sole charge of laying out the fortifications and slaves would perform the labor. It was amusing to hear them sing at their work. One of them, apparently a leader among his brethren would perform the solos, and the rest would join in on the chorus, keeping time al the while, pounding away on the breastworks. The following is a verse of their song:

Possum up a gum stump,
Coonies in the hollow,
Wake up, snakes and June bugs,
I'll gib you half a dollar.

Thanksgiving day came and Christmas, and still found us in the same terrible condition, our rations small, and the cold winds of winter whistling through our prison pen, while death was claiming its poor victims on all sides. How many died at this place I cannot say, As I never found out.

When Christmas of 1864 came we conversed with one another, wondered what our friends were saying, thinking and doing at home, nc doubt enjoying themselves with good roasted turkey or some such savory meal, not knowing our condition, while we were receiving a pint of corn meal and scarcely any fuel to cook it with, the cold winter approaching upon us and no sign of exchange, seeing the poor boys stretched out upon the bare ground, lying spoon fashion, as I have said before, and the nights immensely cold, while the next morning they were dead, their earthly career was ended.

I always thought I would never relate the horrors of my prison life, for they would seem too much to believe, but they are solemn realities of what we endured. Like the immortal words of the poet when he wrote:

But that I am forbid the secrets of my prison house,
I could a tale unfold, whose lightest word would harrow thy soul
Freeze thy young blood.
Make thy two eyes, like stars, start from their spheres,
Thy knotted and combined locks to part,
And each particular hair to stand on end,
Like quills upon the fretful porcupine.

## Corporal John Doudle

Prisoner, Florence South Carolina, and Libby Prison, Richmond, Virginia
January–February 1865

The month of January passed away with no signs of an exchange, and no pity for us whatever, February came and brought rumors of exchange.

On the 11th of February orders came into camp for the first thousand to be ready to move at any time. We could scarcely believe it, as we had been fooled so often. My comrades and I consulted over the matter, and they thought that the Rebels would take us to another bull pen. Comrade Berger and I, as I had said before, were in partnership for a tin cup. While we were talking orders came for us to fall in line. I resolved to go alone, as none of the rest would come, and let Berger have the tin cup.

On the 12th of February 1,000, or supposed to be, marched out of Florence prison and over to the railroad, where we were put on board freight cars and started off but to where, we did not know.

While on the cars I saw the only place that I did know about. It was Pocotaligo Bridge, as I had been there in 1862 when our command, under General Isaac Stevens, was stationed at Beaufort, S.C., when the forces went over the mainland, by Port Royal Ferry, to destroy the bridge, not thinking then that I would ever cross it as a prisoner of war.

We were half starved and almost frozen, as the weather was intensely cold, especially when we came into the State of Virginia, where there was snow on the ground. They made us get off the cars and march in the snow, which caused the blood to run out of our feet. While a great many died on our journey, they tried their best to kill the whole of us.

On the 21st of February we were introduced into a dingy brick building in Richmond, Va. Known to the world as Libby Prison, and I said to myself. "Fooled again." The floors of this place were in a filthy condition. Our rations from the 21st to the 24th was one spoon full of cooked rice. On the evening of the 23rd we were drawn in line in Libby Prison. We were then paroled and signed the following pledge:

We the undersigned, do solemnly pledge our sacred word of honor, that we will
Not take up arms again, in any garrison, fortification, or in the field work of the United States
Or do any police or constabulary duty, or any duty usually performed by soldiers, until
We shall have been duly declared exchanged.

On the morning of the 24th of February, 1865, we left Libby Prison, and were put on board the *Libby Davis*. The vessel was of light draft so it would not strike the torpedoes which the Rebels had in the James River. We saw Fort Darling and the Rebel Gunboats below Richmond, and we landed at Aiken's Landing, 12 miles from Richmond, and [were] set free.

We came to Annapolis via Fortress Monroe, and there we were taken to the barracks. We received our descriptive list from our respected captains, and a couple of months pay and our choice of either going to a hospital or coming home, I preferred the later, and received a furlough for thirty days, as I thought if I was to die, I would die at home, as I was very weak, and suffering with catarrh.

When I was at home one month, Dr. John G. Koehler, then a district physician for this place, went with me to Pottsville to the Provost Marshal, and had my furlough extended another thirty days. When my furlough had expired I went back to camp Parole, Annapolis, and handed in the certificate for my last thirty days furlough.

## Captain Charles E. Brown

In the Field Near Petersburg, Virginia, January 1865–March 1865

In January 1865 a man from Reading and my self volunteered to go out in the videt post and act as sharpshooters. We were compelled to go out before daylight and stay out until dark. My friend got killed while firing early in the day and I had to stay there with him until dark before I could get his remains back to our lines.

At another time I was making a detail in the breast works to go to work that night and while there got into a dispute with one of the men. I stood up to talk with him and a Rebel sharp shooter, seeing my head, fired his gun. The bullet hit about a half of an inch from the top of the breast works. That turned the bullet length wise and glancing off struck me over the left eye inflicting a gash one inch long and rendering me unconscious. The doctor was summoned and after stopping the flow of blood by means of a plaster and restoring me to consciousness, I got my men and went to work that night.

Nearly everyday something would happen. We were getting close towards the end of the war, but we did not know it then. We fought hard all along that line in front of Petersburg. All the troops that can be spared are going to the left and are coming up on the rear of Petersburg. All the troops that can be spared are sent to the left of the breast works, the breast works are fourteen miles from here Good news our troops have broken the Rebel Lines on the left and are coming up on the rear of Petersburg. While fighting here we were compelled to fight very hard.

During this time the Rebels were burning and blowing up everything, it was one explosion after another. All night long the Rebels are leaving our front. Later on one morning we marched to Petersburg. On our march we failed to notice any Rebels. We marched close to the area where General Grant had cut off General Lee and his army. Night over took us and the order to rest was given, it being known that the following day would be a hard one for us all. Our expectations of a hard fight did not materialize. General Grant and General Lee were making terms for the surrender. We had marched to about one half mile from were General Lee surrendered, but could not see Lee. There are Rebel soldiers are going by us here for Petersburg and Richmond, on their way home.

On March 25, Major Samuel Schwenk helped lead a surprise attack with the 50th. The regiment was highly praised for this action.

*Report of Major Samuel K. Schwenk*
*March 29, 1865*
*MAJOR:*
*Pursuant to instructions to forward a report of the operations of this regiment in the action of Saturday, the 25th instant, I have the honor to report that I received orders at 4.30 a.m. to send all the men with arms, except the pickets, to brigade headquarters, and immediately sent ninety men, the whole number in camp with arms, in charge of Capt. Charles E. Brown, Company C, and First Lieut. Wilbur H. Wilcox, Company D, who reported at Second Brigade headquarters at 4.50 a.m. and was assigned a position in an old fort beyond brigade headquarters, and soon afterward occupied old rifle-pits, constructed about 400 yards southeast of Fort McGilvery and running at right angles with the main line, when they at once commenced firing upon the flank of the enemy's advancing line and kept up a brisk fire until the enemy was repulsed and our entire line reoccupied.*

*The casualties were two men very slightly wounded, and Captain Brown reports that all the men behaved very well and fired with great accuracy and effect.*

*Very respectfully, your obedient servant,*
*SAML. K. SCHWENK,*
*Major, Commanding Regiment.*

The final campaign of General Lee's Army of Northern Virginia began March 25, 1865, when he sought to break General Grant's ever-tightening hold at Petersburg. Lee tried unsuccessfully to attack the Federal position at Fort Stedman.

Grant counterattacked a week later at Five Forks. The Confederate line snapped, and Lee's meager forces abandoned Richmond and Petersburg. Although fighting would continue for the next week, it would be to no avail. Lee was beaten and asked for surrender terms on April 9.

## Private George Heebner

Encamped Near Petersburg, April 5, 1865

> Editors, *Miners' Journal*:
> We have taken possession of Petersburg after a siege of nearly ten months. Our brigade was the first to enter the town on the morning of the 2nd. The boys of the different commands are in high spirits in consequence of the last victories and glorious achievements accomplished by the National Army. Our troops now occupy Petersburg and Richmond, and the Rebel army is demoralized. Their loss in the recent engagements is estimated at between 20 to 30 thousand. Including some 60 pieces of artillery. Our regiment itself captured 16 pieces of artillery, two one hundred pounders, four twelve pounders and eight twenty-five pounders, and one thirty-two pounder including some five hundred prisoners which we picked up since our occupation. We are on picket at present on the Boydon Plank Road, running directly to Richmond. Large numbers of deserters and stragglers are roaming through the country, and keep coming into our lines by squads. Secession recruitments are pretty near run out. The civilians express their dissatisfaction, but the greater portion of them is jubilant at our arrival. They had said they had not had a full stomach for the last six months, annul our occupation. The colored population as a general thing are delighted at the appearance of our troops and are rejoicing at the sight of our national standard, which promises them a home and protection. Most of the prisoners captured are taking the oath. Since the establishment of the headquarters in the court house there has been an opportunity afforded to have as much as a pass approved. The officials are so busy engaged that they cannot attend anything but administering the oath to civilians and prisoners. The Rebels plainly see that their efforts are in vain and that their object can never be accomplished.
>
> I remain, very respectfully your obedient servant.
>
> Geo. Heebner.

The 50th Pennsylvania had the honor of being the first Pennsylvania regiment to enter the city of Petersburg, and the first to cross the Appomattox River.

*Major Samuel K. Schwenk*

*Headquarters, Browders Crossing, Virginia, April 8, 1865*

*Brvt. Major C.A. Lounsberry:*

*In conformity with instructions I have the honor to report the operations of this regiment, in the occupation of Petersburg.*

*At daylight on the 3rd instant, we received orders to detach one Company, to garrison battery No. 9 and move into Petersburg. Leaving Co. C under Capt. Charles C. Brown, we advanced and crossed the enemy works at 5 A.M., and marched into Petersburg, capturing two flags and thirty-eight prisoners and halted at the court house.*

*At 8 A.M. we relieved the 211th P.V. and established a picket line along the Appomattox River, which we crossed at 9 A.M. and advanced to Dunlop Station, and sent out scouts and detachments on the turnpike and railroad, captured a Rebel mail, 22 bags of mail, 500 new Enfield Rifle muskets, 200 cavalry sabers, one piece of artillery, a thirty pound Parrott with carriage and caisson, 4 boxes of accoutrements, 550 rounds of artillery ammunition, shell and solid shot, two car loads of grain, sixty hogsheads of tobacco and 114 prisoners. Co. F, under 1st Sgt. Jacob Pauline, occupied Fort Goosneck, and Clifton and took 16 prisoners and eleven pieces of artillery, including two 100 pounders, eight of them spiked, and two magazines full of ammunition, a large Union Flag was taken from the residence of David Dunlop, Esq, which was raised over his house in 1861 and authorities compelled him to take it down in 1861 to save his life and property.*

*In the evening we formed a picket line, running nearly east and west from Chesterfield Battery, via Dunlop Station to the Richmond turnpike. The mail was taken from the enemy by Sergt. Alex P. Garret, and 6 men from Company C. The flags were captured by Sergt. Lucien Pucker, Co. B and private Henry Hummel of Company F.*

*Captain James H. Levan, with companies H and I, crossed the Appomattox River, and advanced about five miles on the Richmond and Petersburg Railroad, recapturing 6 Union Soldiers, and took procession of a Rebel Hospital with two surgeons and thirty-two patients and attendants. Just as the enemy was packing up and making preparations to leave the Regiment reconnoitered the country, and rendered valuable service.*

*First Lieutenant Henry J. Christ, with Co. G, occupied Fort Chesterfield and two batteries, with ten pieces of artillery, and three magazines full of ammunition, advanced three miles on the Richmond turnpike and captured eleven prisoners.*

*Casualties were one man killed and four wounded. During the entire action all the officers and men behaved very well, executing every order with good faith and alacrity, so I cannot justly and consistently, select the names of any particular persons to be mentioned for meritorious services, but must recommend them all as deserving praise for their faithful performance of their duties.*

*Very respectfully your obt. Servt.*
*Samuel K. Schwenk*
*Major Commanding Regiment*

## Captain Charles E. Brown

Near the James River, Virginia, April 1865

On April 10th 1865 the day following Lee's surrender we marched back to the James River. We went into camp at the river and awaited transportation to Washington.

## Anonymous, Company C

Fort Gaines, Washington, D.C., May 13, 1865

Editors, *Miners' Journal*:
We are as yet at Washington, D.C. as a matter of course. How long we are to remain here is uncertain. The rumor among the boys in camp is that we are awaiting the arrival of the different armies which are expected shortly to make their appearance, and then we can look for that grand review which is to take place in this locality.

We do not feel desirous of having reviews, as we had quite enough of them while lying around Petersburg. They cannot muster us out any to soon, and the boys are all anxious to return to their respective homes after four years duration of hardships and privations in the field, and bringing to terms at the point of a bayonet, an almost invincible feat, to a permanent peace.

The debate raging among the boys now is when shall we receive the welcome orders to our final departure towards home? Our camp is at present situated in a pleasant and also healthy locality near Tennally Town, which is about five miles from the city of Washington. We are surrounded on all sides by large fortifications, which present a very formidable appearance. The boys are amusing themselves by daily routine of duty, such as camp guard, picket and fatigue duty, and worse than all drilling four hours a day, which is not admired by any. But in the meantime we feel more comfortable today than we did one year ago on that memorable field at Spotsylvania Court House, where our loss was heavy in killed, wounded and prisoners. A few of the latter are now returning to the regiment (the undersigned being one of them). But a great many of our comrades who were among us then, are now sleeping the last sleep, in and about the prison pens of Andersonville, Ga. and Salisbury, N.C. and many other prisons. Peace be to their ashes; and we their comrades in arms, offer our heartfelt sympathy to their friends and relatives who mourn their loss.

I conclude, hoping happy times may shortly come when we return to our homes and resume our avocations, and enjoy the peace that we have suffered so much the last four years to gain.

I subscribe myself your humble servant,
Nailer.

On May 23 and 24, 1865, over 150,000 Federal soldiers marched in a parade in Washington, D.C., known as the Grand Review. It was hailed as the greatest event in America's history.

On the first day, the Army of the Potomac, commanded by General George G. Meade, marched. The next day, the Armies of Georgia and Tennessee, commanded by General William T. Sherman, marched down Pennsylvania Avenue, past the White House. The event was spread over a two-day period because General Ulysses S. Grant clamed if they marched all armies together the event would stretch all the way to Richmond.

Within a week of the Grand Review both Federal armies, the Army of the Potomac and the Armies of Georgia and Tennessee, were disbanded.

## Captain Charles E. Brown

Washington City, May 1865

While in the camp at the James River we had a good time, as we waited to go aboard the transports down the James River to Fortress Monroe, and then up the Potomac, where we will land at Alexandria. When we got to Georgetown we went into camp. We were lying there a long time all on account of effecting settlement with the government. All officers that held an office of responsibility had to file a certificate in detail of its men to the government. A large number of prisoners came to us here from the Rebel prisons and I got charge of them and had to take them to Washington and get a settlement with the government. It required the greater part of a week for us to get our back pay, while waiting for the big review. At last it came, and it took us about three days until it was all over. At the time there were no paved streets and we were compelled to wade and march through the mud. The prisoners bought a sword for one hundred dollars and presented the same to me, for effecting a settlement for them in Washington. Near the White House was a reviewing stand. Seated thereon, were men of importance in the Nation's affairs, with the exception of poor Abraham Lincoln.

He was dead and buried. Nearly every soldier made a sorrowful remark about him. After the review we went into camp and awaited the transportation to take us to Harrisburg. We went to the railroad station and boarded the train for Pennsylvania.

# 1865

*Seek home for rest, / For home is best.*

—*Thomas Tusser*

## Corporal John Doudle

### Home, Schuylkill Haven, Pennsylvania, June 3, 1865

On the 3rd day of June I received my discharge and came home, as the war was over. All the comrades that were captured with me came out of prison excepting two, Henry Helm and Samuel Agley. Such was my life as a prisoner of war. Peter Dunkle lived through all the prisons, and was only in our lines a day, when he expired. So Helm, Agley and Dunkle died from the sufferings of prison life. Samuel Agley was eaten up by vermin. I hope that the like of this will never occur again.

I cannot finish without giving the boys of Company C, and also the regiment, my heartfelt thanks, as they were as brave a set of boys as ever trod upon Southern soil. We were united and generous to one another, and I must say they treated me with respect. Charles E. Brown, Augustus Mellon, Samuel A. Losch and A.P. Garrett raised themselves from the ranks and became commissioned officers. Although I did not serve under Captain Brown or Lieut. Mellon we had many a march together when they were in the ranks. Theirs are unapproachable records, as they were gallant and brave soldiers, and also must have been good peers which we must forever honor and respect.

I hope when us few survivors that are left will explain the hardships and what we endured on many a weary march on the battlefield, or in the prison pen, to our children, and let it be handed down to our children's children that, when we are laid to rest they will be awake to their duty and trust, and see that our graves will be kept green.

In concluding my history of what I have seen and gone through, I hope that the reader will read it carefully, for "Truth is Truth." Such was the life of a soldier and a prisoner of war. I never missed a day's duty from the 14th of August 1861, until the day I was captured, May 12th 1864, at Spotsylvania Court House, Virginia. There are many incidents which I did not note, but I think I have seen enough.

Corporal John Doudle was urged by the editors of the *Schuylkill Haven Call* newspaper to write a narrative of his experiences during the Civil War under the title "War Stories." Doudle was a citizen of Schuylkill Haven and his narrative is filled with the names and the achievements of Schuylkill Haven people. His excellent narrative was also published in the *Pottsville Daily Republican* during the months of July and August 1908.

Orders were received on June 17, 1865, for Company C to proceed along with the surviving members of the regiment to Gettysburg where they were to participate in a ceremony planned for the Fourth of July. The governor of Pennsylvania was going to dedicate a memorial within the cemetery.

## Captain Charles E. Brown

Harrisburg, Pennsylvania, July 1865

When we arrived in Harrisburg, you can imagine how happy we all were to be back in our own state again, to say nothing of the joy once again to embracing our parents. Here we were to take off our uniforms and start another occupation that was to continue for the remainder of our lives. Of course it was sorrowful for some, to see only a few of the large number that had left this town come home. All that did not come back were left on the battlefields. My brother Benjamin Brown died at Vicksburg, and is buried in the National Cemetery there.

There were five brothers of us, John, Benjamin and Charles were in the army, and my mother had the pleasure of seeing two of her three sons who enlisted alive after the war was over. There were a large number of parents who had sons in the army but did not see them after the war was over; they were left on the field of battle. On July 13, 1865 our regiment was paid off and mustered out of the United States Service. Now we were citizens once again.

They did not muster me out of the United States service. I got orders to take my Company home and there await further orders. On the eighth day of August I got orders to return to Harrisburg. There and then they mustered me out of service and paid me off. The reason they had refused to muster me out earlier was due to the fact that the French had taken Mexico, when we had a Rebellion in our own country.

After the war was over the United States warned the French to get out of Mexico and this country held enough officers and soldiers to drive them out, but the warning was sufficient. England did all she possibly could against us during the war and after the war was over the United States compelled England to pay sixteen million dollars in gold for what she had done against our country.

It is a miracle that I had the pleasure of coming home after four years of service in the Rebellion, with all the narrow escapes I had. During my four years service we had some of the best soldiers in my company that was in the entire army. They either got killed or wounded or taken prisoners. I know of some of our company that had to go to the hospital three different times, suffering with bullet wounds. I hope the public won't look at [this] history as though I was writing it for self praise. I am writing it for the benefit of our company and for the benefit of the town, to show to them what this town did to save their country during the war. I am sorry I could not give a full history. It would be very interesting to give our losses in different battles together with the dates and names of battles.

We were in the siege of Vicksburg and Jackson, Mississippi and the Siege of Knoxville, Tenn. The siege of Richmond and Petersburg, Va. We fought many hard battles in those sieges and the only credit we got was the siege of Vicksburg, Jackson, Knoxville, Richmond and Petersburg.

The fiftieth regiment was in thirty-six regular battles besides being under fire day and night, in those sieges and many skirmishes too numerous to mention. We had a fine Company of soldiers when we went to the battlefield in 1864, as ever listed in an army and our losses were great on our way back to Richmond. On the 30$^{th}$ of May at the battle of Bethesda Church I was fourth sergeant and all our commissioned and non commissioned officers, both above and below me, were either killed or wounded or taken prisoner. That left me in command of the company and I commanded the company every day till I brought the company home to Schuylkill Haven after the war. Thus you can see what a terrible loss we had in our company. William Tyson and I were the only two that were not disabled in some way. He and I were with the company from the sixth day of May, 1864 till the end of the war.

Now the history of my early experience in the war is completed, in a short way as I said I would write it. There were many interesting things that happened during the war that I omitted. I wrote all of the facts as these in several letters from my memory, as I had no data or names or facts on hand at my disposal. Of the large number of the first company that enlisted in 1861, there are only six surviving,

> namely Levi Eckert, William Wildermuth, Henry M. Deibler, Jacob Heim and Peter Paul. In our second enlistment we left with a full company and they sent men to us until the end of the war. During the siege of Petersburg and Richmond, they sent us more men than we could take and they had to go elsewhere, greatly to their dislike.

After the return home of the boys from Company C, the *Schuylkill Haven Call* newspaper constantly requested and even pleaded with Captain Brown to write about his many experiences during the war and, finally, in 1916, he agreed to write. He penned his narrative from March to May, before the involvement of the United States in World War I, and although the war was raging in Europe at the time, he was very aware of what was approaching for the United States. And, in the patriotic spirit he showed all his life, Captain Brown ended his narrative with these thoughts:

## Captain Charles E. Brown

Home, Schuylkill Haven, Pennsylvania, April 1916

> All the soldiers that came to us during the years 1864 and 1865 were all young people and there are a large number still living. I am very proud and thankful that I have been spared and am able to write their history. This history will be for those to read after we have answered the final call.
>
> When I read of the war in Europe [World War I] and learn what the women are doing for their government, taking the place of the men so that the men can shoulder their guns and fight for their country, by their actions, meaning the women, you can see what war in your own country would mean.
>
> Every man, woman and child must do what they can to save their country. When I read about the foreign war I always think about the patriotic ladies and what they did for their country during our war. There are still a large number of these ladies living in our town, and when I see or meet them I always say and think, "There is one of our patriotic ladies that did all she possibly could for our country and the soldiers during our war." I would like to mention those patriotic ladies by name, but it is impossible for me to remember all of them and sooner than slight one single person, I will mention no names, however should anyone ask me were they are I will tell them.
>
> A woman that does all she possibly can for her country in time of war deserves more credit than a man. We had a large number of patriotic ladies in Schuylkill Haven during our war and nothing will afford me greater pleasure than to mention them all.
>
> Benjamin Christ from Minersville recruited and organized the fiftieth regiment and was our colonel for the first three years. He did not reenlist but went home

when his three-year term of service had expired. William Telford of Bradford County was our next Colonel. About a month or so before we came home, Samuel Schwenk became our Colonel. He was from Schuylkill County. Captain D.F. Burket, a Schuylkill Haven man, recruited and organized Company C, and George Brumm, of Minersville, a brother of Judge Brumm, was our first Lieutenant.

A man by the name of Eckle was our second Lieutenant, but I never saw him as he was on detached duty. We had eight or ten in our company on detached duty. Some were in the Signal Corps, some in transportation, and several other departments.

A copy of my last discharge from the army is as follows:

*Charles E. Brown, a Captain of Company C, Fiftieth Regiment of Pennsylvania Veteran volunteers, Said Charles E. Brown was born in Bradford County in the state of Pennsylvania.*

*He is twenty-three years of age, five feet eight inches high, medium complexion, brown eyes, dark hair and by occupation when enrolled, a boatman.*

The regiment was discharged in July 1865, but they held some of the commissioned officers for further orders, and I was one of them. They called me to Harrisburg in August and gave me in full to the tenth day of August and then sent me home a free man. Upon my arrival home I bought a boat from William Kantner. Its name was the *General Sherman*. I then went boating and on the 12th day of January 1867, I was married to Francis Mellon. To us were born four boys and two girls. The two that were born last are still living, namely Warren G. Brown, who is 39 years of age and Arthur C. Brown who is now 37years of age.

Mrs. Brown was 70 years old on the 26th day of September 1916 and I was 74 years of age on the 11th day of December 1915. We are thankful to God that he spared us and granted us privilege to reach such mature years.

With all the narrow escapes that I experienced, God was surely merciful to me. That I am here in the world today is about all I am thankful for. Let us have Peace and hope that God will protect and save us from another war in this our beloved country.

In recognition of the service of the 50th Regiment, Brevet Major General O.B. Wilcox, who commanded the division at different times in the 9th Corps, sent a letter to the members of the 50th at the dedication of their monument at Antietam.

## Brevet Major General O.B. Wilcox

Madison Barracks, Sackett's Harbor, New York, October 11, 1883

The Fiftieth Pennsylvania volunteers first came conspicuously under my notice at the Battle of South Mountain, 14th of September, 1862. It had just come out of the scathing fire of Chantilly, and the Second Manassas , as a part of the Second Brigade of the First Division, Ninth Army Corps. On this day, September 14th, Major Overton commanded the Regiment and Colonel Christ the Brigade, and here was performed the double feat of changing front under heavy enemy fire and checking an incipient panic. This was done well and gallantly under the cool bravery and good management of Colonel Christ and Major Overton, and during the rest of the fight supporting General Cox's Kanawa Division, from that day forward the Regiment was known at my headquarters as " Old Reliable."

At Antietam, when the long impatiently expected orders to advance were brought, the Regiment dashed forward in the most gallant style, and deeply shared with the whole Division the orders for recall, after we had cleaned our own front, and thought we were in sight of Lee's Headquarters wagons.

Again in the Battle of the Wilderness, Ny River and Spotsylvania, the long siege of Petersburg, and the fight for the Weldon Road at Globe Tavern, the Fiftieth shone conspicuously.

The success of Ny river was one of the brilliant little episodes of the war. Our Division, mainly Christ's Brigade, had gained a position overlooking the road by which the rebels in large numbers, supposed to be Longstreet's Corps, were moving. It was at once a saucy and imprudent position, with the river behind us, and was twice charged and the charges repulsed with great determination. In this affair captain Samuel K. Schwenk, with four companies of the Fiftieth, made a fine bayonet charge at a critical moment, which probably saved the day, as the enemy had almost gained the crest of the hill. It was an honor, however, which the 17th and 20th Michigan and 79th New York came into share, although not at the point of the bayonet. This, the bayonet charge, was the peculiar glory of Schwenk and his little battalion of the 50th.

At Spotsylvania, when the enemy made their grand charge on the left of the army, which my Division had the honor to hold, the 50th had to fight their way hand to hand through overwhelming numbers. In order to save their colors, which they did successfully, though with bloody losses.

On the 18th of June, 1864, in the charge in the Suffolk railroad cut in front of Petersburg, the brave "old Roman," Col. Ben Christ, was severely wounded, at the head of his brigade, but all through the rest of the war, As up to this time, the officers and men of "Old Reliable" maintained the enviable reputation they gained in front of South Mountain: Brenholtz, Overton, Schwenk, Brumm, Telford, Adjutant Lewis Crater, Quartermaster John S. Eckel, Captains Daniel F.

Burket, Samuel F. Bossard, Gordon Z. Dimock, Charles Parker , James B. Ingman, George Yeager, Henry E. Clevland, Henry A. Lantz, Charles C. Brown, James H. Levan, George V. Meyer, Jacob Paulus, Henry J. Alspach, Edward F. Weist, Samuel Hesss, Wilbur H. Wilcox, Benjamin R. Lyons, John H. Herring, William H. Blanchford, Henry J. Christ and Edward A. Wilbur and a number of others particularly distinguishing themselves.

Very Respectfully,
(signed)

O.B. Wilcox.
Brevet Major General U.S. Vol's.

Schuylkill Haven Call
*Schuylkill Haven, Pennsylvania*

*On Labor Day 1908 the* [37th] *annual reunion of the 50th P.V.V.I. was held in Schuylkill Haven. At two P.M. the annual business meeting was in the main lodge room of the Yoder building. The meeting was called to order by the president, General Samuel K. Schwenk, of New York, who in a few chosen remarks paid a tribute to the patriotism of Schuylkill Haven and the members of Company C.*

*Among those in attendance were: General Samuel K. Schwenk, wife and niece, of New York; J. Milton Mishler, wife and grandson, Milton Mishler and wife, John F. Philips and wife. Adam Lloyd and wife, Wm. H. Tyson and wife; John Doudle and wife, Z Daubenhour, Edw. Hebner, Geo. Heebner, Levi Eckert, David Dampman and wife, A. Wall and wife, of Phila. G.A. Mishle and wife, Trenton, N.J.; S.S. Hess and wife, Stroudsburg, Pa.; William Williams, Frank Wise Newark, Ohio; Benj. Knarr, Camden N.J. Josiah Wright, Camden N.J. Henry Lebengood and wife, Pottstown, Pa.; H.A. Boyer, Reading; John A. Kepner, wife and daughter, Harrisburg; John S. Kreider, and wife, Lebanon, Pa.; J.H. Zimmerman and J. Starr and wife, Llewellyn; H. Michel, Girardville; E.B. Troutman, Wilkes Barre; C. Osmond and B.S. Bausman, Pottsville; Wm. H. Blanchford and wife Spring City; Lewis Kreider, Reading; Wm. Eckert, wife and two daughters, Monocacy; H.P. Brownback, Pottstown; J. Hoffman, Paxtinos; C.W. Bartlet, Reading; H.I. Christ, Hazelton, M. Wadsworth and wife, son and daughter in law, Phoenixville; C. Swhagel and wife Snyderstown, Pa.; Albert Fisher, frank Hummel, J.J. Hoffman, Paxtinos; Jos Yeager and wife Sunbury; Hiram Focht, wife and daughter, Reading; H.F. Bousman, Pottsville; Aaron Gilbert, Chas. Eller, John Eckert Cressona; and Henry Hill, Peter Paul, David Raudenbush, William Wildermuth, Chas. Schappel, I.W. Tyson. I. Lidermuth, H.H. Deibler, William Schert, John Seiert, and Mr. Mrs A.P. Garrett, Schuylkill Haven.*

*Among members present was Hamilton Seitzinger, of Pottsville, who claims to be the youngest member who carried a musket. There were others as young but they were drummer boys. He enlisted at the age of 14 years and eight months, and after the rebellion he enlisted in the Fourth Regular cavalry and saw service against the Indians in Texas from 1866 to 1869.*

*The business session was opened with prayer by comrade Wm. H. Blanchford. On motion Comrade William Williams the reading of the minutes of the last reunion was dispensed with.*

*Comrade William Williams proposed a change of time of meeting from Labor Day, owing to it being a general holiday, thereby in ways interfering with the reunion. After considerable discussion in motion Comrade S. Hess listed the third Tuesday of September for the date.*

*Comrade I.W. Tyson suggested that the reunion hereafter be held for two days instead of one and President Schwenk said he wished the boys could get together for a month. It was decided that the length of time of the reunion could be decided at the time and place.*

*For the place of the next reunion Comrade Eller suggested Pottsville, Comrade David Dampman suggested Petersburg, Va.; Comrade Eller wanted the reunion in the North, he wanted nothing to do with the "Tar Heel" state of Virginia* [sic]. *General Schwenk suggested that "We took Petersburg once and we can take it again." Comrade Phillips named Phia.; Secretary Mishler suggested Gettysburg; Comrade William Eckert said, "Hold the reunion where the people will take an interest in it, just as they have done here today; this is a great success as our reunion in Schuylkill Haven was some 20 years ago." Comrade Henry Hill, after a little discussion named Spring City and the latter place was unanimously decided upon.*

*Comrades Blanchford and Youngblood, of Spring City, assured the boys of a royal welcome.*

*The annual election of officers resulted in the following being unanimously chosen; President Gen. Samuel Schwenk; vice President, William Williams; Secretary J. Milton Mishler; Chaplain Moses Wadsworth, Surgeon, Dr. M.M. Richey, Auditor, Lewis Crater.*

*At seven o'clock a camp fire was held in the Keystone Hall, and the big room was crowded to the doors. The hall was beautifully decorated with flags and bunting, music was rendered by Bensinger's orchestra.*

*The camp fire was called to order by President Schwenk and was opened with prayer by Chaplin Wadsworth.*

*President Schwenk introduced John R. Jones, Esq. who in a brilliant speech welcomed the battle scarred veterans to Schuylkill Haven. His speech teemed with references to the patriotism of the defenders of the nation during the great Rebellion and the inherent patriotism of this great nation. A brief history of the regiment was sketched. Our heritage is to preserve the nation saved by the heroes of "61 to 65," and the best way to do this is for every man to perform the full duties of citizenship by attending the political primaries and conventions and seeing to it that the best men are placed in positions of trust.*

*The orchestra at this point played a medley of national airs after which President Schwenk thanked Mr. Jones for his eloquent speech.*

*Hon. Mr. Charles Brumm was introduced. Mr. Brumm's speech was almost wholly historic and reminiscent and was one of those magnificent oratorical efforts for which the gifted speaker is known for and the gifted speaker was applauded many times.*

On July 17, 1914, the *Schuylkill Haven Call* remarked in an editorial column that the veterans of the 50th Pennsylvania Volunteers decided to hold their annual reunion in Schuylkill Haven once again. The *Call* stated: "The annual gathering of these veterans has been held in Schuylkill Haven on two previous occasions. The first for the town was held many years ago during the month of February in Metamara Hall. The second was held about five years ago on Labor Day in Keystone Hall. Few of our present day generation are aware of the grand showing this old burg made during the civil war. She did herself proud that she furnished six hundred and forty two of her sons during that long bloody civil war. Of this number 196 enlisted in the fiftieth Pennsylvania Volunteers. In this regiment their was one company that alone was composed of Schuylkill Haven sons, it was Company C. Twice was this company recruited to its full quota from Schuylkill Haven, the first time in 1861 and then filled up again in 1864."

At this time the surviving members of old Company C were Charles E. Brown, Levi Eckert, George Schwenk, Henry M. Deibler, Charles Oswald, William Wildermuth, William Bretz, John Eckert, Aaron P. Gilbert, Edward Heebner, Jacob Hehn, Charles Knarr, Adam Lloyd, William C. Losch, Peter Paul, Albert Reiger, James Saylor, William H. Tyson, Josiah Wright, August Wall and Thomas Wallesia.

The reunion was held on Saturday, September 12, 1914, with a large parade through the streets of Schuylkill Haven and rousing speeches made by members of the regiment and also citizens of the town. The men held their annual business meeting in the Losch Opera House. The town was decorated in the national colors for the men.

At the business meeting of the regiment, Lieutenant Colonel Samuel Schwenk remarked: "It is indeed a very precious privilege to come here to Schuylkill Haven, where so large a number of our regiment were recruited, and from which Mayor Lessig said, such a large percentage of our citizens were sent to war. You may be proud of the soldiers that came from this town."

Schuylkill Haven Call

*Schuylkill Haven, Pennsylvania, November 3, 1916*

*"Only Two Dozen Local Veterans"*

*In conversation with a Civil War Veteran of our town this week we learned that of the 446 residents of Schuylkill Haven that enlisted in the army and navy during the Civil War there are just about an even dozen living and residing here at this date.*

*The Jere Helms Post No. 26, G.A.R. of town has a membership of 21 but seven of the members reside out of town. There are about seven local Civil War veterans who are not affiliated with the G.A.R. Post, making the total number of war veterans here about twenty-four.*

*Four hundred and forty-six of this town's sons enlisted in the different companies and various regiments of the army and in different branches of the navy during the bloody civil strife from 1861 to 1865. One Company C, 50th Regiment P.V.V., there were 164 men from Schuylkill Haven, including the two enlistments. It must be remembered that this one company was, throughout the entire war, an almost all Schuylkill Haven Company.*

*Of the total number of men in Co. C there survive about 40, only a handful being from or residing here at this time, namely Irving Tyson, Charles Brown, William Wildermuth, H.M. Deibler.*

*During the year six members of this company that were former residents of Schuylkill Haven or enlisted in Company C from town, passed away. They were Charles Knarr of Haas, Pa.; Peter Paul of Schuylkill Haven, G. Schwenk of Illinois; A. Williams, of a soldiers home, Franklin Wise, of, Ohio and James Saylor of Philadelphia. There was a total of nine deaths in Company C during the year. There were 33 deaths in the entire membership of the 50th Regiment, leaving about 290 survivors in the regiment at this time.*

*In distance traveled in the variety of their service and in the extremes of heat and cold to which they were subjected, it may be doubted whether any other organizations of Pennsylvania troops parallel or approached the 50th and 45th Regiments. The itinerary of the 50th or the total number of miles traveled by this regiment on rail, foot and water amounted to over 12,000 according to statistics gathered by writers and publishers of histories of the war.*

# A Timeline of the Service of the 50th PVVI

The 50th Pennsylvania Veteran Volunteer Infantry was organized at Harrisburg, Pennsylvania, October 1, 1861, left for Washington, D.C., on October 2, 1861, then moved to Annapolis, Maryland, October 9.

The regiment was first attached to Brigadier General Isaac Stevens's brigade, W.T. Sherman's South Carolina Expedition, and then to the following divisions:

| | |
|---|---|
| April 1862 | District of Beaufort, South Carolina, Department of the South |
| July 1862 | 1st Brigade, 1st Division, 9th Army Corps, Army of the Potomac |
| September 1862 | 2nd Brigade, 1st Division, 9th Army Corps, Army of the Potomac |
| April 1863 | Army of the Ohio |
| June 1863 | 3rd Brigade, 2nd Division, 9th Army Corps, Army of the Tennessee |
| August 1863 | 2nd Brigade, 1st Division, 9th Army Corps, Army of the Ohio |
| April 1864 | 2nd Brigade, 3rd Division, 9th Army Corps, Army of the Potomac |
| September 1864 | 2nd Brigade, 1st Division, Army of the Potomac, to July 1865 |

# *A Timeline of the Service of the 50th PVVI*

The regiment participated and was engaged in the following campaigns, skirmishes and battles:

| | |
|---|---|
| October 21–November 7, 1861 | Sherman's Expedition to Port Royal, South Carolina. On the voyage south, aboard steamer *Winfield Scott*, shipwrecked off coast of North Carolina. |
| December 6, 1861 | Occupation of Beaufort, South Carolina |
| January 1, 1862 | Port Royal Ferry, Coosaw River, South Carolina; serve duty at Port Royal Island until July 1862 |
| February 10, 1862 | Barnwell's Island, South Carolina (Company D skirmished with the enemy.) |
| May 29, 1862 | Pocotaligo, South Carolina |
| June 7, 1862 | Camp Stevens, South Carolina |
| July 14–18, 1862 | Move to Hilton Head, South Carolina, then to Newport News, Virginia |
| August 3–6, 1862 | Move to Aquia Creek and Fredericksburg, Virginia |
| August 6–16, 1862 | Operations in support of Major General John Pope |
| August 16–September 2, 1862 | Pope's Campaign in Northern Virginia |
| August 24, 1862 | Sulphur Springs |
| August 29, 1862 | Battle of Groveton |
| August 30, 1862 | Battle of Bull Run |

| | |
|---|---|
| September 1, 1862 | Battle of Chantilly (The 50th was one of the first regiments engaged in the battle.) |
| September 6–24, 1862 | Maryland Campaign (Movements prior to the Battle of Antietam) |
| September 14, 1862 | Battle of South Mountain, Maryland |
| September 16–17, 1862 | Battle of Antietam |
| September 19–October 2, 1862 | March to Pleasant Valley; serve duty there until October 25 |
| October 25–November 19, 1862 | Move to Falmouth, Virginia; remain at Falmouth until February 12, 1863 |
| December 12–15, 1862 | Battle of Fredericksburg |
| January 20–24, 1863 | Burnside's second campaign |
| January 20–22, 1863 | "Mud March" or "Burnside's Quagmire" |
| February 12–14, 1863 | Move to Newport News, Virginia. After days of endless drilling, special notice was given the regiment for its precision on the drill field. |
| March 21–26, 1863 | Move to Kentucky; serve duty at Paris, Kentucky until April 27. The 9th Corps reassigned to the Army of the Ohio. |
| April 27–29, 1863 | Move to Nicholasville, Lancaster and Stanford, Kentucky |
| May 6–8, 1863 | Move to Somerset |

| | |
|---|---|
| June 4–10, 1863 | Move through Kentucky to Cairo, Illinois. The 9th Corps assigned the duty of preventing Joseph Johnson army from attacking the rear of General Grant's army. |
| June 14–17, 1863 | Move to Vicksburg, Mississippi |
| June 17–July 4, 1863 | Siege of Vicksburg, Mississippi |
| July 5–10, 1863 | Advance on Jackson, Mississippi; remain at Milldale until August 12; perform reconnaissance movements for the purpose of developing the enemies position |
| July 10–17, 1863 | Siege of Jackson (This was a severe campaign on the men and officers of the 50th.) |
| August 12–23, 1863 | Move to Covington, Kentucky |
| August–October, 1863 | Burnside's campaign in east Tennessee |
| October 10, 1863 | Action at Blue Springs, Tennessee; the regiment is assigned with the 23rd Army Corps and is hotly engaged. |
| October 27, 1863 | Erect winter quarters at Clinch Mountain |
| November 4–December 23, 1863 | Knoxville Campaign; fast-paced movement toward Campbell Station |
| November 16, 1863 | Campbell's Station (This was the decisive battle of the Knoxville Campaign.) |
| November 17–December 5, 1863 | Siege of Knoxville (At this point, the regiment has been marching and fighting since November 14; the boys commence in digging pits and entrenchments for the siege.) |

| | |
|---|---|
| December 5–26, 1863 | Pursuit of Longstreet's army to Blaine's Crossroads |
| January 1, 1864 | Re-enlist at Blaine's Crossroads; short furlough |
| April 23, 1864 | Move to Annapolis, Maryland; return to the Army of the Potomac |
| May 4–June 12, 1864 | Rapidan Campaign |
| May 5–7, 1864 | Battle of the Wilderness |
| May 8–12, 1864 | Battle of Spotsylvania |
| May 9, 1864 | Battle of Nye River |
| May 12–21, 1864 | Battle of Spotsylvania Court House |
| May 12, 1864 | Assault on the Salient; the 50th regiment suffers heavy casualties |
| May 23–26, 1864 | North Anna River |
| May 24, 1864 | Ox Ford |
| May 26–28, 1864 | Line of the Pamunkey |
| May 28–31, 1864 | Totopotomoy; movement toward Cold Harbor |
| June 1–12, 1864 | Battle of Cold Harbor; the regiment is in the thickest part of the battle |
| June 1–3, 1864 | Fight at Bethesda Church |
| June 16–18, 1864 | Move to Petersburg |

| | |
|---|---|
| June 16, 1864–April 2, 1865 | Siege of Petersburg |
| July 30, 1864 | Mine explosion at Petersburg |
| August 18–21, 1864 | Battle of Weldon Railroad |
| September 29–October 2, 1864 | Poplar Springs Church and Peeble's Farm |
| October 8, 1864 | Reconnaissance on Vaughan or Squirrel Level Road (name not given in records) |
| October 27–28, 1864 | Battle of Boydton Plank Road, Hatcher's Run |
| March 25, 1865 | Fight and skirmishing at Fort Stedman, Petersburg, Virginia |
| March 28–April 9, 1865 | Appomattox Campaign |
| April 2, 1865 | Assault on and fall of Petersburg; the beginning of the last battles of the war |
| April 3–9, 1865 | Pursuit of Lee to Burkesville |
| April 21–28, 1865 | Moved to City Point, then to Washington, D.C. |
| May 23, 1865 | Grand Review |
| July 4, 1865 | Present at the laying of cornerstone at Gettysburg |
| July 30, 1865 | Mustered out |

# The Boys of Company C

## Officers

### Captains

### Daniel F. Burket

Residence Schuylkill Haven, Pennsylvania
Harbor Master, Schuylkill Canal
Mustered in September 9, 1861
Mustered out December 31, 1864 on expiration of term
Buried in First Union Cemetery, Schuylkill Haven

On returning from service in the 5th Pennsylvania, a three-month regiment, Burket set up a recruiting office in the town hall in Schuylkill Haven in early August 1861. He recruited men for three years. Burket's father had been a soldier in the War of 1812. Burket' s young son also served in the Civil War, enlisting as a drummer boy. During his service in the war Burket was wounded in the left shoulder during the battle at Second Bull Run.

### Charles E. Brown

Residence Schuylkill Haven, Pennsylvania
Boatman
Dark complexion, gray eyes, black hair, 5'9"
Mustered in September 9, 1861
Mustered out July 30, 1865 as a veteran
Buried in the Union Cemetery, Schuylkill Haven

Charles Brown first lived in the lower portion of the flats in Schuylkill Haven near the "Eck" in a small log house. He first remembered being employed as a boy of ten years old in the tobacco factory of Clouser & Kearcher, earning wages of twenty-five cents per week.

He took up boating when he was quite young, the occupation he followed until the outbreak of the Civil War. Returning from the war he again took up boating and was later made weigh master at the landing in town and was also captain of the wreck boat *Petril*. When the Schuylkill Canal was discontinued Brown went to New York where he operated boats for a time between New York and Philadelphia and Connecticut.

Brown's community service included membership on a special police force with Captain Linden of the Pinkerton Detective Agency and Marshal Heisler of Minersville during the rise and popularity of the violent secret organization of coal miners, the Molly Maguires, between 1868 and 1878. He was employed in the Bast Rolling Mill as a watchman, and also as watchman in the First National Bank and Schuylkill Haven Trust Co. Brown finished his working career as the turnkey for the Schuylkill County Almshouse.

Charles Brown possessed an enviable war record. He quickly rose through the ranks from private to corporal, corporal to sergeant, then to first lieutenant on November 26, 1864, and finally to captain of the company on January 15, 1865. At the battle of Antietam Brown was commended for his bravery while saving the life of Lieutenant Colonel Samuel Schwenk, who was seriously wounded and lay for many hours on the battlefield apparently dead. During the hottest part of the battle, Corporal Brown and Private James Levan of Company C worked their way on their hands and knees to where Schwenk lay and dragged him to a place of safety. Charles Brown was also awarded the Medal of Honor for capturing the flag of the 47th Virginia Infantry at Weldon Railroad, Virginia, August 19, 1864.

After the war Charles Brown was active in the 50th Regiment Association and was associated with General Samuel Schwenk who preceded him in death by only a year. Shortly before his death at the age of seventy-eight, Brown attended a meeting of the Veterans Volunteers in New York. He had also offered his services to his government in World War I.

On March 31, 1911, the *Schuylkill Haven Call* newspaper described Brown's heroic actions in battle and his reception of the Medal of Honor:

> *Captain Charles E. Brown, who served throughout the Civil War in the Fiftieth Pennsylvania Volunteers, won a Congressional medal of honor in a gallant manner in front of Petersburg, August 18, 1864. His heroic action in capturing a Confederate flag was witnessed and applauded by the Ninth Corps to which he belonged.*
>
> *After a long and fatiguing march all of the night of August 17, the Ninth Corps reached its objective point just as day was breaking, only to be fiercely attacked by a large force of Confederates, and driven back some distance. When our artillery came up and opened with great spirit and effect upon the advancing Southerners, forcing them back to their works in confusion.*

*The sudden discomfiture of the enemy encouraged the Ninth Corps to make a charge, which was successful. In the desperate melee in mounting the Confederate works, many hand to hand conflicts took place—a notable one being between Charles Oswalt, and Joseph Long, of the Fiftieth Pennsylvania Regiment, and a number of bold Confederates. When Captain Brown saw the severe struggle in which his two comrades were engaged, he picked up a Belgian rifle still in the death grip of a prostrate Confederate, and started to aid them, but before he reached the scene, his men had killed their opponents.*

*At this juncture, Captain Brown discovered a Confederate color-sergeant, with his torn flag and two of his guard making their way through abattis. They were proceeding slowly and with considerable difficulty, owing to the formidable obstructions, so Captain Brown concluded to give pursuit. Discreet and noiseless in his movements, he was upon the fugitives ere they were aware of his presence. Leveling his captured gun at the distance of a few paces, he ordered them to throw down their arms and surrender, an invitation they lost no time in accepting.*

*Getting in their rear, Captain Brown picked up the surrendered battle flag, ordered his prisoners to march towards our lines, distant about two hundred yards. The Captain took the precaution to keep his prisoners well covered with his gun, which to his horror, he subsequently discovered to be unloaded. As Captain Brown neared his command, waving the coveted prize, the colors of the Forty-Seventh Virginia, he was heartily cheered by his comrades who had given him up for lost. His three prisoners, on being transferred to the keeping of the provost guard, bitterly lamented the fate that had befallen them, especially mourning the loss of their flag, which they said had been presented to their regiment by Richmond ladies, to whom they pledged their lives in its defense. They regretted they had not saved their flag before it fell into "Yankee hands."*

*General Wilcox, commanding the division to which Captain Brown belonged, on learning of the latter's gallantry, seized him by the hand and complimented him upon his action, declaring he would at the first opportunity report the matter to the war department.*

*In December, 1864 Captain Brown was surprised to receive an order to report with his company at General Burnside's headquarters. With his little command he marched over in "fightin trim," expecting to be assigned to some special duty, perhaps a dangerous undertaking. Drawing his command up in front of General Burnside's log cabin, Captain Brown reported his arrival and awaited orders. Directly the popular and magnificent commander of the Ninth Corps, accompanied by his staff, appeared in front of Captain Brown and his company, both full of expectancy. The compliment of a salute by the command being politely acknowledged by General Burnside, he said: "Captain Brown, one of the greatest pleasures of my life is to say to you that I have been deputized by the President of the United States to present on behalf of Congress a medal of honor, for the distinguished gallantry displayed by you in not only capturing a confederate battle flag, but its holder and two armed guards, whose duty it was to defend the emblem. The heroism displayed by you in your single-handed action last August is characteristic of the true hearted American soldier. Your act will ever be incentive to others. I heartily congratulate you upon your brilliant action, and in presenting you with this coveted medal, the highest honor that can be bestowed by the government whose existence you are aiding in preserving, I express the hope that you may be spared for many years to come, to enjoy the commendation of the government and the esteem of your comrades and fellow citizens."*

*For years after the war Captain Brown ran a canal boat between New York and Philadelphia, but his modesty being equal to his bravery he seldom alluded to the clever manner in which he captured three armed Confederates and a battle flag with an empty gun.*

*Written by General J. Madison Drake*
*Historian Army and Navy Medal of Honor Legion.*
*Taken from Easton Sunday Call, February 12th, 1911.*

Charles Brown was very active in veteran's affairs in his county and community, and felt a strong duty to uphold the honor of his fellow soldiers and company members—especially those who were there from the beginning. On November 16, 1916, Brown penned a letter to the editor of the *Schuylkill Haven Call*, in reference to the definition of a veteran.

## *A NEW DEFINITION FOR A WAR VETERAN*

*To the Editor:*

*I want to give the definition of a veteran soldier. Up to the time that we re-enlisted at Blaine's Crossroads, East Tennessee, the War Department called our regiment the 50th Regiment Pennsylvania Volunteer Infantry. After we re-enlisted for three years or during the war on the 13th day of January, 1864, then they called us the 50th Pennsylvania Veteran Volunteer Infantry regiment.*

*Now that leaves four veterans living that served four years in Co. C 50th Regiment Pa. V.V. Inf. Namely Capt. Charles E. Brown, Schuylkill Haven, Sergeant Levi Eckert, Manyunk, Corporal William Wildermuth, Schuylkill Haven, and Corporal Henry Deibler, of Schuylkill Haven.*

*Now the men that enlisted in Co. C in 64 and 65 are all short term men. Some of them were volunteers. Some of them were drafted and some were substitutes. Now I see you call some emergency men Civil War Veterans that were not from their home over 30 days and they were never in the U.S. service, and never saw a Rebel.*

*Now there are only four soldiers living that served in Company C 50th Regiment. All the rest enlisted in 1864 and 1865. I am anxious to give every soldier that was enlisted in Company C all the credit that belongs to him, but when they claim as much credit as a soldier that served four years, then I will call them down.*

*This is in answer to what you had in the Call last week about the veterans of Company C.*

*Charles Brown*
*Late Captain Co. C*
*50th Pa. Vet. Vol. Inf. Regiment*
*Schuylkill Haven.*

On February 21, 1919, the *Schuylkill Haven Call* newspaper ran this obituary for Charles E. Brown:

## *ANOTHER VET CALLED HOME*

*Capt. Charles E. Brown, one of this town's most honored citizens and a civil war veteran, who gave to his country the very best service, died suddenly at his home on St. John Street at 7:30 o'clock, Thursday morning. Death was apparently caused by a stroke. He arose early in the morning and after coming down stairs to look at the fires, lighted his pipe as he was often wont to do and did odd jobs around the house. He then went up stairs to inquire how his wife, who had been in ill health, felt. Without warning, he fell to the floor and was dead when picked up.*

*Captain Brown, as he was more familiarly called, was 78 years of age. He came to this town when three years of age. He was born in Fernville, Bradford County. He followed boating prior to his enlisting in the army. Upon his return and being mustered out he again took up boating which occupation he followed until its abandonment in this section. He then followed the occupation in New York and Connecticut.*

*He was a member of the First M.E. church. For several terms he served this town as a school director. He was a member of the Medal Of Honor Legion. He was of a quiet, unassuming disposition. Despite his excellent war record and his many thrilling experiences during the war he was always somewhat reticent to relate them or to mention his particular feats of bravery.*

*To survive him he leaves a widow and two sons, Warren of Schuylkill Haven and A.C. Brown of Chicago, and also a sister, Mrs. Theodore Stitzer of Mahanoy City, and one brother, William Brown of Cressona and two grand children. His funeral will take place Monday, afternoon at his later home, at 1:30 o'clock.*

*Mr. Brown possessed an enviable war record. In June 1861, he with a number of Schuylkill Haven young men enlisted at their country's call for volunteers. They were sent to Harrisburg, where they waited until August before they were properly equipped and put into service. He was a member of Company C, 50th Regiment, Pennsylvania Volunteer Infantry. Two thirds of the men in his Company were Schuylkill Haven boys. They were under the command of Captain Burket of Schuylkill Haven. The first year of service Mr. Brown was a private. The second year he was made Corporal. For eight months he served as Sergeant and one month as a Lieutenant of his Company. It was at this time he was given a Medal of Honor by congress for meritorious conduct. Shortly after this Captain Burket was wounded in the left shoulder and was placed in the Invalid Corps. Lieut. Brown then succeeded him to his captaincy, which he held until the end of the war.*

*Captain Brown put in a solid four years of war, from August 8, 1861 to August 8, 1865. He was in the thick and thin of battle at all times and in most of the biggest and most important engagements of the war. He never was severely wounded but had many narrow escapes, bullets going through his hat, coat and trousers, shoe and equipment and oftentimes either scratching or bruising the skin. At one time the soles of his shoes were shot away. Three times during the war he was captured by the confederates and each time made his escape.*

*Among the many thrilling experiences captain Brown had during the war, one of particular importance and one showing his bravery was on the occasion of capturing a Confederate flag, a sergeant and two color privates with an empty gun. Captain Brown discovered these men near the breast works of his Company and although he was wearing a sword and had no gun at the time, he picked up a Belgian rifle lying near by and made for the Rebel, not knowing at the time that his gun was not loaded. He commanded them to surrender and they did so. For this act he was given special citation by his commander in chief and was given a medal by the government during the war. This medal was highly prized by him.*

## Lieutenants

### George W. Brumm

Residence Minersville, Pennsylvania

Watchmaker

Mustered in September 9, 1861

Mustered out 1865

Brumm was assigned as the first lieutenant of Company C and later was promoted to captain and transferred to Company F on March 17, 1864.

## William H. Hiney

Residence Tremont, Pennsylvania

Brick Maker

Mustered in September 9, 1861

Killed in action; died July 8, 1864, of wounds received in action June 1, 1864

Hiney was initially assigned as a sergeant in Company C, later promoted to second lieutenant on October 21, 1862, then to first lieutenant on March 17, 1864. Hiney re-enlisted with the regiment on March 17, 1864 at Warrenton Junction, Virginia.

## John S. Eckel

Residence Tremont, Pennsylvania

Clerk

Mustered in April, 1, 1862

Mustered out 1865

Eckel enlisted in Tremont, Pennsylvania. He was promoted from quartermaster sergeant to second lieutenant on March 17, 1864, then to first lieutenant and finally to quartermaster of the company.

## Samuel A. Losch.

Residence Schuylkill Haven, Pennsylvania

Boatman

Light complexion, blue eyes, light hair, 5'5"

Mustered in September 9, 1861

Mustered out July 30, 1865

Buried in Union Cemetery, Schuylkill Haven

Losch enlisted as a corporal on August 14, 1861, at Schuylkill Haven and was later promoted to sergeant. He re-enlisted with the regiment at Blaine's Crossroads in 1864 and on March 17, 1865, he was promoted to second lieutenant, then to first lieutenant on April 1, 1865.

## John F. Saylor

Residence Schuylkill Haven, Pennsylvania

Boatman

Mustered in September 9, 1861

Resigned July 29, 1862

Saylor enlisted in Schuylkill Haven as a second lieutenant but resigned his commission in July of 1862.

## August Mellon

Residence Schuylkill Haven, Pennsylvania
Boatman
Dark complexion, black eyes, black hair
Mustered in September 9, 1861
Mustered out July 30, 1865

Mellon enlisted in Schuylkill Haven on August 14, 1861, as a corporal and was promoted to sergeant, then to second lieutenant on June 17, 1865. Mellon received a gunshot wound to his right leg during the 1864 campaigns in Virginia. He re-enlisted with the company at Blaine's Crossroads.

### Non-commissioned Officers

## William H. Mennig

First Sergeant
Residence Schuylkill Haven, Pennsylvania
Boatman
Mustered in August 14, 1861
Not listed on muster out roll

## David Raudenbush

First Sergeant
Residence Schuylkill Haven, Pennsylvania
Carpenter
Light complexion light, blue eyes, sandy hair
Mustered in September 9, 1861
Mustered out July 30, 1865
Buried in Union Cemetery, Schuylkill Haven

Raudenbush enlisted at Schuylkill Haven on August 14, 1861, was assigned as a corporal and was later promoted to first sergeant. On July 1, 1864, Raudenbush was wounded in the right leg above the knee by a musket ball at the Wilderness and listed as missing during the 1864 campaigns. He re-enlisted with the regiment at Blaine's Crossroads.

## William Hill

First Sergeant
Residence Schuylkill Haven
Boatman

Dark complexion, blue eyes, black hair
Mustered in September 9, 1861
Killed in action May 6, 1864, in the Wilderness Campaign

Hill was the company's earliest elected first sergeant. He was promoted to second lieutenant prior to being killed in action. Hill re-enlisted with the regiment at Blaine's Crossroads.

## Levi Eckert

Sergeant
Residence Schuylkill Haven, Pennsylvania
Boatman
Light complexion, blue eyes, light hair, 5'4"
Mustered in September 9, 1861
Mustered out July 30, 1865
Buried in Union cemetery, Schuylkill Haven

Eckert enlisted on August 14, 1861, at Schuylkill Haven and was promoted to corporal, then to sergeant on November 24, 1864. He re-enlisted with the company at Blaine's Crossroads. Eckert was wounded during the campaigns in Virginia in 1864.

## Henry Hill

Sergeant
Residence Schuylkill Haven, Pennsylvania
Boatman
Dark complexion, black eyes, black hair, 5'9"
Mustered in September 9, 1861
Mustered out July 30, 1865
Buried in Union Cemetery, Schuylkill Haven

Hill enlisted at Schuylkill Haven on August 14, 1861. He was promoted to corporal, then to sergeant on March 20, 1865. He re-enlisted at Blaine's Crossroads with the regiment. Hill received a gunshot wound in the left leg during the campaign in 1864. Hill was awarded the Medal of Honor for his actions during the battle of the Wilderness, May 6, 1864. The citation, issued on September 23, 1897, reads:

> *This soldier, with one companion, would not retire when his regiment fell back in confusion after an unsuccessful charge, but instead advanced and continued firing upon the enemy until the regiment re-formed and regained its position.*

On August 2, 1909, the *Pottsville Daily Republican* printed the obituary of Henry Hill.

*Death of Henry Hill*
*A Civil War Veteran:*
*Voted Medal, By Congress, for Conspicuous Bravery:*
*Henry Hill, of Schuylkill Haven, a veteran of the Civil War, and for many years employed at the county prison in the capacity of night watchman and turnkey, died yesterday afternoon at his home, following an illness of about two weeks, aged 66 years.*

*Mr. Hill was a native of Pottsville, though he spent the greater part of his life at Schuylkill Haven. The earlier years of his life were spent as a boatman on the Schuylkill Canal and at Philadelphia. He enlisted as a private as a member of Company C 50th Regt. Penna. Volunteer Infantry, Sept. 9, 1861 and was promoted to Sgt. At the expiration of his three years he re enlisted, serving until the end of the war. He participated in bloody seven days fight through the Shenandoah Valley and took part in the fights at Spotsylvania, Beaufort, Cold Harbor Chantilly, Antietam, Fredericksburg and the Wilderness. In the last fight he was severely wounded by a bursting enemy shell. Congress voted him a medal for the display of bravery in battle. The deceased was a member of St. Johns Reformed Church, Schuylkill Haven. Henry spent most of his post war years as the turn key and night watchman of the Schuylkill County Prison. His widow (Sara A. Hein) Hill and the following sons and daughters survive. John, Fred, Daniel, Miss Susie, Mrs. Joseph Michael of Schuylkill Haven and Samuel of Wilkes Barre.*

*The funeral was held Thursday afternoon and proceeded from his late home on Market St., to St. Johns Reformed Church where services were held; the funeral was very largely attended. The Citizens Band, G.A.R. and P.O.E. of A attended in body. The pall bearers were his sons Samuel, Daniel, John, Fred, Charles and Clyde. Interment was made at Union cemetery, Schuylkill Haven.*

## George Schwenk

Sergeant
Residence Schuylkill Haven, Pennsylvania
Boatman
Dark complexion, gray eyes, sandy hair, 5'6"
Mustered in September 9, 1861
Mustered out July 30, 1865

Schwenk enlisted on August 14, 1861, at Schuylkill Haven. He re-enlisted at Blaine's Crossroads in 1864. He was promoted to corporal then to sergeant on March 20, 1865, and mustered out with the company in July 1865. Schwenk was wounded during the fight at Second Bull Run.

## Samuel Hoffman

Sergeant
Residence Schuylkill Haven, Pennsylvania
Boatman
Light complexion, blue eyes, black hair, 5'6"
Mustered in September 9, 1861
Mustered out July 30, 1865

Hoffman enlisted at Schuylkill Haven on August 14, 1861. He was promoted through the ranks to sergeant. In 1865, he re-enlisted with the company at Blaine's Crossroads. Hoffman received a gunshot wound to the left arm during the Second Bull Run campaign.

## James H. Levan

Sergeant
Residence Minersville, Pennsylvania
Carpenter
Mustered in September 9, 1861
Mustered out July 1865
Buried in Union Cemetery, Minersville

Levan was enlisted as a sergeant in Company C but was promoted to captain of Company I on November 26, 1864, where he served with distinction as the company commander. As a private, Levan was commended for his bravery in saving the life of Lieutenant Colonel Samuel Schwenk during the battle of Antietam. He, along with Corporal Charles E. Brown, crawled on hands and knees while under fire to bring back a seriously wounded Schwenk.

## Alex P. Garrett

Sergeant
Residence Schuylkill Haven, Pennsylvania
Barber
Light complexion, gray eyes, light hair, 5'9"
Mustered in September 9, 1861
Mustered out July 1865

Garrett enlisted in Schuylkill Haven on August 14, 1861. He was promoted to corporal, sergeant, then sergeant major of the regiment on March 20, 1865. Garrett received a gunshot wound in his back.

## Henry M. Deibler

Corporal
Residence Schuylkill Haven, Pennsylvania

Boatman
Light complexion, blue eyes, dark hair
Mustered in September 9, 1861
Mustered out July 30, 1865

Deibler enlisted in Schuylkill Haven on August 14, 1861, and was promoted to corporal. He re-enlisted with the regiment at Blaine's Crossroads. Deibler was captured and listed as missing during the Second Bull Run campaign, but was exchanged and returned to his company. He was again wounded on May 9, 1864 during the campaign at the Nye River.

## George W. Cake

Corporal
Residence Schuylkill Haven, Pennsylvania
Boatman
Dark complexion, black eyes, dark hair, 5'8"
Mustered in September 9, 1861
Absent in arrest at muster out

Cake enlisted on August 14, 1861, in Schuylkill Haven and re-enlisted at Blaine's Crossroads. He was wounded during the campaign from May to June of 1864. Why he was under arrest at muster out is unknown.

## Jacob Scheck

Corporal
Residence Tremont, Pennsylvania
Boatman
Light complexion, blue eyes, light hair, 5'8"
Mustered in September 9, 1861
Mustered out July 30, 1865

Scheck enlisted in Schuylkill Haven on August 14, 1861. He was promoted to corporal November 26, 1864. Scheck re-enlisted with the regiment at Blaine's Crossroads in 1864.

## Charles Oswald

Corporal
Residence Schuylkill Haven, Pennsylvania
Boatman
Light complexion, blue eyes, black hair, 5'6"
Mustered in September 9, 1861
Mustered out July 30, 1865

Oswald enlisted in Schuylkill Haven on August 14, 1861, and was promoted to corporal. He re-enlisted at Blaine's Crossroads and was wounded in the May to June campaign of 1864. Oswald is buried in the International Order of Odd Fellows cemetery in Pottsville. Oswald was also involved in the hand-to-hand fight with a Rebel soldier that led to Captain Charles E. Brown's heroic action that earned him the Medal of Honor.

## Isaac Eckert

Corporal
Residence Schuylkill Haven, Pennsylvania
Boatman
Light complexion, blue eyes, black hair, 5'5"
Mustered in September 9, 1861
Mustered out July 30, 1865
Buried in Union Cemetery, Schuylkill Haven

Eckert enlisted in Schuylkill Haven on August 14, 1861. He re-enlisted with the regiment at Blaine's Crossroads in 1864 and was promoted to corporal March 20, 1865.

## Wiliam Wildermuth

Corporal
Residence Schuylkill Haven, Pennsylvania
Boatman
Light complexion, gray eyes, dark hair, 5'6"
Mustered in September 9, 1861
Mustered out July 30, 1865

Wildermuth enlisted in Schuylkill Haven on August 14, 1861. He re-enlisted at Blaine's Crossroads in 1864 and was wounded during the May through June 1864 campaign with a gunshot wound to the right leg. He was promoted to corporal on May 16, 1865.

Wildermuth was one of the last four members of Company C alive in 1916, and still living in Schuylkill Haven.

## Fredrick Scheck

Corporal
Residence Tremont, Pennsylvania
Boatman
Dark complexion, gray eyes, dark hair, 5'8"
Mustered in September 9, 1861
Mustered out July 30, 1865

Scheck enlisted at Schuylkill Haven on August 14, 1861. He re-enlisted with the regiment at Philadelphia in 1864, and was promoted to corporal on July 1, 1865.

## Gotlieb Burkert

Corporal
Residence Washington Township, Schuylkill County, Pennsylvania
Boatman
Light complexion, 5'4"
Mustered in September 9, 1861
Mustered out July 30, 1865

Burkert enlisted in Schuylkill Haven on August 14, 1861, and re-enlisted with his regiment at Blaine's Crossroads in 1864. During the May through June campaign of 1864 he received a gunshot wound in the right leg.

## John Doudle

Corporal
Residence Schuylkill Haven, Pennsylvania
Boatman
Light complexion, black eyes, sandy hair, 5'5"
Mustered in September 9, 1861
Prisoner, captured at Spotsylvania Court House, 1864
Mustered out.

Corporal John Doudle is one of the main contributors to this book. His history of Company C up to his capture and of his own time spent in Andersonville prison is an excellent narrative. Doudle enlisted at Schuylkill Haven on August 14, 1861, and was promoted to corporal. He was captured on May 12, 1864, and sent to Andersonville, Georgia. He was discharged by general order on June 3, 1865.

Doudle died in Philadelphia on June 16, 1910. The following day, the *Schuylkill Haven Call* ran his obituary.

> *John Doudle of Philadelphia, a former resident of town, died at his home on Sunday and was buried on Friday Morning. Mr. Doudle was a veteran of the Civil War having served as a Corporal of Co. C 50th P.V. He enlisted from Schuylkill Haven on August 14, 1861. On May 12, 1864 at Spotsylvania Court House, he was captured by the Rebels together with twelve other Schuylkill Haven men and suffered imprisonment at Andersonville and Libby Prison from which place he was paroled in Feb. 24th, 1865. A most entertaining history of his experiences was published in the* Call *during the summer of 1908. Mr. Doudle is survived by his widow and three sons and three daughters, Frank, Will, Agnes and Florence at home and David and Mrs. McVeigh, all of Philadelphia. He was a brother of the late Alex Doudle of town and had a host of friends here.*

## George H. Hoffman

Corporal

Residence Schuylkill Haven, Pennsylvania

House and sign painter

Mustered in September 9, 1861

Discharged on surgeon's certificate

Hoffman enlisted in Schuylkill Haven on August 14, 1861. He was probably discharged due to illness, but no record was located.

## Robert Bechtel

Corporal

Residence Haven Bay, Pennsylvania

Boatman

Mustered in September 9, 1861

Not listed on muster out roll.

Bechtel enlisted in Schuylkill Haven on August 14, 1861. He was transferred to the signal corps, which is the reason he was not on the muster out rolls.

## Benjamin Brown

Corporal

Residence Schuylkill Haven, Pennsylvania

Boatman

Mustered in September 9, 1861

Died at Vicksburg, July 30, 1863

Brown enlisted in Schuylkill Haven on August 14, 1861. He was the older brother to Captain Charles E. Brown of the company. Brown is buried in the Vicksburg, Cemetery, plot G 5639.

## William H. Genslin

Musician

Residence Northhampton County, Pennsylvania

Musician

Light complexion, blue eyes, brown hair, 5'1½"

Mustered in March 12, 1864

Mustered out July 30, 1865

Genslin was one of three musicians enrolled in the company. He enlisted at Harrisburg in 1864.

## Celestine McKibbons

Musician
Residence Montgomery County, Pennsylvania
Laborer
Dark complexion, hazel eyes, brown hair, 5'
Mustered in March 14, 1864
Mustered out July 30 1865

McKibbons enlisted in Harrisburg on March 14, 1864. He also was one of the three musicians Company C had during the war.

## Jeremiah Helms

Musician
Residence Schuylkill Haven, Pennsylvania
Tailor
Mustered in September 9, 1861
Wounded in action September 17, 1862; died September 24, 1862

The youngest of three brothers who fought in the Civil War, Jeremiah Helms enlisted in Schuylkill Haven on August 14, 1861, against his parents' wishes. During the battle of Antietam, Jere Helms, as he was known to the men of Company C, set down his drum and took up a musket to charge with his company. He was mortally wounded by a musket ball to the head and died several days later.

Mr. Peter Helms, Jere's father, traveled by carriage to Sharpsburg where he retrieved the body of his youngest son. The sad story of this young patriot was written in the *Pottsville Miners' Journal* on October 12,1862.

> *On last Tuesday a week, Jeremiah Helms, the youngest son of Mr. Peter Helms of Schuylkill Haven, and a member of Company C, 50th regiment P.V. was interred at Myerstown, Lebanon County, his former residence, in the presence of a large concourse of mourners and friends. Rev. Mr. Yengst preached a sermon upon the following text. Found in the 11th Chapter, 25th verse of St. John. "Jesus said unto her. I am the resurrection and the life, he that believeth in me, though he was dead, yet shall he live."*
>
> *His father brought his Corpse home from the late battlefield of Antietam, where he was mortally wounded on the 17th ult. while nobly battling with the enemy in defense of those dear rights which every freeman should enjoy. He was shot through the head with a Minnie ball in line of the eyes. He was perfectly sensible for the first seven days of his suffering, and able to walk about. Thus he lingered, with out a murmur, bearing his pain like a true soldier, with Christian fortitude, until the morning of the 27th, only the day previous to his father's arrival, when he breathed his last and became another victim to this cursed Rebellion and sacrifices at the star of his country's choicest blessing, liberty and freedom. He fell a*

*noble hero martyr to the cause he so much loved to defend. His comrades bear testimony of his true soldiery conduct, always cheerful and prompt in performance of his duty. He fought well at the battles of Pocatalico, S.C. Bull Run, Chantilly, Va. and South Mountain and Antietam Md. He prevailed for some time upon his parents to go to war: they could not at first consent to his going on account of his youth, but seeing that he was fired with a zeal of patriotism that was pure and noble, permission was given when he enlisted in Company C 50th Regt. P.V. at the age of 16 years. He is the youngest of three brothers, all of whom have enlisted in defense of the Union, at the respective ages of 16, 18, and 20 years.*

*After the battle of Bull Run he was heard in earnest prayer, upon bended knees in his tent. In his last letter, which was after the Battle of South Mountain, he wrote his parents not to feel uneasy about him, that he was fighting for the Lord, as well as for the protection of the Stars and Stripes, and his parents to attend a "Camp Meeting" in serving the Lord. His brother James, who is a member of the 48th P.V. visited him during his suffering, when he told him that he should return to his regiment and do valiant service, that he was beyond recovery. He also told his nurse the same, Morgan Pugh of Minersville, and that by his kind and unceasing attentions towards him he (Pugh) only prolonged his suffering, as he could not recover.*

*He seems to have been resigned to his fate, and satisfied to die, as a proud defender of his insulted country.*

On February 8, 1867, the Jere K. Helms Post 26 of the Grand Army of the Republic was formed in honor of the young boy from Schuylkill Haven who gave his life in the defense of freedom. The post was started by his oldest brother, fellow veteran, Captain James K. Helms, and assisted by fellow Company C member Lieutenant Samuel A. Losch from Schuylkill Haven. The post had 221 members.

On May 19, 1906, the following article appeared in the *Schuylkill Haven Call* about the Jere Helms GAR Post No. 26:

*The Schuylkill Haven Post is named after Jere Helms the youngest brother of the late James K Helms of town and Peter D. Helms of Pottsville, the present Post commander. Jere Helms was sworn into the U.S. service at Harrisburg, Pa. September 9, 1861, as a drummer boy in Co. C Capt. D.F. Burket, 50th Reg. P.V.V. He was then a boy of 15 years of age…he remained with the Regt. during all of their engagements, up to the battle of Antietam, Md. September 17, 1862, when he discarded his drum, picked up the gun and ammunition of a soldier who had been killed and in spite of the protest of Major George W. Brumm, (a brother of Hon, C.N. Brumm) who told him to take charge of his horse while the fight was going on, he went into battle.*

*Young Helms was in the thickest of the fight, when charging up a hill he was mortally wounded, being shot through the head right back of the eyes. The boy was shot in sight of Captain Brown, Henry Hill, and Samuel A. Losch who picked him up and carried him from the field and put him into a room in a near by farm house, the old Sherrick House, together with about 30 more wounded soldiers. A man from Company C, by the name of Morgan Pugh was detailed to stay back with young Helms until he either got better or died. The man Pugh was faithful to his charge, yet with all his care young Helms died seven days after the battle and he was buried in Myerstown, Lebanon Co., Pa. Thus perished one of the noblest and bravest boys that ever left our town.*

## Privates

### Samuel Agley

Residence Schuylkill Haven, Pennsylvania
Boatman
Light complexion, gray eyes, sandy hair, 5'9"
Mustered in August 14, 1961
Died while a prisoner; date unknown

Agley re-enlisted at Blaine's Crossroads on January 1, 1864.

### Lafayette Baker

Residence Schuylkill Haven, Pennsylvania
Boatman
Light complexion, blue eyes, light hair, 5'11"
Mustered in September 9, 1861
Mustered out July 30, 1865
Buried in First Union Cemetery, Schuylkill Haven

### Elias Berger

Residence Schuylkill Haven, Pennsylvania
Boatman
Mustered in August 14, 1861
Mustered out May 12, 1865, credited to date March 9, 1865

Berger was held in Andersonville prison from May 12, 1864 to March 5, 1865.

### Augustus Berger

Residence Schuylkill Haven
Boatman
Mustered in August 14, 1861
Killed in action at Antietam, September 17, 1862

## George W. Brosins

Residence Mahantongo Township, Pennsylvania
Farmer
Mustered in September 9, 1861
Deserted September 19, 1861

## Elias Burget

Residence Schuylkill Haven, Pennsylvania
Boatman
Mustered in September 9, 1861
Deserted January 25, 1863

## Jonathan Brenner

Residence Tremont, Pennsylvania
Miner
Mustered in September 9, 1861
Wounded at Antietam; died September 17, 1862

## Garrett Carrigen (Kerrigan)

Residence Montoursville, Pennsylvania
Boatman
Light complexion, blue eyes, sandy hair, 5'6"
Mustered in September 9, 1861
Mustered out July 30, 1865

## Peter Dankle

Residence Lehigh County, Texas
Tailor
Mustered in September 14, 1861
Died while a prisoner at Andersonville, Georgia.

## Emanuel Eckle

Residence Tremont, Pennsylvania
Moulder
Light complexion, gray eyes, sandy hair, 5'4"
Mustered in August 14, 1861
Killed in action at Cold Harbor, Virginia, June 3, 1864

Eckle's hometown was Tremont, Pennsylvania.

## William Emerick

Residence Washington Township, Pennsylvania
Boatman
Mustered in August 14, 1861
Discharged on surgeon's certificate, date unknown

Emerick was from Washington Township.

## Thomas Ellis

Residence Ohio
Puddler
Mustered in September 9, 1861
Discharged on surgeon's certificate, date unknown

## Henry Eilerding

Residence Harrisburg, Pennsylvania
Farmer
Mustered in September 9, 1861
Discharged on surgeon's certificate, date unknown

## George Freistine

Residence Lebanon and Pottsville, Pennsylvania
Boatman
Mustered in August 14, 1861
Deserted at Fredericksburg, January 25, 1863

Freistine is buried at the Charles Baber Cemetery in Pottsville.

## Peter Fitzimons

Residence Adams County, Pennsylvania
Laborer
Mustered in August 14, 1861
Died of disease, date unknown

## Richard Fohl

Residence Schuylkill Haven, Pennsylvania
Boatman
Mustered in September 9, 1861
Wounded at Antietam, died September 17, 1862

## Frank Fenstamacher

Residence Schuylkill Haven, Pennsylvania
Boatman
Mustered in September 9, 1861
Wounded, date unknown
Not listed on muster out roll

## Peter Fickenshee

Residence Schuylkill Haven, Pennsylvania
Laborer
Mustered in September 9, 1861
Discharged on surgeon's certificate, date unknown

## Christian Gulliver

Residence Montoursville, Pennsylvania
Boatman
Dark complexion, blue eyes, sandy hair, 5'7"
Mustered in September 9, 1861
Mustered out July 30, 1865

Gulliver was wounded slightly in the left arm at the battle of the Nye River in 1864.

## John Graff

Residence Tremont, Pennsylvania
Laborer
Mustered in August 14, 1861
Mustered out September 29, 1864
Wounded in action at Antietam, September 17, 1862

Graff was transferred to Company K on September 22, 1864.

## Jacob Getler (Guertler)

Residence Schuylkill Haven, Pennsylvania
Boatman
Dark complexion, blue eyes, light hair, 5'5"
Mustered in September 9, 1861
Killed in action in Petersburg, Virginia, June 17, 1864

## Aaron P. Gilbert

Residence Schuylkill Haven, Pennsylvania
Boatman

Mustered in September 9, 1861
Discharged on surgeon's certificate, date unknown

## Robert Gilmore

Residence Schuylkill Haven, Pennsylvania
Laborer
Mustered in September 9, 1861
Deserted at Camp Curtin, September 10, 1861

## George Heebner

Residence Schuylkill Haven, Pennsylvania
Boatman
Dark complexion, black eyes, light hair, 5'7"
Mustered in September 9, 1861
Mustered out July 30, 1865

## Jacob Hehn

Residence Schuylkill Haven, Pennsylvania
Boatman
Light complexion, hazel eyes, light hair light, 5'7"
Mustered in September 9, 1861
Mustered out July 30,1865

Hehn was discharged for wounds received in action, then re-enlisted February 22, 1864. He mustered out with the company.

## William Hoffman

Residence Schuylkill Haven, Pennsylvania
Boatman
Light complexion, blue eyes, dark hair, 5'7"
Mustered in September 9, 1861
Wounded at the Wilderness May 6, 1864, transferred to the Veteran Reserve Corps

## Jacob Harbst

Residence Schuylkill Haven, Pennsylvania
Farmer
Mustered in September 9, 1861
Not listed on muster roll

## Lewis Hohl

Residence Schuylkill Haven, Pennsylvania

Baker

Mustered in September 9, 1861

Deserted September 18, 1861

## George Hiney

Residence Tremont, Pennsylvania

Brickmaker

Mustered in September 9, 1861

Killed in action at the battle of Second Bull Run, July 29, 1862

## Stoughton Keighnor (Keihnes)

Residence Schuylkill Haven, Pennsylvania

Boatman

Light complexion, blue eyes blue, light hair, 5'8"

Mustered in September 9,1861

Mustered out July 30, 1865

## Charles Knarr

Residence Schuylkill Haven, Pennsylvania

Boatman

Mustered in September 9, 1861

Mustered out September 29, 1864 on expiration of term

## Benjamin Knarr

Residence Schuylkill Haven, Pennsylvania

Boat Builder

Mustered in April 20, 1862

Mustered out April 19, 1865 on expiration of term

## Jonas W. Kramer

Residence Schuylkill Haven, Pennsylvania

Shoemaker

Mustered in September 9, 1861

Discharged for wounds received in action, date unknown

## George Klinger

Residence Schuylkill Haven, Pennsylvania

Farmer

Mustered in September 9, 1861

Discharged on surgeon's certificate, date unknown

## Josiah Lehman

Residence Tremont, Pennsylvania

Boatman

Dark complexion, blue eyes, black hair, 5'6"

Mustered in September 9, 1861

Died from wounds received at Spotsylvania Court House May 12, 1864. Lehman was buried May 27, 1864 at Alexandria, Virginia, grave number 1,945.

## John Little

Residence Schuylkill Haven, Pennsylvania

Boatman

Mustered in September 9, 1861

Discharged on surgeon's certificate, date unknown

## Thomas Lloyd

Residence Jeansville, Luzerne County, Pennsylvania

Miner

Mustered in September 9, 1861

Killed in action at Spotsylvania Court House, May 12, 1864

## Joseph Long

Residence Schuylkill Haven, Pennsylvania

Boatman

Light complexion, blue eyes, dark hair, 5'5"

Mustered in September 9, 1861

Killed in action December 31, 1864 in Petersburg

In August of 1864 Long was one of two soldiers involved in a hand-to-hand fight with Rebels that resulted in Captain Charles Brown receiving the Medal of Honor.

## Lewis Long

Residence Schuylkill Haven, Pennsylvania

Boatman

Mustered in September 9, 1861

Discharged on surgeon's certificate, date unknown

## Henry B. Miller

Residence Tremont, Pennsylvania

Machinist

Mustered in September 9, 1861

Mustered out July 30, 1865

## George Moyer

Residence Schuylkill Haven, Pennsylvania

Farmer

Dark complexion, black eyes, sandy hair, 5'6"

Mustered in September 9, 1861

Mustered out July 30, 1865

## Edward Marland

Residence Glenn Carbon, Pennsylvania

Miner

Mustered in September 9, 1861

Mustered out July 30, 1865

## Daniel Mussic

Residence Schuylkill Haven, Pennsylvania

Boatman

Mustered in September 9, 1861

Died from disease, date unknown

## Dennis Melley

Residence Schuylkill Haven, Pennsylvania

Miner

Mustered in September 9, 1861

Transferred to the regular army, date unknown

## John Martin

Residence Schuylkill Haven, Pennsylvania

Laborer

Mustered in September 9, 1861

Discharged for wounds received in action, date unknown

## Patrick Malloy

Residence Minersville, Pennsylvania
Miner
Mustered in September 9, 1861
Discharged on surgeon's certificate, date unknown

## Charles Meckenstorm

Residence Tremont, Pennsylvania
Shoemaker
Dark complexion, gray eyes, black hair
Mustered in September 9, 1861
Deserted from Camp Dick Robinson, April 9, 1863

## Patrick McCullough

Residence Minersville, Pennsylvania
Miner
Light complexion, gray eyes, black hair
Mustered in September 9, 1861
Mustered out July 30, 1865

## Daniel McGlenn

Residence Beaver Meadows, Pennsylvania
Peddler
Mustered in September 9, 1861
Killed in action at Antietam, September 17, 1862

## Franklin O'Donnell

Residence, Schuylkill Haven, Pennsylvania
Boatman
Mustered in September 9, 1861
Mustered out September 29, 1864 on expiration of term

## Isreal Oswald

Residence, Schuylkill Haven, Pennsylvania
Blacksmith
Light complexion, blue eyes, dark hair
Mustered in September 9, 1861
Transferred to the Veteran Reserve Corps January 1, 1865
Buried in Jerusalem Cemetery, Schuylkill Haven.

## Edward Oswald

Residence Schuylkill Haven, Pennsylvania
Boatman
Mustered in September 9, 1861
Not listed on muster out roll
Buried in Schuylkill Haven

## Morgan Pugh

Residence Minersville, Pennsylvania
Miner
Mustered in September 9, 1861
Mustered out September 29, 1864, on expiration of term

After the battle of Antietam, Pugh was assigned the duty of staying behind at the Sherrick Farm to render as much help and care he could to the dying drummer boy Jere Helms.

## William Patton

Residence Schuylkill Haven, Pennsylvania
Boatman
Mustered in September 9, 1861
Not listed on muster out roll

## Peter Paul

Residence Schuylkill Haven, Pennsylvania
Boatman
Light complexion, blue eyes, brown hair, 5'4½"
Mustered in September 9, 1861
Mustered out July 30, 1865
Buried in Union Cemetery, Schuylkill Haven

Paul was wounded with a gunshot wound to the right shoulder. His obituary appeared June 2, 1916, in the *Schuylkill Haven Call.*

### Vet Peter Paul Answers Taps

*Peter A. Paul, a veteran of the Civil War and one of the town's eldest and most respected citizens died Wednesday morning at 12:45 o'clock. Deceased was born at a little place called Bear Ridge, near Cumbola, of German parents. At a very early age, he with other members of the family were thrown upon their own resources and compelled to make their own way in life. At the age of 11 years he went with an uncle at Port Carbon, but a yecr later came to the father and mother of William J. Saylor, Jr. Here he was reared to manhood. At the age of 25 he married Emma Rebecca Frehafer, who was one year his junior.*

*The death of Mr. Paul followed a lingering illness of 16 years. During this period he was afflicted with rheumatism and sat continuously in a chair. The last two weeks of his illness he was compelled to take to his bed. He was conscious almost to the last and only a few minutes before his demise, recognized his wife of 50 years.*

*He enlisted twice and during his first engagement was wounded. The bullet entered the shoulder and was extracted near his hip. The bullet is still in possession of the family. For a period of 15 years following his return from the military he was a signal man for the railroad Company at the Mine Hill crossing. Some 15 years ago he was stricken blind with cataracts and remained in that condition for some three months. He was finally relieved after being a patient in one of the Philadelphia hospitals.*

*The war record of Mr. Paul is one any citizen could feel justly proud of. He was following the occupation of a boatman at the out break of the war. On September 28, 1861 he enlisted from Schuylkill county and was mustered in as a private in Capt. D.F. Burket's Company C 50th P.V. He served three years under Col. B.C. Christ and was assigned to the fourth division of the Ninth Army Corps, Army of the Potomac. He participated in the following battles: Pocotaligo, May 29, 1862; Second battle of Bull Run, August 30, 1862; battle of Chantilly, September 1, 1862; It was in the last battle that he was injured by a gun shot wound in the right shoulder and was sent to the hospital at Mt. Pleasant, Washington, D.C.*

*He was later transferred to Baltimore, Pt. Lookout, and Alexander, finally being transferred to the second battalion of the Invalid Corps. He was engaged in duty in the defense of Washington D.C. and honorably discharged October 28, 1864; at the expiration of his enlistment, on February 21, 1865, he again enlisted for a period of one year or until the end of the war. The second enlistment was in Co. C 50th P.V.V. under command of Capt. Charles Brown and Col. Welford. During his second enlistment he participated in the siege and fall of Petersburg, April, 1865. He returned to Washington D.C. and was discharge July 30, 1865.*

## George Reed

Residence Schuylkill Haven, Pennsylvania
Boatman
Light complexion, black eyes, sandy hair
Mustered in September 9, 1861
Mustered out July 30, 1865

Reed captured a Rebel flag at Jackson, Mississippi. He was not awarded the Medal of Honor for this accomplishment because the capture did not take place during action. It was removed from a building.

## John Ryan

Residence Schuylkill Haven, Pennsylvania

Boatman

Dark complexion, gray eyes, black hair, 5'7"

Mustered in September 9, 1861

Mustered out July 30, 1865

Ryan re-enlisted Blaine's Crossroads and was one of the oldest members of Company C to finish out the war.

## Michael Riley (Reilly)

Residence Schuylkill Haven, Pennsylvania

Laborer

Dark complexion, gray eyes, black hair, 5'4"

Mustered in September 9, 1861

Killed in action during the Wilderness Campaign, May 6, 1864

## Philip Reisher

Residence Schuylkill Haven, Pennsylvania

Mason

Mustered in September 9, 1861

Discharged on surgeon's certificate, date unknown

## James Saylor

Residence Schuylkill Haven, Pennsylvania

Boatman

Mustered in September 9, 1861

Mustered out September 29, 1864 on expiration of term

Saylor was demoted from sergeant to private, but the reason is unknown.

## Franklin Sharon

Residence Schuylkill Haven, Pennsylvania

Boatman

Mustered in September 9, 1861

Killed in action at Spotsylvania Court House, May 12, 1864

Sharon re-enlisted with the company at Blaine's Crossroads.

## Lucian Schwartz

Residence Schuylkill Haven, Pennsylvania

Boatman

Mustered in September 9, 1861
Died of disease, date unknown

## George Simpson

Residence Schuylkill Haven, Pennsylvania
Boatman
Mustered in September 9, 1861
Died of wounds received in action, date unknown

## William Williams

Residence Schuylkill Haven, Pennsylvania
Boatman
Fair complexion, blue eyes, dark hair, 5'6"
Mustered in September 9, 1861
Mustered out July 30, 1865

Williams was captured May 12, 1864, and held prisoner at Andersonville. Williams had also been held by the provost guard at the Pottsville jail for his actions while on furlough. On September 24, 1909, the *Schuylkill Haven Call* printed this story:

> *At the outbreak of the Civil War, Mr. Williams, who was a native New Yorker by birth, "Just blew into town," as he says and enlisted in old Company C 50th P.V.V. The rolls of which bear the names of some of Schuylkill Haven's most prominent citizens both of present times and days gone by. While home on a furlough Mr. Williams and a couple of comrades, while trying to get a square deal for a comrade, were arrested by the provost guard and drummed up to the Pottsville jail. The streets were lined with soldiers of the 96th Regiment, then encamped on Lawton's Hill and they naturally wanted to know what was up. When the facts were known the boys of the 96th made a demand upon the jailer for the imprisoned soldiers with the ultimatum that if they were not released the regiment would storm the jail and release them. Mr. Williams and his companions were speedily set free and the 96th boys hired a carriage and four white horses and headed by the regimental band, the released prisoners were escorted back to Schuylkill Haven.*

## Samuel Wesner

Residence Schuylkill Haven, Pennsylvania
Laborer
Mustered in September 9, 1861
Mustered out July 30, 1865

Wesner re-enlisted with the company at Blaine's Crossroads.

## Patrick Williams

Residence Schuylkill Haven, Pennsylvania

Miner

Dark complexion, blue eyes, dark hair, 5'6"

Mustered in September 9, 1861

Died as a prisoner, date unknown

Williams re-enlisted with the company at Blaine's Crossroads.

## William Wagner

Residence Schuylkill Haven, Pennsylvania

Farmer

Light complexion, blue eyes, dark hair, 5"6"

Mustered in September 9, 1861

Killed in action, August 19, 1864

Buried in the 9th Army Corps Cemetery, Meade Station, Virginia

Wagner re-enlisted with the company at Blaine's Crossroads.

## Alex Williams

Residence Schuylkill Haven, Pennsylvania

Mustered in September 9, 1861

Discharged on surgeon's certificate, date unknown

## Franklin Wise

Residence Schuylkill Haven, Pennsylvania

Boatman

Mustered in September 9, 1861

Discharged on surgeon's certificate for wounds received in action at Second Bull Run, August 30, 1862; date of discharge unknown

# Enlistments

# 1864

Many of the men, who joined the 50th Regiment in 1864 were either drafted men or men who went in as a substitute for another drafted man. On February 1, 1864, President Lincoln issued a call for 500,000 men, which were assumed to include the 300,000 from the October 17, 1863 call. March 14, 1864, brought an additional call for 200,000 men.

## George Bowsman

Residence Pottsville, Pennsylvania
Boat builder
Dark complexion, gray eyes, brown hair
Mustered in February 19, 1864
Mustered out July 30, 1865
Drafted

## David Berger

Residence Schuylkill Haven, Pennsylvania
Laborer
Light complexion, gray eyes, light hair, 5'7"
Mustered in February 19, 1864
Mustered out July 30, 1865
Drafted
Buried in First Union Cemetery, Schuylkill Haven

Berger was wounded in action on May 6, 1864 at the Wilderness.

## William Beeker

Residence Pottsville, Pennsylvania
Mustered in February 22, 1864
Mustered out July 30, 1865
Drafted

## Volney Belle

Residence Berks County, Pennsylvania
Laborer
Fair complexion, blue eyes, light hair, 5'8"
Mustered in February 23, 1864
Discharged by general order, July 11, 1865
Drafted

## Jacob Benedict

Residence Pottsville, Pennsylvania
Boatman
Light complexion, gray eyes, black hair, 5'1"
Mustered in February 19, 1864
Killed in action at Spotsylvania Court House, May 12, 1864
Drafted

## Albert Bertold

Residence Berks County, Pennsylvania
Laborer
Dark complexion, hazel eyes, brown hair
Mustered in March 4, 1864
Killed in action at Cold Harbor Virginia, June 3, 1864

## Charles Burket (Burkhart)

Residence Berks County, Pennsylvania
Boatman
Fair complexion, gray eyes, dark hair
Mustered in February 22, 1864
Killed in action near Petersburg, Virginia, August 19, 1864
Drafted

## Alpheus Combs

Residence Schuylkill Haven, Pennsylvania
Farmer
Light complexion, hazel eyes, brown hair, 5'7"
Mustered in April 16, 1864
Mustered out July 30, 1865
Buried in Union Cemetery, Schuylkill Haven

## Rolandus Correll

Residence Schuylkill County, Pennsylvania
Teamster
Dark complexion, gray eyes, brown hair, 5'2"
Mustered in April 19, 1864
Mustered out July 30, 1865

## Peter Dilcamp (Delcamp)

Residence Schuylkill Haven, Pennsylvania
Boat Builder
Light complexion, gray eyes, dark hair, 5'10"
Mustered in March 8, 1864
Discharged by general order, August 16, 1865
Buried in Union Cemetery, Schuylkill Haven
Drafted

## John N. Eckert

Residence Schuylkill Haven, Pennsylvania
Boatman
Fair complexion, gray eyes, sandy hair, 5'8"
Mustered in February 29, 1864
Mustered out July 30, 1865
Buried in Union Cemetery, Schuylkill Haven

## William Eckert

Residence Schuylkill County, Pennsylvania
Boatman
Light complexion, gray eyes, brown hair, 5'2"
Mustered in April 6, 1864
Mustered out July 30, 1865

Eckert was wounded in action at the Wilderness, May 6, 1864.

## John Eckert

Residence Schuylkill Haven, Pennsylvania
Boatman
Fair complexion, gray eyes, sandy hair, 5'2"
Mustered in February 22, 1864
Mustered out July 30, 1865
Buried in Union Cemetery, Schuylkill Haven.

Eckert was captured May 12, 1864, at Spotsylvania Court House and sent to Andersonville, Georgia.

## Daniel Ebert

Residence Berks County, Pennsylvania
Boatman
Fair complexion, gray eyes, dark hair, 5'4"
Mustered in February 22, 1864
Killed in action at Nye River, Virginia, May 9, 1864

## Peter Fritz

Residence Pottsville, Pennsylvania
Laborer
Dark complexion, blue eyes, dark hair, 5'1½"
Mustered in August 22, 1864
Died of wounds received in action at the Wilderness, May 6, 1864

## John Fritz

Residence Berks County, Pennsylvania
Boatman
Fair complexion, hazel eyes, sandy hair, 5'2"
Mustered in February 22, 1864
Killed in action when hit with a shell in front of Petersburg, Virginia, April 2, 1865

## William D. Guertler

Residence Schuylkill County, Pennsylvania
Stone Cutter
Dark complexion, gray eyes, dark hair, 5'10"
Mustered in April 16, 1864
Mustered out July 30, 1865

Guertler was captured on May 12, 1864, and sent to Andersonville. He was also wounded in action with a gunshot wound in the right hand and received a four-dollar pension.

## Jerome Hoffman

Residence Schuylkill Haven, Pennsylvania
Boatman
Florid complexion, blue eyes, brown hair
Mustered in March 3, 1864

Mustered out July 30, 1865
Buried in Union Cemetery, Schuylkill Haven

## Edward Heebner

Residence Pottsville, Pennsylvania
Boatman
Light complexion, hazel eyes, black hair
Mustered in February 19, 1864
Mustered out July 30, 1865

## Romandes Harner

Residence Schuylkill Haven, Pennsylvania
Boatman
Light complexion, hazel eyes, brown hair, 5'1"
Mustered in April 4, 1864
Mustered out July 30, 1865
Buried in Union Cemetery, Schuylkill Haven

## William Haines

Residence Pottsville, Pennsylvania
Mustered in February 19, 1864
Mustered out July 30, 1865

## Henry Hehn

Residence Schuylkill Haven, Pennsylvania
Boatman
Light complexion, hazel eyes, light hair, 5'11"
Mustered in February 22, 1864
Died while a prisoner at Andersonville, date unknown
Buried at Fortress Monroe, Virginia

## William J. Koch

Residence Schuylkill Haven and Pottsville, Pennsylvania
Boatman
Light complexion, hazel eyes, black hair
Mustered in February 19, 1864
Mustered out July 30, 1865
Buried in Union Cemetery, Schuylkill Haven

## Adam Lloyd

Residence Schuylkill Haven, Pennsylvania
Boatman
Light complexion, hazel eyes, brown hair
Mustered in February 19, 1864
Mustered out July 30, 1865

On May 6, 1864, at the battle of the Wilderness, Lloyd was wounded in the left leg by a gunshot wound. He received a two-dollar monthly pension for his wound in 1882.

## George W. Lloyd

Residence Schuylkill Haven and Pottsville, Pennsylvania
Boatman
Light complexion, hazel eyes, black hair
Mustered in February 9, 1864
Discharged by general order July 11, 1865
Buried in Union Cemetery, Schuylkill Haven.

Lloyd was wounded on May 6,1864, at the battle of the Wilderness.

## William G. Losch

Residence Pottsville, Pennsylvania
Boatman
Complexion light, eyes blue, hair brown
Mustered in February 19, 1864
Mustered out July 30, 1865

## John Lendal

Residence Schuylkill County, Pennsylvania
Laborer
Light complexion, hazel eyes, dark hair, 5'7"
Mustered in February 22, 1864
Discharged on surgeon's certificate, date unknown

## John B. Martz

Residence Pottsville, Pennsylvania
Boatman
Light complexion, gray eyes, black hair, 5'7"
Mustered in February 29, 1864
Mustered out July 30, 1865

## Daniel Martz

Residence Reading, Pennsylvania

Laborer

Dark complexion, gray eyes, brown hair

Mustered in February 10, 1864

Discharged by general order, May 16, 1865

Martz was wounded by gunshots in the right foot and right arm. It was quoted he was bleeding from fifteen different places on his body. In 1880 he received a pension of four dollars a month.

## Samuel Martz

Residence Pottsville, Pennsylvania

Blacksmith

Medium complexion, gray eyes, brown hair, 5’8”

Mustered in February 19, 1864

Killed in action at the battle of the Wilderness May 6, 1864

Martz was hit by a shell during battle. Charles Brown was near him when he was hit and watched as his heart bounded along the ground.

## Jonathan Mc Harque

Residence Berks County, Pennsylvania

Farmer

Florid complexion, gray eyes, dark hair, 6’1”

Mustered in March 20, 1864

Mustered out July 30, 1865

McHarque was wounded at the battle of the Wilderness. May 6,1864.

## Albert Reiger

Residence Schuylkill County, Pennsylvania

Boatman

Dark complexion, gray eyes, brown hair, 5’6”

Mustered in April 19, 1864

Mustered out July 30, 1865

## Edward Reiger

Residence Schuylkill County, Pennsylvania

Boatman

Fair complexion, blue eyes, light hair, 5’6”

Mustered in February 22, 1864

Mustered out July 30, 1865

## Thomas Rupp

Residence Schuylkill County, Pennsylvania
Boatman
Light complexion, blue eyes, light hair
Mustered in February 22, 1864
Mustered out July 30, 1865

## John Reed

Residence North Manheim Township, Pennsylvania
Laborer
Fair complexion, gray eyes, light hair
Mustered in February 19, 1864
Killed in action May 25, 1864

## Frank Reinheimer

Residence Ashland, Pennsylvania
Boat builder
Dark complexion, hazel eyes, brown hair
Mustered in June 24, 1864
Not listed on muster out roll

## Paul Sheck

Residence Pottsville, Pennsylvania
Laborer
Mustered in July 5, 1864
Mustered out June 30, 1865
Sheck enlisted as a substitute.

## Samuel Schwenk

Residence Schuylkill County, Pennsylvania
Farmer
Dark complexion, dark eyes, dark hair, 5'6"
Mustered in February 22, 1864
Mustered out July 30, 1865

Schwenk was first a member of Company C of the 151st PVI and re-enlisted in the 50th Regiment.

## Adam Schwab

Residence Schuylkill County, Pennsylvania
Boatman
Dark complexion, dark eyes, dark hair, 5'3"
Mustered in February 23, 1864
Mustered out July 30, 1865

Schwab was born in Germany.

## Daniel Sullivan

Residence Reading, Pennsylvania
Laborer
Fair complexion, blue eyes, light hair, 5'6"
Mustered in March 28, 1864
Discharged on surgeon's certificate, date unknown

## William Sirles

Residence Macongie, Pennsylvania
Moulder
Dark complexion, hazel eyes, brown hair, 5'8"
Mustered in February 11, 1864
Mustered out November 18 1864

Sirles was transferred to Veteran Reserve Corps because of wounds.

## Charles Sheppell

Residence Berks County, Pennsylvania
Blacksmith
Dark complexion, dark eyes, dark hair
Mustered in February 22, 1864
Mustered out December 24, 1864

Sheppell was transferred to Veteran Reserve Corps for wounds received at the battle of the Wilderness, May 6, 1864.

## William H. Tyson

Residence Berks County, Pennsylvania
Boatman
Light complexion, light eyes, light hair, 5'9"
Mustered in February 22, 1864
Mustered out July 30, 1865

Tyson was wounded in the right hand.

## Irving W. Tyson

Residence Schuylkill Haven, Pennsylvania
Boatman
Light complexion, hazel eyes, dark hair, 5'9"
Mustered in February 22, 1864
Discharged by general order June 8, 1865

Tyson was wounded in the right hand at the battle of the Wilderness May 6, 1864. He went back to boating on the canal after the war and also worked for thirty years a railroad man at Philadelphia. After he retired he returned home to Schuylkill Haven and was a well-respected citizen. He was the last surviving member of the Jere Helms G.A.R. Post No. 26. Tyson always claimed he voted for "Honest Abe Lincoln while in the field with the army."

## Charles Williams

Residence Port Clinton, Pennsylvania
Boatman
Florid complexion, gray eyes, light hair, 5'2'
Mustered in February 19, 1864
Mustered out July 30, 1865
Buried in Port Clinton Cemetery, Pennsylvania

Williams was wounded in the collarbone.

## Josiah Wright

Residence Montgomery County, Pennsylvania
Laborer
Dark complexion, blue eyes, brown hair, 5'10"
Mustered in March 11, 1864
Mustered out July 30, 1865

Wright was wounded at the battle of the Wilderness, May 6, 1864.

## Levan J. Warner

Residence Pottsville, Pennsylvania
Boatman
Medium complexion, gray eyes, brown hair, 5'3"
Mustered in February 19, 1864
Killed in action at the battle of the Wilderness, May 6, 1864

# Enlistments 1865

## Lewis Boyer

Residence Schuylkill Haven, Pennsylvania

Pottsville

Laborer

Dark complexion, hazel eyes, black hair

Mustered in February 26, 1865

Mustered out July 30, 1865

## William Bretz

Residence Schuylkill County, Pennsylvania

Boatman

Light complexion, gray eyes, light hair

Mustered in January 26, 1865

Mustered out July 30, 1865

## David Block

Residence Pottsville, Pennsylvania

Plasterer

Medium complexion, blue eyes, dark hair, 5'6"

Mustered in January 16, 1865

Mustered out July 30, 1865

## Henry Burns

Residence Schuylkill Haven, Pennsylvania

Boatman

Medium complexion, hazel eyes, light hair, 5'9"

Mustered in March 27, 1865

Mustered out July 30, 1865

## Franklin Burns

Residence Schuylkill Haven, Pennsylvania
Boatman
Light complexion, blue eyes, brown hair, 5'5"
Mustered in March 27, 1865
Mustered out July 30, 1865
Buried in Union Cemetery, Schuylkill Haven

Burns was wounded by a gunshot in the left side at Petersburg, Virginia. In 1880 he received a two-dollar pension.

## William Byrne

Residence Schuylkill Haven, Pennsylvania
Boatman
Medium complexion, dark eyes, black hair
Mustered in March 27, 1865
Mustered out July 30, 1865

## Charles Eiler

Residence Schuylkill County, Pennsylvania
Farmer
Light complexion, gray eyes, brown hair, 5'2"
Mustered in April 6, 1865
Mustered out July 30, 1865
Buried in Cressona Cemetery

## Marks E. Eckert

Residence Schuylkill County, Pennsylvania
Blacksmith
Medium complexion, blue eyes, light hair, 5'5"
Mustered in February 27, 1865
Mustered out July 30, 1865

## Franklin Fisher

Residence Schuylkill County, Pennsylvania
Plasterer
Light complexion, blue eyes, light hair, 5'8"
Mustered in January 16, 1865
Discharged by general order June 9, 1865

Fisher was wounded in April of 1865, near Petersburg, Virginia.

## Mahlon Garber

Residence Schuylkill County, Pennsylvania
Laborer
Fair complexion, light eyes, light hair
Mustered in April 6, 1865
Mustered out August 16, 1865on expiration of term

Garber was listed as being sick from July 1, 1865, until his muster out.

## Thomas Haus

Residence Leigh County, Pennsylvania
Painter
Dark complexion, gray eyes, dark hair, 5'6"
Mustered in February 13, 1865
Mustered out July 30, 1865

## William Koch

Residence Mt. Manheim, Pennsylvania
Boatman
Dark complexion, hazel eyes, brown hair, 5'2"
Mustered in February 6, 1865
Mustered out July 30, 1865
Buried in Union Cemetery, Schuylkill Haven

## Isaac Knarr

Residence Schuylkill Haven, Pennsylvania
Carpenter
Light complexion, blue eyes, gray hair
Mustered in February 6, 1865
Mustered out July 30, 1865

## George Knarr

Residence Pottsville, Pennsylvania
Boatman
Ruddy complexion, hazel eyes, brown hair
Mustered in January 21, 1865
Mustered out July 30, 1865

## Charles Karney

Residence Schuylkill Haven, Pennsylvania
Laborer
Medium complexion, blue eyes, light hair, 5'4"
Mustered in March 13, 1865
Mustered out July 30, 1865

## Andrew Krebs

Residence Schuylkill County, Pennsylvania
Teamster
Light complexion, hazel eyes, dark hair, 5'5"
Mustered in April 6, 1865
Mustered out July 30, 1865

## Jacob Lindermuth

Residence Schuylkill County, Pennsylvania
Mustered in February 6, 1865
Mustered out July 30, 1865

## William E. Machlin

Residence Pottsville, Pennsylvania
Mustered in March 1, 1865
Mustered out July 30, 1865

Machlin enlisted as a substitute.

## William Mercer

Residence Schuylkill County, Pennsylvania
Boatman
Fair complexion, blue eyes, light hair
Mustered in February 6, 1865
Mustered out July 30, 1865

## Lewis B. Reber

Residence Pottsville, Pennsylvania
Farmer
Light complexion, blue eyes, light hair, 5'6"
Mustered in February 13, 1865
Mustered out July 30, 1865

## John Smith

Residence Eldred Township, Schuylkill County, Pennsylvania
Laborer
Light complexion, gray eyes, dark hair, 5'7"
Mustered in January 16, 1865
Mustered out July 30, 1865

## John Sweeny

Residence Mt. Mannheim, Pennsylvania
Boatman
Dark complexion, gray eyes, brown hair, 5'3½"
Mustered in February 6, 1865
Mustered out July 30, 1865

## Lewis Seaman

Residence Schuylkill County, Pennsylvania
Blacksmith
Dark complexion, gray eyes, brown hair, 5'7"
Mustered in April 6, 1865
Mustered out July 30, 1865

## John Seifert

Residence Schuylkill County, Pennsylvania
Laborer
Fair complexion, hazel eyes, light hair, 5'6"
Mustered in April 6, 1865
Mustered out July 30, 1865

## William B. Seifert

Residence Schuylkill County, Pennsylvania
Laborer
Medium complexion, hazel eyes, light hair, 5'7"
Mustered in April 6, 1865
Mustered out July 30, 1865

## Arthur Venable

Residence Carbon County, Pennsylvania
Shoemaker
Light complexion, hazel eyes, brown hair, 5'5"
Mustered in February 13, 1865
Mustered out July 30, 1865

## Augustus Wall

Residence Schuylkill County, Pennsylvania
Boatman
Dark complexion, gray eyes, brown hair, 5'6"
Mustered in February 6, 1865
Mustered out July 30, 1865

# Engagements and Casualties

## Casualties in Company C

In the battles of Second Bull Run and Chantilly

### Killed:

George W. Kinley
Edward Haemer

### Wounded:

D. Berkert
Jonas Kremer
George Simpson
Peter Powell
Samuel Hoffman
Garret Garrigan
Benjamin Knarr
Dennis Mellery
John Martin
George Schwenk

### Missing:

Jacob Guertler
Charles Knarr
Franklin Wise
Edward Marl
Henry M. Diebler

In the battles of South Mountain and Antietam

## Killed:

Richard Fahl
Daniel McGlenn

## Wounded:

Augustus Berger
Jeremiah Helms
Jonathan Branner
Samuel Agley
John Graif
William Patten
Franklin Fenstermacher
Jacob Hahn

In the battles of the Wilderness and subsequent engagements up to June 6,1864

## Killed:

Wm. H. Hill
Michael Riley
Levan J. Warner
Sam. Martz
Dan. Evert
Jacob Benedict
Thomas Lloyd
Franklin Sharer
John Reed
Emanuel Eckert
Albert Bartolet

## Wounded:

Levi Eckert
Wm. Eckers
Peter Fritz
Christ Gulliver
Wm. Hoffman
George Lloyd

Adam Lloyd
John Mehargue
Charles Shappell
Adam Lehwab
Irvin Tyson
Josiah Wright
D.T. Burke
Augustus Mellon
Chas. Oswald
William Wildermuth
Henry M. Diebler
Josiah D. Lehman
Gottlieb Burket
Henry Hill
William H. Hiney
George Cake
William Koch
Lafayette Baker
John Eckert,
Jacob Hehn

## Missing:

David Raudenbush
John Doudle
Samuel Agley
Elias Berger
Peter Dankle
Wm. Guertler
Henry Hehn
Wm. Hains
Garrett Kerrigan
Dan. Sullivan
William Williams

## Summary of Casualties

| Date | Location of Engagement | Wounded in Action | Killed in Action | Missing in Action |
|---|---|---|---|---|
| November 7, 1861 | Port Royal, SC | No casualties | | |
| December. 6, 1861 | Beaufort, SC | 1 WIA | | |
| January 1, 1862 | Port Royal Ferry, SC | 2 WIA | | |
| May 29, 1862 | Pocotaligo, SC | 11 WIA | 2 KIA | |
| August 24, 1862 | Sulphur Springs, VA | No casualties | | |
| August 29, 1862 | Bull Run, VA | 17 WIA | 5 KIA | 6 MIA |
| August 31, 1862 | Centreville, VA | 14 WIA | 4 KIA | 6 MIA |
| September 1, 1862 | Chantilly, VA | 32 WIA | 7 KIA | 1 MIA |
| September 14, 1862 | South Mountain, MD | 2 WIA | | |
| September 17, 1862 | Antietam, MD | 31 WIA | 9 KIA | |
| December 11–13 1862 | Fredericksburg, VA | 1 WIA | | |
| July 4, 1863 | Siege of Vicksburg, MS | No casualties | | |
| July 10–17, 1863 | Jackson, MS | 1 WIA | | |
| October 10, 1863 | Blue Springs, TN | 2 WIA | | |
| November 14, 1863 | Hough's Ferry, TN | No casualties | | |
| November 15, 1863 | Lenoir Station, TN | No casualties | | |
| November 16, 1863 | Campbell's Station, TN | 3 WIA | 1 KIA | |
| November 17–December 5, 1863 | Siege of Knoxville, TN | 6 WIA | 3 KIA | |
| May 6, 1864 | Wilderness, VA | 58 WIA | 10 KIA | 1 MIA |
| May 9, 1864 | Nye River, VA | 56 WIA | 5 KIA | |
| May 12, 1864 | Spotsylvania Court House, VA | 46 WIA | 20 KIA | 114 MIA |
| May 25, 1864 | North Anna, VA | 2 WIA | 1 KIA | |

| Date | Location of Engagement | Wounded in Action | Killed in Action | Missing in Action |
|---|---|---|---|---|
| June 1, 1864 | Bethesda Church, VA | 2 WIA | | |
| June 3, 5–7, 1864 | Cold Harbor, VA | 12 WIA | 7 KIA | 1 MIA |
| June 17–18, 1864 | Petersburg, VA | 23 WIA | 9 KIA | |
| June19-29, 1864 | Petersburg rifle pits | 11 WIA | 8 KIA | |
| July 30, 1864 | explosion of mine | 16 WIA | 1 KIA | 1 MIA |
| August 19, 1864 | Weldon Railroad, VA | 9 WIA | 8 KIA | 3 MIA |
| September 30, 1864 | Peagrams Farm, VA | 3 WIA | 2 KIA | 7 MIA |
| October 27, 1864 | Hatchers Run, VA | 4 WIA | | |
| November 30, 1864–March 24, 1865 | Ft. McGilvey | 4 WIA | 2 KIA | |
| March 25, 1865 | Ft. Stedman, VA | 2 WIA | | |
| April 2, 1865 | assault on Petersburg, VA | 1 WIA | 1 KIA | |
| Miscellaneous killed and wounded in action while on picket | | 1 WIA | 8 KIA | |
| | | 373 WIA | 113 KIA | 141 MIA |

Total: 627 Casualties

# Selected Bibliography


Bates, Samuel P. *History of the Pennsylvania Volunteers, 1861–5*. Privately printed, 1869.

*Civil War Files of Schuylkill County*. In the collection of the Historical Society of Schuylkill County.

Crater, Lewis. *History of the Fiftieth Regiment, Penna. Veteran Volunteers, 1861–65*. Reading, PA: Coleman Printing House, 1884.

Letters to the editor, *Pottsville Miner's Journal*, 1860–65.

Munsels, W.W. *History of Schuylkill County PA*. George McNamara, 1881.

*Official Records of the War of the Rebellion*. Series 1, Vol. 6, Vol. 12, Vol. 19, Vol. 21, Vol. 24, Vol. 30, Vol. 31, Vol. 36, Vol. 42, Vol. 46.

Pennsylvania at Antietam. Report of the Antietam Battlefield Memorial Commission of Pennsylvania, 1906.

Pennsylvania State Archives, descriptive lists of the 50th Pennsylvania Regiment.

*Pottsville Daily Republican*, June 1908.

*Schuylkill Haven Call*, June 1916.

Wallace, Francis B. *Memorial to the Patriotism of Schuylkill County in the American Slave holder's Rebellion, 1865*. Pottsville, PA: Benjamin Bannan, 1865.